SAN LEANDRO H

THE
MODERN ERA
THROUGH
WORLD
WAR II

FROM THE 18TH CENTURY TO 1945

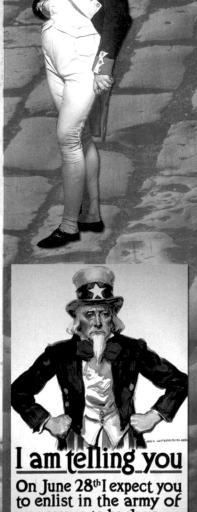

THE
MODERN ERA
THROUGH
WORLD
WAR II

FROM THE 18TH CENTURY TO 1945

ARTHUR KNEBEL AND HERMANN-JOSEF UDELHOVEN

I am telling you

On June 28th I expect you to enlist in the army of war savers to back up my army of fighters.

GERMANY
BERLIN 1936
1–16th AUGUST

OLYMPIC GAMES

Rosen
PUBLISHING

New York

This edition first published in 2013 by:

The Rosen Publishing Group, Inc.
29 East 21st Street
New York, NY 10010

Library of Congress Cataloging-in-Publication Data

Knebel, Arthur.
The modern era through World War II/Arthur Knebel, Hermann-Josef Udelhoven.
   p. cm.—(Witness to history—a visual chronicle of the world)
Includes bibliographical references and index.
ISBN 978-1-4488-7224-4 (library binding)
1. History, Modern—18th century—Juvenile literature. 2. History, Modern—19th century—Juvenile literature. 3. History, Modern—20th century—Juvenile literature. 4. World history—Juvenile literature. I. Udelhoven, Hermann-Josef. II. Title.
D299.K54 2012
909.08—dc23

2012011122

Manufactured in the United States of America

CPSIA Compliance Information: Batch #S12YA: For further information, contact Rosen Publishing, New York, New York, at 1-800-237-9932.

Copyright © 2005 Peter Delius Verlag, Berlin
Publisher: Peter Delius

All images from akg-images Berlin/London/Paris and from dpa Deutsche Presse Agentur, Hamburg. For detailed copyright information, please see *The Contemporary World: From 1945 to the 21st Century.*

The publishers would like to express their special gratitude to the team at akg-images Berlin/London/Paris who have made their incredible picture archive accessible and thus the extraordinary illustrations of this book possible.

Contents

The Storming of the Bastille: The start of the French Revolution **p. 12**

The French Emperor
Napoleon Bonaparte **p. 16**

World War I: Man and animal wear gas
masks **p. 96**

Lenin, the head of the Bolshevik October revolution in Russia **p. 136**

World economic crisis: the stock market crash of "Black Thursday" **p. 163**

Advertisement for the international associations of the Nazi SS **p. 171**

The Modern Era
1789–1914

In Europe, the revolutionary transformation of the ruling systems and state structures began with a bang: In 1789 the French Revolution broke out in Paris, and its motto "Liberté, Egalité, Fraternité"—Liberty, Equality, Brotherhood—took on an irrepressible force. A fundamental reorganization of society followed the French Revolution. The ideas behind the revolution were manifest in Napoleon's *Code Civil*, which he imposed on many European nations. The 19th century also experienced a transformation of society from another source: The Industrial Revolution established within society a poorer working class that stood in opposition to the merchant and trading middle class. The nascent United States was shaken by an embittered civil war. The economic growth that set in following that war was accompanied by the development of imperialist endeavors and its rise to the status of a Great Power.

Liberty Leading the People, allegory of the 1830 July revolution that deposed the French monarchy, with Marianne as the personification of liberty, contemporary painting by Eugène Delacroix.

First edition of the Napoleonic code, March 21, 1804

George Stephenson's "Rocket" steam engine

Everyday poverty in a laborer's cottage

The Civic Age

Criticism of authority and tradition on all levels grew with the rationalist and emancipatory ideas of the Enlightenment. The French Revolution of 1789 broke up the old order of the three estates and, with its motto of ❹ "Freedom, Equality, Brotherhood," laid the foundations for a new pan-European social order based on the principles of personal freedom and equality before the law. In the course of the 19th century, the middle class, often champions of liberalism, increasingly came to dominate public life.

Red "cap of liberty" and the motto: "Unity, indivisibility of the Republic, liberty, equality, brotherhood or death," French revolutionary poster, 1792

Path to the Political Emancipation of the Citizen

Napoleon ended the French Revolution with his coronation as ❻ emperor of France in 1804 and, through military conquest, set about reordering continental Europe according to his own vision. Although he was ultimately defeated at the Battle of Waterloo in 1815, and the other powers attempted to restore the pre-revolutionary conditions in the 1815 Congress of Vienna, Napoleonic rule left deep traces across Europe. The ideas spread by the revolution and the Napoleonic reforms that followed made a return to the old structures of rule impossible. With Napoleon's ❶ civil code, the areas of Europe he conquered experienced a civic law that

Emperor Napoleon, portrait by Jean-Auguste-Dominique Ingres

shaped the demands of later nationalist and liberal movements for constitutional protection of citizens' rights.

The tensions between the old ruling powers and bourgeois movements demanding a political voice eventually culminated in the European revolutions of 1848. The threat of civil disorder was initially successful in forcing through constitutional reform, but the movements lacked unity, and much was clawed back once order was restored. The 1848 revolutions nonetheless marked the entry of the middle class into the ranks of those seeking to preserve social order. The middle classes tried to imitate the ❺ lifestyle of the aristocracy. Bourgeois society and the workers would never again find themselves on the same side of the barricades.

Ball held at the Court of Vienna

Changes in Society and the Economy

At the beginning of the 19th century, industrialization, which had already begun in Great Britain in the 18th century, gathered pace in many parts of the European continent with inventions such as the ❷ steam engine. The implementation of new technologies created a rapid transformation of working and living conditions, often initially for the worse. With the emergence of a growing pool of undifferentiated "wage labor," a new stratum—the working class—was formed. The industrial workers lived in workers' quarters in the expanding cities marked by squalid conditions. As economic conditions in the countryside continued to deteriorate, rural workers lost their livelihood and moved into the cities to seek work. Many people also emigrated, particularly to America. They fled from ❸ poverty and the increasingly authoritarian backlash that followed the 1848 revolutions.

The emerging industrial labor force was often politicized and organi-

Karl Marx

Steel mill, painting by Adolph Menzel

Battle of Verdun, 1916

zed. The demands of the workers were often related to wages and hours, but in many places they also joined movements with demands including universal male suffrage and the relief of poverty. More systematic political ideologies, notably anarchism and socialism as expounded in the popular *Communist Manifesto* by ❼ Karl Marx and Friedrich Engels, vied for influence among the urban working class. By contrast, although many radical leaders had bourgeois origins, the middle class as a whole became increasingly conservative, identifying its interests with the preservation of property rights.

The expanding economies of the ❽ Industrial Revolution demanded access to new sources of raw materials and markets outside Europe. At the same time, the flood of labor to the cities and the lack of regulation contributed to appalling urban working and living conditions.

Nation-States and Imperialism

In addition to the Industrial Revolution, increasing nationalism—in the form of imperialism—became a major source of great power engagements outside Europe, especially in the later decades of the century. This made a decisive contribution to the outbreak of World War I. In the second half of the 19th century, nations increasingly linked their emerging identities with competition for world power. As well as bringing power and prestige to a nation, colonies were a source of valuable raw materials, markets for industrial goods and, in some cases, strategically vital naval bases. Influence in the world meant economic power. Furthermore, imperialism was underpinned by the presumptions of 19th century social science, which lent intellectual cover to imperialist ventures. At its simplest imperialism was perceived, or at least presented, in paternalistic terms. The self-image of British imperialism, for example, was that of the world's greatest empire nurturing the development of subject peoples around the globe until such time as they would be ready to govern themselves—although of course only Britain would be able to determine when this might be.

Once Tunisia had been occupied by France, and Egypt by Great Britain, at the beginning of the 1880s, the contest between the European powers for territories began. The United States, which made its own colonial acquisitions in the Pacific, accelerated US hegemony in Central and South America with the 1823 Monroe Doctrine. The Great Powers also included the new Italian state and the German empire. The overlapping of interests, particularly in what became known as the "scramble for Africa," led to open conflict. At the Berlin Congo conference of 1884, an agreement was reached as to the spheres of interest of the Great Powers in Africa, considerably reducing the costs of imperialism to the point where a carving-up became viable.

However the European powers also followed an alliance policy that anticipated the fault lines and

German cartoon: "German imperialism soars," the British lion prevents the German imperial eagle from flying

fronts of World War I. The first military conflict of the Great Powers after the Vienna Congress was the Crimean War of 1853–1856. Great Britain and France fought on the side of the Ottoman Empire against Russia in the Black Sea region. This strained relations between Austria and Russia, as the weak Austro-Hungarian Empire sought to remain neutral despite its alliance with Moscow. The expansionist drives of the Great Powers inevitably created conflicts. Great Britain and France had overlapping claims in Asia and Africa that threatened to turn into a major war. However, neither side could afford such a course, and the *Entente Cordiale* (French: "friendly understanding") of 1904 secured an alliance between Great Britain and France. ❿ Imperial Germany then sought to catch up with Britain and France by acquiring its own colonial empire, and this competition led to an ⓫ arms race. By the beginning of the ❾ First World War in 1914 the major powers were thus entangled in a complex web of alliances and a growing competition for colonial empire.

Cartoon on the naval arms race: "In the kitchen of the feet chef"

THE FRENCH REVOLUTION 1789–1799

The French Revolution had far-reaching consequences not only for France but for all of Europe as it challenged the fundamental institutions that shaped the political structure of Europe. It was an attempt to establish in common laws the equality of all persons regardless of their origin. The Revolution led by the bourgeoisie had as its goals the abolition of aristocratic rule, a constitution, and intellectual freedom. It stressed social mobility without class barriers ("Let ability win through!") and strove for a moral society, the nation, in which the common good took precedence over self-interests: "Liberty, Equality, Brotherhood!" Radicalism, however, along with outside pressure, transformed at times the rule of virtue into a despotism of its own kind.

The storming of the Bastille on July 14, 1789

2 Cockade in the colors of the Tricolore

■ Beginning of the Revolution

The internal crisis of the monarchy brought about the convening of the Estates General in 1789. At the same time, the destitute masses revolted in Paris.

In May 1789, King Louis XVI summoned together representatives of the three estates, aristocracy, clergy, and bourgeoisie, to bring France's catastrophic financial situation under control. The third estate, the bourgeoisie, composed 98 percent of the population and carried the tax burden but in fact had few rights. On June 20, 1789, to counter the attempt of the king and the aristocracy to dissolve the National Assembly, the members took the **4** "Tennis Court Oath" not to disband and announced their opposition. The king, how-

3 National Guard planting a liberty tree, gouache, ca. 1790

ever, installed an ultra conservative government, after which the people of Paris revolted and on July 14, 1789, stormed and destroyed the **1** Bastille—a prison and symbol of the power of the state. The Revolution had started.

Two days later the National Assembly forced the king to accept the revolutionary Tricolore in the **2** national colors blue-white-red as symbol of the "alliance of king and people." A revolutionary fervor spread throughout the country. On August 8, 1789, the rights of man were declared and every-

where **3** "liberty trees" were planted in celebration.

Freedom of the press made possible a flood of new newspapers and pamphlets. Diverse opinions and parties developed. The National Assembly carried out judicial and constitutional reforms and abolished the feudal system in France. The new system of census voting provoked a major confrontation because it allowed only the wealthiest taxpayers to take part in the political process. The poor and peasants, who had been involved in the events since the beginning, fought for universal suffrage.

At first, the monarchy was retained as the form of government. Most of the members of the Assembly, above all **5** the powerfully eloquent leader of the early revolutionary phase, Honoré Gabriel Riqueti Comte de Mirabeau, supported a constitutional monarchy based on the English model.

The National Assembly takes the Tennis Court Oath in Versailles on June 20, 1789

Declaration of Man and of the Citizen, 1789

"Men are born and remain free and equal in rights. Social distinctions can only be founded on communal utility."
(Article 1)

above: Declaration of Man and of the Citizen, 1789

5 Mirabeau during the session of the Estates General on June 23, 1789

| Jun 20, 1789 | "Tennis Court Oath" | Aug 26, 1789 | Declaration of Man and of the Citizen | Jul 14, 1790 | Celebration of the constitutional consecrati |
| Jul 14, 1789 | Start of the revolution with storming of the Bastille | Oct 5, 1789 | Bread March by the women of Paris | | |

■ Phase of Radicalization

Between 1791 and 1792 the Revolution became more radical when it faced massive resistance to its ideas in France and abroad. Some French provinces were in open revolt, and the revolutionary masses in Paris became even more active.

The Sans-culottes

The sans-culottes ("without kneebreeches") saw themselves as true revolutionaries. They rejected the wigs and kneebreeches of the aristocracy and were recruited from the ranks of wage-earners and urban proletariats who fought early on and in the foremost ranks. The journal that served as their voice was the "Père Duchesne" of the social revolutionary J.-R. Hébert.

Armed sans-culotte in uniform

6 Battle between the French Revolutionary Army and the Coalition Army in Valmy on September 20, 1792

The radicalization of the Revolution was triggered by the undiplomatic behavior of the king, as well as outside pressure. **7** Even after Louis XVI swore upon the constitution at the celebration of the inauguration of the constitution at Champ de Mars, he attempted unsuccessfully to block it. He fled from Paris in June 1791 with his family, but his flight was stopped near Varennes and the king was taken prisoner.

The radical parties of the Revolution demanded the abolition of the monarchy and the declaration of a French republic. In 1791, the majority of the nobility fled from France and as emigrants worked against the Revolution from abroad, seeking support from powerful parties throughout Europe. Internationally, fear of the revolutionary forces taking power in France grew. In February 1792 the emperor of Austria and the king of Prussia formed a pact against the Revolution.

The "Girondists" now became the leading party. They were political moderates but supported the war that began in April 1792.

The initial battles ended devastatingly for the Revolutionary Army. Only after the Austro-Prussian commanding general threatened Paris with conquest and destruction in July 1792 did a patriotic zeal seize the entire country. The *sans-culottes* controlled the events; **8** ten thousand French citizens armed themselves and marched off

to war. **6** 50,000 revolutionary soldiers defeated the allied troops near Valmy on September 20, 1792 and in November 1792 the Revolutionary Army marched into Belgium and Germany.

The revolutionary momentum was now directed against the king, who had been held in Temple since August 1792. After the discovery of his clandestine correspondence, he was sentenced to death as a "treasonable conspirator, rebel, and public enemy," and **9** guillotined publicly in Paris on January 21, 1793.

7 Louis XVI and Marie Antoinette swear upon the constitution

8 Arming of the people at the Hôtel des Invalides

9 Execution of Louis XVI on the Place de la Concorde in Paris

■ The Jacobins verses the Girondists

The issue of a war against the German Empire sparked a struggle for power between the pro-war Girondists and the anti-war Jacobins.

Jean-Paul Marat gives a speech

Since the middle of 1792, a struggle for control over the direction of the Revolution had been playing out between the moderate Girondists and the radical clubs of the Cordeliers and ❷ Jacobins — named after their meeting place in a monastery in the rue St. Jacob. The leaders of the Girondists were Jean-Pierre Brissot and the minister of the interior, Jean-Marie Roland. They argued for the war and the export of the Revolution to the rest of Europe. They particularly attempted to check the mob rule of the streets of Paris after the storming of the Tuileries Palace in August 1792. On the radical side stood tribunes of the people. Among these was the leftist social revolutionary Jacques René Hébert, mouthpiece of the sans-culotte movement, and also, notably, the "friend of the people," ❶ Jean-Paul Marat, a radical speaker who described himself as "the eye of the masses." These radicals created a fermenting, turbulent, and violent climate within the city, which was particularly apparent when the slaughter of the enemies of the Revolution in Sep-

tember 1792 ("September Massacres") was tolerated by Justice Minister Danton. In March 1793, the radicals succeeded in establishing the dreaded Revolutionary Tribunal. In summary trials, they proceeded with extreme severity against actual and supposed enemies of the Revolution. Concurrently, the war on the borders continued.

The arrest of Hébert, who was then freed by the people, and the charge against Marat by the Girondists, precipitated a conflict in which the Girondists were defeated by the Jacobins in June 1793. Shortly thereafter, the representatives of the Département Gironde were executed or forced to commit suicide. The reign of the Jacobins began and Marat, as the leader of the people, joined them. However, the "friend of the people" was violently stabbed to death in his bath on July 13, 1793, by the Girondist Charlotte Cor-

Jean-Paul Marat:

"500 or 600 chopped-off heads would have secured peace, liberty and happiness for you. A misunderstood humanitarianism made your arms lame and hindered you from administering the blows. It will cost the lives of millions of your brothers."

above: Portrait of Jean-Paul Marat

day d' Armont. The cult surrounding Marat, now the "Martyr of Liberty," became a weapon against all anti-revolutionaries. The revolts against the Jacobin reign, which first broke out in Vendée and in Lyon, led to bloody civil war in some provinces and ruthless verdicts from the victorious Jacobins throughout the whole country.

Club of Jacobins, January, 1792

Women in the Revolution

Women from all levels of society saw the Revolution as an opportunity for political participation. Manon Roland de la Platière, a member of the bourgeoisie and the wife of the Girondist minister of the interior, hosted a salon for supporters of the Revolution in Paris. From the start, for example during the storming of the Bastille, women were to be found in the front ranks of the revolutionary masses. They were ridiculed by their opponents as "soldiers in skirts" but played a significant role in the French Revolution, particularly in the sans-culotte movement.

above: Armed revolutionary
right: Manon Roland de la Platière

1792–93	Power struggle of Girondists and Jacobins	Jun 2, 1793	Girondists defeated	1793–94	Power struggle between Danton and Robespierre
Mar 1793	Revolutionary Tribunal established	Jul 13, 1793	Murder of Marat	Apr 5, 1794	Danton executed

■ The Reign of Terror

Jacobin rule culminated in the "Reign of Terror"; the dictatorship of Robespierre—who had eliminated his former comrades-in-arms—and the Committee of Public Safety. The rule of the Directory after the fall of Robespierre is seen as the end of the Revolution.

3
Georges Danton

4
Maximilien de Robespierre

5
Louis Antoine de Saint-Just

filled "Festival of the Supreme Being." The Terror raged for three months until it climaxed in a ❼ tumultuous scene in the National Convention on July 27, 1794. Robespierre and his comrades were overthrown and sent to the guillotine.

While Paris celebrated the end of the Reign of Terror, the Revolutionary Army pushed further into the German Rhineland and the Netherlands. The ruling "Directory," which was made up of former Jacobins supporting the president of the Convention, Paul Barras, did away with the Revolutionary Tribunals. In October 1795, ❽ General Bonaparte, a favorite

of Barras, put down an uprising against the Convention. From this point on, Napoleon Bonaparte increasingly strove for power. After the fall of the Directory in November 1799, he became, with the title of First Consul, sole ruler of France.

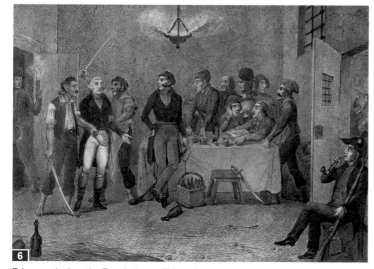

6
Prisoners before the Revolutionary Tribunal

7
The overthrow of Robespierre, July 27, 1794

Diverse currents existed within the Jacobin cause. At first there was a power struggle between ❸ Georges Danton, who wanted to stem the reign of mob violence, and ❹ Maximilien de Robespierre, who stood for a radical change in all social conditions. Robespierre, president of the Jacobin club since July 1793, prevailed. By execution he eliminated first the remaining radicals around Hébert in March 1794, and then, in April of the same year, the moderates around Danton. Robespierre

established the dictatorship of the Committee of Public Safety. This was dominated by a triumvirate of Robespierre, ❺ Louis Antoine de Saint-Just—the most radical mind of the Revolution— and the speaker of the Committee of Public Safety, Georges Couthon. This phase of the revolution is known as the Reign of Terror. Mass executions and ❻ Revolutionary Tribunal trials were on the agenda. In June 1794, Robespierre attempted to create a Cult of Reason in Paris with a pomp-

8
Napoleon puts down the Royalists' revolt against the Directory's constitution

| Apr 5, 1794 | Beginning of the "Reign of Terror" | May 25, 1795 | Revolutionary Tribunal abolished | Nov 9, 1799 | Napoleon becomes First Consul |
| Jul 27–28, 1794 | Overthrowing and execution of Robespierre | Aug 22, 1795 | Beginning of the ruling "Directory" | | |

NAPOLEONIC DOMINATION 1792–1814

Revolutionary France turned almost all of Europe against it. Between 1792 and 1806, it faced changing coalitions in four wars, and triumphed each time. Led by ❶ Napoleon, France gained dominion over the majority of Europe and brought its liberal ideas and laws to the occupied countries. But Napoleonic rule was ambivalent. It fostered civil emancipation, but suppressed opposition and national self-determination. This dictatorship cloaked as a democracy soon aroused the resistance of the occupied states. When France's string of victories reached an end in Russia in 1812, the other European powers also rebelled. The Battle of Waterloo in 1815 sealed Napoleon's fate. This was followed by a period of restoration, but the seeds of liberalism had been planted and began to germinate.

Napoleon Bonaparte Crossing the Alps, painting by Jacques Louis David, 1801

■ The French Revolutionary Wars and the First Napoleonic Wars

At first, France was merely defending itself against the shifting coalitions of European powers, but under Napoleon's leadership it soon sought domination over Europe.

Napoleon's Egyptian campaign, 1798

In the War of the First Coalition (1792–1797), the *levée en masse* ("general mobilization") and above all Napoleon's decisive action in the Italian campaign led to a French victory over the armies of Austria, Prussia, Great Britain, Spain, and the Netherlands.

Two years later, after his failed ❸ Egyptian campaign, Napoleon deposed the Directory with a coup d'état to place himself at the head of France. He defeated Austria in the War of the Second Coalition (1798–1802) at Marengo and forced an accommodation at Lu-

6 Battle of the Three Emperors

néville, bringing the left bank of the Rhine permanently into France.

In order to stem Napoleon's ambition and maintain a balance of powers in Europe, the British prime minister ❷ William Pitt the Younger continually forged new coalitions against France. In the War of the Third Coalition (the first of the Napoleonic Wars),

5 Continental Blockade: French soldiers search merchants in Leipzig for British goods, 1806

Admiral Nelson was able to destroy the French fleet at ❹ Trafalgar on October 21, 1805. This defeat caused France long-term losses in overseas trade. Nevertheless, Napoleon won the decisive ❻ Battle of the Three Emperors on December 2, 1805, at Austerlitz, ensuring the defeat of the Third Coalition, consisting of

Great Britain, Sweden, Austria, and Russia. On December 26, 1805, Napoleon dictated the Treaty of Pressburg and organized the founding of the Confederation of the Rhine that was to bring an end to the Holy Roman Empire. In a countermove against Great Britain, Napoleon also later imposed the economic ❺ blockade of the Continental System.

When Prussia demanded Napoleon's withdrawal from the region on the east side of the Rhine, the War of the Fourth Coalition broke out, which the French won in the battles at Jena and Auerstedt on October 14, 1806. Follo-

2 Cartoon: Napoleon and the British Prime Minister William Pitt the Younger carve up the world between them, 1805

4 The naval battle of Trafalgar, 1805

wing these battles they ❼ occupied Berlin and with the subsequent Treaty of Tilsit, Prussia was virtually divided into two.

7 Napoleon marches through the Brandenburg Gate in Berlin, October 27, 1806

| 1792–97 | War of the First Coalition | 1800 | Battle of Marengo | Oct 21, 1805 | Battle of Trafalgar | Dec 26, 1805 | Treaty of Pressburg |
| 1798–1802 | War of the Second Coalition | Feb 1801 | Treaty of Lunéville | Dec 2, 1805 | "Battle of the Three Emperors" at Austerlitz |

■ The Loss of Hegemony over Europe

In 1810 Napoleon stood at the height of his power and ruled Europe. The wars with Spain and Russia, however, caused his fall.

8

The Executions on Principe Pio Hill, executions of rebellious civilians by French soldiers in May 1808, painting by Francisco Goya, 1814

9

Napoleon watches Moscow burn, 1812, wood etching, 1879

Napoleon marched through Spain to Portugal, occupying Spanish cities and installing his brother Joseph Bonaparte as king, having inveigled the Spanish royal family to Bayonne and held them there. On the second of May, 1808, the people rebelled. The ❽ Spanish War of Independence was waged primarily as a guerrilla war and lasted five years, until the Spanish, aided by a powerful British army under the command of Arthur Wellesley, Duke of Wellington, and later victor over Napoleon, were able to expel the invaders at the end of 1813. This victory proved to other nations that resistance against French occupation could be successful. Austria's leading minister, Count Johann Philipp von Stadion, believed in 1809 that the time was ripe for a revolt against France, but Napoleon's ❿ victory at Wagram only caused Austria further loss of territory. The ⓫ Tyrolean uprising was part of the Austrian revolt that was quickly crushed after initial successes; its leader, Andreas Hofer, was shot in 1810 in Mantua. In order to bring peace to the French-Austrian front, Napoleon forced a marriage between himself and ❿ the emperor's daughter, Marie Louise.

In the same year, Russia refused to accept the Continental System aimed at isolating Great Britain, whereupon Napoleon invaded Russia in June 1812 with his Grande Armée of more than 600,000 soldiers, only about half of which were French. The French reached Moscow in September. The Russians retreated, leaving only "scorched earth" behind, thus minimizing French gains. This tactic proved truly effective only after the Battle of Borodino, one of the most merciless of the 19th century, the ❾ torching of Moscow, and the refusal of peace negotiations. Napoleon's army was suffering such privations that he was forced to retreat in the winter, losing most of his army. The myth of Napoleon's invincibility was gone.

> *Archduke Charles of Austria in his speech:*
> ## "To the German Nation," 1809:
> *"We fight for Germany, for independence and to restore the national honor that is our due. Germans, recognize your position! Take help where it is offered; contribute to your own saving; Be worth our respect! Only the German who forgets himself is our enemy."*

10 Marie Louise, daughter of the Austrian Emperor

11 Tyrolean freedom fighters led by Andreas Hofer

12 Battle of Wagram on July 5-6, 1809

Oct 14, 1806	Dual battles of Jena and Auerstedt	**1809**	Battle of Wagram	**1812**	Napoleon invades Austria
ca. 1806	Continental System imposed	Jul 1807	Treaty of Tilsit	1810	Tyrolean uprising	Sep 1812	Battle of Borodino

■ The Napoleonic Code

Napoleon's domination of Europe was founded not only on his success in war but also on his equally innovative—and restrictive—domestic policies.

In the same year as the ❶ coup d'état of November 1799, which led to the introduction of the Consulate, a new constitution, tailor-made for and approved by Napoleon, came into force. Napoleon had himself elected ❷ first consul and in 1802 secured the office for life. Two years later, he discarded the consulate entirely and had himself ❹ crowned emperor of the French in November 1804.

Napoleon determined to centralize power, reorganize the economy, and make a concordat with Pope Pius VIII, which recognized Catholicism as the religion of the majority of the French People but accepted the nationalization of

1 The Directory is dissolved in a coup d'état in 1799, contemporary depiction

sential civil rights. Enacted in 1804 and still in force today, Napoleon's ❸ *Code Civil* (the Napoleonic code) guarantees individual equality before the law, personal freedom, the right to property, and a regulated civil wedding as well as divorce.

Napoleon also reorganized the constitutions and civil laws of the territories he conquered in accordance with this code. Ironically, the rights and laws he himself introduced allowed resistance against the Napoleonic occupation to grow.

3 The *Code Civil*, 1804

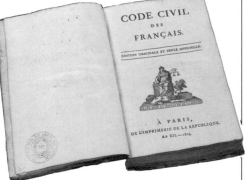

2 Napoleon and his co-consuls

Church property. He introduced civil service (with life-long job security); reformed the educational system, civic administration, and courts; and centralized the government while preserving es-

The Rise of Napoleon Bonaparte (1769–1821)

Born on August 15, 1769, in Ajaccio, Corsica, Napoleon was marked out early for a military career. He graduated as a lieutenant of artillery in 1785 and quickly rose through the ranks. He was promoted to brigadier general in 1793, after he had assumed command of an artillery brigade and recaptured Toulon from the English. In 1795 he crushed a royalist revolt in Paris and was rewarded with appointment as commander of the Army of the Interior. In 1796, he was given command of the army in Italy. His marriage to the aristocratic Joséphine de Beauharnais in 1796 gave Napoleon access to politically influential people.

The Consulate Constitution

The Constitution of 1799 was the fifth French constitution since the start of the French Revolution. It called for a Senate appointed by the first consul, a Tribunate, and the Corps Législatif. The three consuls were elected by the Senate for ten years. The legislative body, the heart of a democratic constitution, was subordinate to the first consul; it could vote only on bills presented to it. Only the first consul could propose new laws. The first consul also appointed all officials, judges, and officers.

4 Napoleon crowns Joséphine Empress of France in Notre Dame Cathedral following his own coronation, detail from painting by Jacques-Louis David, 1806–07

■ The Empire

Napoleon's domestic rule was characterized by repressive measures.

Human and political rights were often greatly restricted in the day-to-day politics of the Napoleonic consulate and empire. It was government not of the people but for the people, but even elementary liberties were suppressed. Napoleon's

7
Germaine de Staël, painting

8
Execution of the bookseller Johann Philipp Palm, 1806, chalk lithograph

❺ minister of police, Joseph Fouché, established a modern secret service. The right of assembly was limited; assemblies had little power in any case, and freedom of the speech and press were held in check by censorship. But perhaps most people preferred unity and the return of prosperity after so many years of disorder. The most prominent example was the expulsion of writer and publicist ❼ Germaine de Staël because of her criticism of Napoleon. The legal system was abused up to and including judicial murder, as was the case in the scandalous execution in 1804 of the Duke of Enghien. In Nuremberg, publisher ❽ Johann Philipp Palm was shot in 1806 for printing an anti-French pamphlet. Despite all this, Napoleon, who maintained that he wanted to save the Revolution and stand by its ideals, long continued to be supported by the French people even after he proclaimed the Empire.

5   Joseph Fouché

When Napoleon founded the ❾ Legion of Honor in 1802, he laid the cornerstone for a new social elite, who through their devotion to him would ensure his rule. Social standing, rank, or religion, however, played no role in admission. After being crowned emperor in 1804, Napoleon changed the Legion of Honor into an order of merit that is conferred to this day in France.

Artistic expression of this time

6   Napoleon's desk in Malmaison

is exemplified by the paintings of Jacques-Louis David and by the ❻, ❿ classical Empire style. Egyptian forms inspired architecture, interior design, and fashion all over Europe.

9
Napoleon awards the Cross of the Legion of Honor, painting by J.-B. Debret, 1812

The Murder of the Duke of Enghien

After a failed assassination attempt in 1803, Napoleon dealt with suspected royalist conspirators with uncompromising severity. He made an example of the Bourbon descendant Louis-Antoine-Henri, duke of Enghien (1772–1804), who was living in exile in Germany. Napoleon had the young duke illegally dragged from his castle in Baden and placed before a military court. No evidence was presented, but a guilty verdict was passed. On March 21, 1804, Enghien was shot in Vincennes near Paris.

The Duke of Enghien, lithograph, ca. 1830

10
Empress Josephine's chamber in the imperial residence of Malmaison, near Paris

■ The Dissolution of the Holy Roman Empire

One result of the wars against Napoleon was the end of the Holy Roman Empire. Many Catholic lands and estates in Germany were secularized, and independent regions were assigned to other territories. Austria was also weakened.

View over Lunéville, lithograph, 19th century

Ruins of the Cistercian Abbey of Heisterbach in the German Rhineland, destroyed during the secularization, painting by Steuerwaldt, 1863

Early industrial zone in Westphalia, early 19th c.

In February 1803 the Imperial Diet of the Holy Roman Empire met in ❹ Regensburg for the last time. The result was a political and legal reorganization that was summarized in the "Diet's Recess." The German princes who had lost territories west of the Rhine in the Treaty of ❷ Lunéville in 1801 were compensated. Most of the Catholic estates were confiscated and secularized. The independence of the 41 free territories of the empire was decreased, their subordination coming under the emperor's direct authority. In this way, the territories directly subordinate to the empire dropped from 1000 to about 30. All of the free imperial cities lost their exceptional status except Bremen, Hamburg, Lbeck, Augsburg, Nuremberg, and Frankfurt. This was the end of the Holy Roman Empire after so many centuries. It was incompatible with the new Napoleonic empire and threatened his own ambitions for a world empire.

Of the property of the Catholic Church, a total of four archdioceses, 18 dioceses, and about 300 monasteries, ❶ convents, and abbeys were secularized—the most significant reduction of Church property and influence since the Reformation. Those profiting most from this were primarily the rising middle class and the sovereign princes. Merchants and factory owners were able to acquire property easily and cheaply. In this respect, the reorganization benefited the nascent process of ❸ industrialization. In foreign affairs, the Diet's Recess achieved not only France's intentions but also those of Russia, who had an interest in weakening the Habsburg Austrian Empire. Prussia now equaled Austria's influence in thc German territories, and the influence and autonomy of the smaller states increased without the loss of their independence to France.

Reforms in Bavaria

The Imperial Diet's Recess presented the German states with numerous possibilities for political reform. One example was the policies of the statesman Earl Maximilian of Montgelas. He obtained a significant expansion of Bavaria and modernized the country. He centralized the administration and made every effort to integrate the new territories into old Bavaria through an "awareness of the Bavarian state." Unified regional courts were created, a religious edict guaranteed the equality of the Protestants, compulsory education was introduced, the privileges of the nobility were abolished, and a liberal penal code was created. Although the constitution, drawn up by Montgelas in 1808, provided for general political equality, Bavaria remained a conservative absolute monarchy.

Earl Maximilian of Montgelas

Imperial hall in the Regensburg Town Hall where the Imperial Diet met

■ The Confederation of the Rhine

The union of 16 German states in the Confederation of the Rhine signified the end and breakup of the Holy Roman Empire, leading Emperor Francis II to abdicate.

Following the Battle of Austerlitz and the resulting Treaty of Pressburg of December 26, 1805, Austria's position was further undermined. Prussia had remained neutral, and in 1806 Bavaria and ❺ Württemberg, now allies of France, were upgraded to ❻ kingdoms. Napoleon compelled 16 southern and western German states to form the Confederation of the Rhine on July 12, 1806, which then declared its members sovereign and separate from the Holy Roman Empire. To finish this process of disintegration, Napoleon coerced Francis II into relinquishing the title of Holy Roman emperor. He would now be merely emperor of Austria. In 1809, the Peace of Vienna reduced the extent of Austrian territory even further. Following Napoleon's marriage to the archduchess Marie Louise, Austria briefly became an ally of Napoleon until she joined the Grande Alliance, which wrecked Napoleon's power at Leipzig in 1814. On August 6, 1806, the Holy Roman emperor abdicated without a successor, and the Holy Roman Empire that

5

Napoleon I visits King Frederick of Württemberg in Stuttgart, 1806, wood engraving, early 20th century

6

"Napoleon bakes kings," English caricature, 1806

7

Treaty of Tilsit: Napoleon, Czar Alexander I, and Frederick Wilhelm II

had existed for more than 800 years was history.

Prussia was also affected by the process of disintegration once Bonaparte became arbiter of the distribution of Europe after his

victory at Austerlitz. After the battles of Jena-Auerstedt, ❽ Eylau, and Friedland, followed by the ❼ Treaties of Tilsit in 1807, Prussia lost all of its territories west of the Elbe. The remaining territories that had previously belonged to the Holy Roman Empire became the Confederation of the Rhine, as part of the Kingdom of Westphalia under King Jerome Bonaparte and Grand Duchy of Berg. The central and northern German states then merged, so the majority of Germany was now controlled by the French. The people did not reject Napoleonic domination because the reforms introduced on the model of the French Revolution created

Emperor Francis II, abdication speech, 1806

"We, Francis the Second, by God's grace chosen as Roman Emperor at all times increasing prestige of the Empire, hereditary empire of Austria… King of Germania, Hungary, Bohemia, Croatia, Dalmationa, Slavonia, Galicia, Lodomeria, and Gerusalem, Hereditary King of Austria… proclaim… that we see the empire's main office and honor through the collation of the confederal Rhenian states as erased and are freed from all duties against the German Empire, and hereby humbly lay down the Emperor's crown and the government of the empire."

above: Francis II, Holy Roman Emperor who became Francis I, Emperor of Austria

much new freedom in trade and the economy.

The reapportionment of Germany and the dissolution of the Holy Roman Empire through the Diet's Recess opened the way for many German territories to proceed with urgently needed political and legal modernization and economic industrialization.

8

Third Coalition War, Battle of Eylau, February 7–8, 1807

1

Napoleon during his exile on the Island of Elba

■ The Napoleonic Wars

From 1813 to 1815 the European powers fought against Napoleon, finally liberated Europe from French rule, and re-established independent nations.

Napoleon's defeat in Russia in 1812 triggered the wars of liberation in Europe. ❷ General Graf Yorck von Wartenburg, who had led Napoleon's Prussian troops, changed sides and secured Russia's neutrality in the ❹ Convention of Tauroggen. A little later, in February 1813, the Russian–Prussian alliance was sealed in Kalisz. Thereupon Prussia immediately started mobilizing its state militia, supported by the territorial reserve and the ❺ volunteer corps. King Frederick William III hesitated, but on March 27, 1813, he officially declared war on France. He encouraged his fellow countrymen with the stirring appeal "*An Mein Volk*" ("To my people"). Although the wars of liberation were fought by regular troops, patriotic poets such as Theodor Körner declared them wars of the German people against foreign rule. By fostering a nascent nationalism he called citizens to arms.

At this time, the Order of the ❸ Iron Cross, which survives to this day as the signet of the German armed forces, was instituted.

The Prussian forces were joined by Austria in August and Bavaria in October and the allied armies of Austria, Prussia, and Russia won a decisive victory over Napoleon in the Battle of Nations, so called due to the number of soldiers and nations involved, at Leipzig on October 16–19, 1813. Napoleon was forced to withdraw across the Rhine. The Confederation of the Rhine thereupon joined the coalition, which marched into France and in March 1814 occupied Paris. Napoleon was forced to abdicate and went into ❶ exile on the island of Elba. The ensuing Treaty of Paris reduced France to its previous borders of 1792 and restored the Bourbons to power, giving the throne to Louis XVIII.

3   "Iron Cross" medal

2

General Graf Yorck von Wartenburg

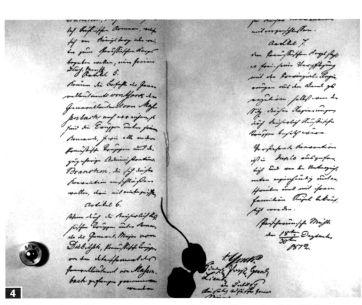

4

The Convention of Tauroggen document, signed on December 30, 1812

The Battle of Nations at Leipzig

The Battle of Nations at Leipzig was probably the largest battle of history before World War I and broke Napoleon's hold on Europe. The main engagement took place, after various indecisive skirmishes, on October 18, 1813, when the Württemberg and Saxon troops joined the allies. Contemporary reports tell of the great suffering of the vast numbers of wounded, for whom there was not adequate care. Approximately 100,000 soldiers died.

The Battle of Nations at Leipzig

5

The volunteer corps, the "Black Troops," follow Major Lützow into battle

Dec 30, 1812	The Convention of Tauroggen	Mar 27, 1813	Declaration of war against France	Mar 31, 1814	Occupation of Paris
Feb 1813	Treaty of Kalisz	Oct 16–19, 1813	Battle of Nations at Leipzig	Apr 6, 1814	Napoleon's abdication

■ The Congress of Vienna

Napoleon returned to power once more in 1815, but was finally defeated for good at Waterloo. Following the Napoleonic wars, the Congress of Vienna, presided over by the Austrian Prince von Metternich, sought to reestablish a new order in Europe.

6
Field Marshal von Blücher and the Duke of Wellington greet one another at Waterloo

Napoleon was not willing to resign himself to exile. He fled Elba, landed near Cannes in March 1815, raised troops, and again seized power in Paris with his army—but for only a short time, the "Hundred Days." The allies swiftly responded to Napoleon's return. They confronted him in Belgium and defeated him a final time under the leadership of ❻ Field Marshal von Blücher and the Duke of Wellington in the ❽ Battle of Waterloo on June 18. Napoleon was exiled permanently to St. Helena, where he died on May 5, 1821. King Louis

XVIII, who had fled during the Hundred Days, returned. By a second Treaty of Paris, France was forced to make reparations and accept further loss of territory.

The ❿ Congress of Vienna had been in session since September 1814 with the goal of territorially reorganizing Europe and establishing a balance of powers. With the exception of the Ottoman Empire, the ❼ leading statesmen of all European nations were participating. The negotiations were dominated by Prince Klemens von Metternich, the Austrian chancellor and chairman of the congress; Prussian chancellor Karl August von Hardenberg; the British foreign minister, Viscount Castlereagh; Czar Alexander I; and the French representative, ❾ Charles-Maurice de Talleyrand-Périgord, who was able to ensure that his country had a say in the matters. Ho-

wever, France was forced to relinquish territories it had seized. In addition, the Kingdom of the Netherlands was founded, Switzerland was recognized as an independent and neutral state, and Russia, Prussia, and Austria were able to increase their territories. Italy remained divided into individual states. This concord was so successful that Europe enjoyed almost 40 years of peace.

A component of the Congress of Vienna was the Confederation Act, signed by 41 German states on June 9, 1815. A German confederation, in which Prussia and Austria assumed leadership, took the place of the Holy Roman Empire, which was dissolved in 1806.

Wilhelm Freiherr von Humboldt on the Congress of Vienna:

The business however is not going well ... Generally this is because the people that are the main negotiators, are, each for particular reasons, not suited to the business. So everyone goes his own way or at least tries to and the great linking power or reason is often searched for in vain.

7 Metternich, Castlereagh, and Hardenberg

8
The defeat of Napoleon's troops at the Battle of Waterloo on June 18, 1815

9
Charles Maurice de Talleyrand-Périgord

10
Proceedings at the Congress of Vienna

top: Wilhelm Freiherr von Humboldt
above: Caricature of the Congress of Vienna

May 30, 1814	First Treaty of Paris	**Mar 1815**	Napoleon in Cannes	**Jun 18, 1815**	Battle of Waterloo
Sep 1814–Jun 1815	Congress of Vienna	**Jun 9, 1815**	Signing of the Confederation Act	**May 5, 1821**	Napoleon's death in St. Helena

THE INDUSTRIAL REVOLUTION BEGINS IN EUROPE CA. 1750–1848

The most momentous change experienced by Europe in the 19th century was the Industrial Revolution. What started merely as an important ❶ technological innovation led ultimately to a huge social transformation. After the Congress of Vienna, the European powers sought a restoration of the political and social structures of the pre-Napoleonic Era. However, the Metternich System, the fundamental principle of politics in Europe, soon failed. A liberal Western Europe found itself standing opposite a conservative Central and Eastern Europe. Despite many suppressive measures, democratic movements arose throughout Europe. These culminated in the revolutions of 1848.

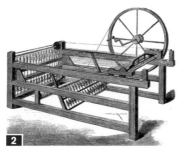
Painting of the steam hammer by its inventor James Nasmyth

■ New Working and Living Conditions

Industrialization spread to all of Europe in the course of the 19th century and destroyed the remains of the old social and cultural order.

The Industrial Revolution is the name by which the huge social, economic, and technological shift that transformed Europe from an agrarian to an industrial

Adam Smith, *The Wealth of Nations*, writing about the interests of the individual businessman

Whoever offers to another a bargain of any kind, proposes to do this. Give me that which I want, and you shall have this which you want. . . We address ourselves, not to their humanity but to their self-love, and never talk to them of our own necessities but of their advantages.

above: The Scottish moral philosopher and political economist Adam Smith

A "Spinning Jenny," the first multi-spool spinning wheel invented by James Hargreaves, 1764

society is known. Feudalism was replaced by capitalism. This social change took place over the course of the 19th century, gradually spreading from west to east. It took place particularly early in England, where the supply of raw materials imported from all over the empire favored the process.

A flood of technological innovations had arisen as a result of

The first all-purpose steam engine, designed by James Watt, 1765

the new scientific discoveries of the mid-18th century. The ❷ spinning machine, the mechanical loom, the puddling process for steelmaking, the steamship, and the threshing and reaping machines decidedly transformed the basis for many types of production. Thanks to ❸ James Watt's all-purpose ❹ steam engine, many things could be done faster, more cheaply, and with fewer mistakes.

In addition to this, a new organizational structure of the work process due to the division of labor in the factories emerged. As ❺ huge factories were in the hands of entrepreneurs with access to capital, mass production of goods—which became increasingly cheaper—was possible. The traditional restrictions set by the trade guilds were replaced by the open freedom of trade that guaranteed the industrialists independence from all regulations except those

The English inventor James Watt

of the marketplace. According to economic liberalism, as formulated by economist Adam Smith, the egoism of the individual, guided "as if by an invisible hand," would provide a model for growth. This was cut short, however, as the beginning of World War I consumed the resources of Europe.

Borsig's manufacturing plant near Berlin, 1847

| 1764 | Spinning machine invented | 1785 | Beginning of the Industrial Revolution | 1796 | First blast furnace in Germany |
| 1765 | Steam engine invented | 1786 | First factory in Manchester | 1822 | Invention of first mechanical loom |

◼ The Consequences of Progress

The negative aspects of economic growth soon came to light. The "social question" was a major political problem that extended well beyond the 19th century.

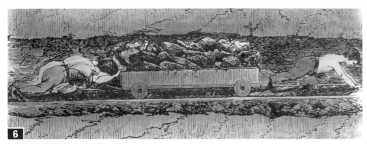

6 Child labor in an English coal mine

7 The emblem of the "German Metalworkers Association," a trade union

New transport possibilities such as the ❾ railroads extended accessible markets beyond national boundaries, and pressure from competition increased. Factories were constantly forced to lower their production costs. The profit margins shrank, resulting in lower wages and longer working hours. The use of cheaper ❻ child labor increased dramatically. Workers ❿ sank into more desperate poverty, while the industrialists and property owners benefited from the economic growth. The gulf between the social classes became ever wider. This led, for example, to the ⓫ "Weavers' Revolt" of 1844, during which 3,000 Silesian weavers stormed the textile factories.

Another problem was the migration of huge segments of the population to the cities. Through "enclosure," by which land held in common could be fenced in by big landowners for their private use, many small farmers became impoverished and were forced to move to the city. This affected millions of people all over Europe, who then had to fight for their survival as laborers, uneducated and with no rights. They formed an "industrial reserve army" and competed against each other for work, no matter how low the wage or how extreme the conditions. To counteract this desperate situation, the labor movement developed. ❼ ❽ Trade unions, associations, and political parties were organized to create a legal basis to fight for legislation that would regulate the "Manchester School" of laissez-faire liberalism. The craftsmen and industrial laborers who participated in the liberal revolutions of the 19th century, particularly those of 1848, were for the most part socialists. Social policy became one of the important topics of domestic politics in all industrialized nations, forming the basis for political parties.

8 Flag of the cigar makers trade union in Berlin, 1858

Karl Marx

Karl Marx, philosopher and economist

Karl Marx was born in 1818 in Trier, Germany. He was chief editor of the liberal newspaper Rheinische Zeitung, *which was banned in 1843. In Paris in 1844 he met Heinrich Heine, Pierre-Joseph Proudhon, Mikhail Bakunin, and Friedrich Engels, with whom he would work for the rest of his life. Marx and Engels collaborated on* The Communist Manifesto, *undoubtedly the most influential book of the workers' movement, published in 1848. After the revolutions of 1848, Marx was forced to emigrate to London, where he stayed until his death. He wrote many papers, including the program for the first International Workingmen's Association. The first volume of his* Das Kapital *was published in 1867. Marx was certainly the most well-known and significant person of the socialist movement and probably its most brilliant mind.*

9 Passenger train on the first route in England

10 Cottage industry in a basement flat, Berlin

11 The "Weavers' Revolt" in Silesia, 1844

1830	Opening of first railroad line	**1837**	First Morse telegram sent	**1848**	*The Communist Manifesto* published
1834	Founding of the German Tariff Union	**1844**	Weavers' Revolt	**1867**	*Das Kapital* by Karl Marx

■ Restoration and Revolution in Europe 1815–1830

Metternich bound almost all the European states into a "Holy Alliance" that was meant to ensure the restoration of the old political order.

Austria's foreign minister and later chancellor, Prince von Metternich pursued the restoration of an authoritarian, monarchical state order in Europe and hereby the retraction of the civic freedoms won since 1789. His "system" was recorded in the 65 articles of the Confederation Act of 1815. This supplemented the final communiqué of Vienna, which the ❷ Diet of the German Confe-

Congregation of the Congress of Vienna, colored etching, 1815

deration ratified in Frankfurt on July 20, 1820, as the Basic Law of the German Confederation. The restoration strategy expressed therein was endorsed by the conservative powers of Central and Eastern Europe—the ❸ Holy Alliance of Austria, Prussia, and Russia. On September 26, 1815, at the ❶ Vienna congress, the treaty was signed by ❹ Czar Alexander I of Russia, Emperor Francis I of Austria, and King Frederick William III of Prussia. All of the Euro-

pean states—with the exceptions of Great Britain, the Vatican, and the Ottoman Empire—later joined this alliance.

After the murder of the poet August von Kotzebue (1761–1819), who had ridiculed the nationalist fraternities, Mettenich issued the Carlsbad Decrees. These stipulated censorship of the press and banned fraternities. The fight against Metternich's "repressive" politics welded together liberal and nationalist forces and drove them to ally with progressive forces, particularly in France.

The German Confederation: assembly of the diet in Frankfurt, color drawing, 1816

Depiction of the Holy Alliance, showing the heads of state of its members: Russia, Austria, and Prussia

Prince von Metternich

Klemens Wenzel von Metternich (1773–1859) fled from the French occupation of the Rhineland at the age of 21. He settled in Vienna, where he soon began a successful career in foreign affairs. He was a decisive participant in the organization of the wars of liberation and became a lea-

ding figure at the Congress of Vienna in 1814–15. There he worked for the creation of a balance of powers in Europe by means of the "Metternich System." This was intended to avoid new wars and, at the same time, provide for the restoration of the pre-revolutionary social order. The German Confederation and the Holy Alliance, as well as the Carlsbad Decrees, served these purposes. Later he lost influence and was driven from office in 1848

at the beginning of the March Revolution in Vienna. However, he continued to seek a voice in domestic and foreign affairs.

top: Klemens Wenzel von Metternich
below: Caricature of the Carlsbad Decrees entitled "The spirit of our age"

The Holy Alliance, 1814: Emperor Francis II receives Czar Alexander I and King Frederick William III in Vienna

The Failed Policies of the Congress and the Growing Liberal Movement

With the Quadruple Alliance, Metternich organized an alliance of great powers that, it was thought, would establish a balance of interests. This was unsuccessful in the long run, however. France was soon forced to revise its domestic Restoration policies.

At Metternich's prompting, Austria, Prussia, Russia, and Great Britain—the Quadruple Alliance—met at various conferences to balance their interests and claims in order to secure the restoration. In 1820 a right of intervention against national and international liberal movements—an extremely conservative policy—was passed, contrary to the desires of Great Britain, which was increasingly supporting liberalism in Europe.

The Quadruple Alliance, as well as the Holy Alliance, finally shattered as a result of the differing attitudes toward, among other things, the ❻ Greek struggle for independence from the Ottoman Empire. Great Britain, France, and Russia intervened in favor of the Greeks, while Prussia and Austria stayed out of it, having no interest in weakening the Ottoman Empire. In the ❼ naval Battle of Navarino in 1827, the British destroyed the Turkish fleet and made Greek sovereignty possible in 1829.

Louis XVIII, the brother of king Louis XVI who was executed in 1793, came to the throne after the

❺ Frederick Ludwig Jahn

fall of Napoleon. The Bourbons—who favored the restoration of absolutism—were once again rulers of France. Initially Louis XVIII attempted to heal the country through a policy of reconciliation, but after 1815 came increasingly under the influence of his reactionary brother, the count of Artois, who succeeded him in 1824 as Charles X and sought to reestablish the absolutist rule of the king. This lasted only until 1830, however, when the ❽ July Revolution, a rebellion of the Parisian population, forced the abdication of ❾ King Charles X, on August 2.

This success imbued the democratic movement in the whole of Europe with the confidence that a liberal constitution could be implemented in each country. Although liberal and nationalistic politicians and intellectuals, such as the

writer Ernst Moritz Arndt and ❺ Frederick Ludwig Jahn, were persecuted, the Restoration was not able to suppress the spreading aspiration for democratic freedom and national unity, the repealing of all censorship measures, and the granting of a political voice for a self-confident and increasingly educated middle-class. These aspirations paved the way for the Europe-wide revolutions of 1848, and were the reason for the failure of the Restoration movement in Europe.

❻ The Greek struggle for independence 1821–1829

❼ The naval battle of Navarino

❽ The 1830 July Revolution in Paris

Liberalism

David Ricardo, English economist and banker

In response to the conservatism of the European governments the liberalism of the middle classes strengthened. Based on the principles of the Enlightenment, political liberalism holds the freedom of the individual to be the central principle for a just government, and rejects the idea of a government that demands a subservient mentality and enslavement to authority from its citizens. The rule of law and civil rights are guaranteed through the principle of a balance of powers between legislative, executive, and judiciary officials. Economic liberalism—as represented by, for example, Adam Smith and David Ricardo—favors absolute free trade and rejects both customs barriers and the intervention of the state in the economy, even when done in the interest of the greater social good.

❾ Charles's X embarcation to England on August 15, 1830 after the July Revolution

Jul 20, 1820 Confederation Act becomes basic law of the German Confederation		**1830** July Revolution in Paris
1819 Carlsbad Decrees ban duelling societies	**1827** Battle of Navarino	**Aug 2, 1830** Charles X abdicates

■ The 1848 Revolutions in Europe

It was from France, with the "February Revolution" of 1848, that the impetus for a liberal uprising emanated. The movement affected all of Europe, except for Great Britain and Russia.

When the "banquet campaign," a series of radical political meetings, was forbidden in February 1848, ❸ street fighting broke out between the army and the opposition in the streets of Paris. It culminated in the ❺ storming of the Palais Royal and the forced abdication and flight of Louis Philippe, the "Citizen King." The Second Republic was declared and a provisional government set up under ❶ Alphonse de Lamartine. The Second Republic was dominated by liberals and moderate socialists. The general right to work and universal male suffrage were proclaimed. When he was ousted and the new conservative National Assembly closed the national workshops for the unemployed, which had only just been opened, the ❹ first socialist uprising in Europe broke out in June 1848 and was brutally put down by the government, which promptly established a military dictator-

1

Alphonse de Lamartine

ship. In December 1848 the majority of French voters, hoping for security and order, elected Louis Napoleon, the nephew of Napoleon Bonaparte, to be the new president of the republic. Within three years he had established himself as a dictator through a coup d'état, and at the end of 1852 had himself crowned Emperor Napoleon III. Both in his policies and in his manner he consciously sought to echo his famous uncle. This attempt proved futile and failed to bring the popularity and approval that he desperately sought.

In Vienna, uprisings of workers and students forced the government to abolish the census in March 1848, to enlarge the electoral franchise in the constitution, and to dismiss Chancellor Metternich, who subsequently fled. Within the multinational state of Austria, as liberals fought over their ideals, the non-German nationalities

pushed for independence. The Czechs rebelled against the Habsburgs in the Pentecostal Uprising of Prague. The Hungarian nobility also pushed their claim for autonomy. When ❷ Lajos Kossuth called for an insurrection and proclaimed a Hungarian government in March 1848, the Austrian government agreed to a new parliamentary constitution. A year later, Hungary declared independence under Kossuth but was defeated and dissolved by the Austrians with Russian assistance. In March 1849 the new Emperor

2

Lajos Kossuth

Franz Joseph I imposed a constitution for Austria-Hungary that established a bicameral Parliament with a lower house elected by wealthy property owners.

3

Barricades in the streets of Paris during the February Revolution, 1848

4

Aftermath of a workers' riot in Paris, June 1848

5

Parisian crowd storms the Palais Royale

■ Uprisings in Italy and the March Revolution in Germany

In Italy and Germany, national unification was at the center of revolutionary demands. While the ⓫ uprisings in Italy were suppressed by the authorities, the ❻ March Revolution in Germany led to the first democratic constitutional convention—but this failed to realize its aims.

In Italy the revolutionary movement strove not only for democratic reforms but also for the creation of an Italian national state in a country which did not yet have a very strong national consciousness. As early as January 1848, riots in the Two Sicilies forced ❼ King Ferdinand II to allow a constitution. Later, however, "King Bomba," as Ferdinand was known, shelled the Sicilian towns in order to suppress the rebellion. Elsewhere in Italy, the struggle against Austrian occupation failed, and the revolts of November 1848 in Rome were crushed by French and Austrian troops at the

❻
Crowds waving the German colors during street fighting in Berlin, 1848

❼
Ferdinand II, king of the Two Sicilies, portrait, 19th century

request of Pope Pius IX.

In the German states the February Revolution in Paris had also inspired revolutionary forces. The populace, particularly in the southwest of the country, began demanding democratic rights, in response to which many of the smaller states established middle-class liberal "March ministries." The Prussian king Frederick William IV decided to make liberal concessions. As he was announcing these to a crowd of people in front of the Berlin Palace, his guards opened fire. This led to heavy ❿ street fighting in which 300 people died. Frederick William honored those ❽ who fell in March by riding through the city wearing a sash in black, red, and gold—the colors of the democratic movement. However, the identification of the government

with the people did not last long: The new liberal ministry was replaced by a conservative one in November 1848. The ❾ German National Assembly met in Frankfurt in May 1848 and drew up a liberal constitution for a united Germany. Their work was dismissed contemptuously by the Prussian king, confirming the total failure of the 1848 revolution, and with it the liberal democratic path to German unification. Instead it would have to rely on the force of Prussian arms and the leadership of Chancellor Bismarck.

❽
Funeral of those killed during March 1848 in Berlin

❾
German National Assembly meets in St. Paul's Church in Frankfurt on May 18, 1848

❿
Manning the barricades in Berlin during street fighting on March 18–19, 1848

⓫
Suppression of riots in the city of Naples, 1848

Reasons for the Failure of the 1848 Revolution

Many of the demands of the revolutionaries of 1848 were satisfied over the two decades that followed, but in the immediate aftermath all agreed that the Europe-wide protests had been in vain. The disunity of the participants themselves is perhaps the most important reason for this failure. Idealistic and possessed of a wide variety of aims, from democracy and national self-determination to cheaper bread, there was never any real coherence to their program. The revolutionaries also underestimated the resolve and ruthlessness of their governments, which violently suppressed the crowds while also successfully dividing them with concessions.

Riots by the Charles V bridge in Prague, 1848

May 18, 1848 | German National Assembly meets	**Nov 1848** | Insurrection in Rome crushed	**Dec 1852** | Louis Napoleon crowned Emperor
Jun 1848 | Workers' uprising in Paris	**Dec 1848** | Louis Napoleon elected president of France	

German States: The Reshaping of Austria and Prussia 1815–1871

1

Berlin Concert Hall, built in 1818 on the Gendarmenmarkt, designed by Karl Friedrich Schinkel

After the Congress of Vienna, Austria sought to exert its influence throughout Europe: Metternich's policy of restoring the pre-revolutionary order decisively shaped European politics and made it possible for the Habsburgs to avoid giving way to demands for reform. The situation in ❶ Prussia was different; the humiliating defeat at the hands of Napoleon led to sweeping reforms of the military and bureaucracy aimed at strengthening the state. Therefore the largest German nations developed very differently and eventually became rivals. This explains why Bismarck was able to unify Germany in the 1860s without Austrian support but with the widespread acceptance of the people.

■ Austria: Weakness and Internal Stagnation

The conservative Metternich system sought stability in Europe but left the Austrian empire itself lagging behind the more modern European states.

With the onset of ❹ industrialization, the increasingly self-confident middle classes in Europe demanded participation in the political process, while the social protest movements called for relief from poverty and deprivation. But ❷ Metternich's restoration policy, which sought to build up a conservative consensus throughout Europe after the revolutionary wars of Napoleon Bonaparte, stifled any socio-political liberalization. However, mere repression was not sufficient to hold back popular demands for reform, but Metternich was not far-sighted enough to see that other approaches had to be sought. In 1835 he was confronted

2

Prince Klemens Wenzel von Metternich

by a rival, Minister of State Franz von Kolowrat-Liebsteinsky, who was able to reduce Metternich's influence without implementing the reform policies he had intended, which were blocked by the

intensely conservative bureaucracy.

The ❸ multiethnic nature of the Austrian state made it vulnerable to the rise of conflicting nationalisms. In the 1830s, the Pan-Slavic movement emerged in the Slavic states ruled by the Habsburgs. It asserted the ethnic identity of the Slavs and demanded more influence for them in the empire. In Hungary nationalist sentiment grew after 1815 and independence movements emerged.

"Austro-Slavism"

The Slavic nationalist movement that developed out of Pan-Slavism in the 19th century, especially in the Austrian Empire, was called "Austro-Slavism." The Czechs in particular wanted to be recognized as equal to the Germans and Hungarians within the multinational state.

Historian Frantisek Palacky led the first Slavic Congress in March 1848 in Prague and was later a member of the Austrian upper chamber and the Bohemian provincial parliament.

Frantisek Palacky

He promoted Czech national identity through his Journal of the Bohemian Museum and the papers he wrote on Bohemian history. Palacky is considered the father of modern Czech nationalism.

above: Separation of the German Bohemians from the Czech population in Prague during the revolution of 1848

3

Clash of the Czech demonstrators and Imperial troops in Prague on June 12, 1848

4

The Austrian southern railway from Vienna to Baden, watercolor, 1847

1809 | Grammar schools established across Prussia

1813 | Military school founded in Berlin

1807 | Prussian Reform Edict

1810 | Friedrich Wilhelm University founded in Berlin

■ The Prussian Reforms

The Prussian elite reacted to defeat at the hands of Napoleon at Jena and Auerstedt in 1806 with a program of reforms that transformed the absolutist monarchy into a modern bureaucratic state.

5

Count Neithardt von Gneisenau

During the Napoleonic Wars, Prussia's weaknesses had been exposed, and comprehensive reforms were considered necessary. Generals ❺ von Gneisenau and von Scharnhorst began by restructuring the Prussian army. Through reducing the length of military service, they quickly created a conscript army with about 150,000 reservists, and those outside the aristocracy were given the chance to become career offi-

cers. Corporal punishment was abolished. In 1813 compulsory military service was introduced and a general military school, later directed by the famous military strategist ❻ Karl von Clausewitz, was established in Berlin.

❼ Baron vom und zum Stein and his successor Prince von Hardenberg reformed the outdated state administration along similar lines. They reorganized the governmental departments and gave greater autonomy to the individual municipalities. The ❽ Prussian Reform Edict of 1807 abolished serfdom and strengthened property rights. Restrictions on

7 The reformers Scharnhorst, Hardenberg, and Baron vom und zum Stein

movement and employment were repealed, the power of the guilds was broken, and laws discriminating against the Jews were abolished. In order to train the personnel needed for the state administration, Minister of Education Wilhelm von Humboldt reorganized the Prussian education system and created a model admired and copied across Europe. The state supervised the entire system, providing each child with a general education that emphasized patriotism and duty to the state. From 1809, grammar schools and other educational institutions were established nationwide, and in 1810 the ❾ Friedrich Wilhelm University (present-day Humboldt University) was founded in Berlin. The reorganization of land ownership and the priority attached to the development of the army created the foundation for Prussia's emergence as a major power that would dominate Germany.

6

Karl von Clausewitz

Baron von Humboldt

After serving as Prussian minister of education, Wilhelm von Humboldt (1767–1835) became ambassador to Austria in 1810 and so participated in the Congress of Vienna. After this he served as ambassador to Great Britain. In 1819 he left the state service and worked independently as a scholar. Humboldt dedicated himself primarily to philology, studying many languages, both living and dead, from Europe to East Asia. Alongside his translations of the classic works of antiquity, he published papers reflecting on political philosophy and developed his own theory of education.

above: Baron Wilhelm von Humboldt, lithograph, 1827

8 Prussian Reform Edict of 1807, part of the Stein-Hardenberg Reforms

Friedrich Wilhelm University, opened in 1810, located in the former palace of Prince Henry built by J. Boumann between 1748 and 1755, watercolor, 1860

1815	Congress of Vienna	**Mar 13, 1848**	Austrian Chancellor Metternich resigns
1813	Military conscription introduced in Prussia	**Mar 1848**	First Slavic Congress held in Prague

■ Restoration Policy of the German Confederation

After the Napoleonic Wars, Chancellor Metternich sought to build a conservative consensus in the German Confederation. The Carlsbad Decrees were introduced to discourage radicalism and dissent and, though much resented by liberal intellectuals, were effective in the short term.

The Thinkers Club, cartoon satirizing the restrictions placed on the freedom of speech and of the press by the Carlsbad Decrees

First page of the Confederation Act of June 8, 1815

On June 10, 1815, 37 sovereign German princes and four free cities signed the ❷ Confederation Act of 1815, by which—supplemented by the 65 articles of the final act of the Congress of Vienna of July 20, 1820—the constitution of the German Confederation was to be regulated. The confederation was considered the successor to the Holy Roman Empire, which had been dissolved in 1806.

All participating states remained independent and sent their representatives to the ❸ Diet, which met in Frankfurt and was chaired by the Austrian chancellor, Prince von Metternich. His goal was to align the foreign policies of the individual states and pursue policies favorable to Austria, which meant main-taining Austrian influence there. Under discussion was the shape of a new unified German Reich. The "lesser German solution" envisioned a German state without Austria and with Prussian supremacy. The "greater German solution" would have included Austria, but also the deep-seated rivalry between the two major powers Austria and Prussia.

In the failed March Revolution of 1848, German patriots were roused to open demonstration of their dissatisfaction with the existing state of affairs. This unrest alarmed many of the smaller German states, and forced them to concede liberal reform measures. In the aftermath, the German Confederation was temporarily abandoned. From this point on, until the Seven Weeks' War of 1866, the struggle between Prus-sia and Austria lay at the heart of German politics.

The German Confederation attempted to suppress the nationalist movements that were growing in strength in many German cities. The student fraternities, or "dueling societies," were considered to be hotbeds of violent radicalism, and they were therefore prohibited under the ❶ Carlsbad Decrees of 1819.

Meeting of the Diet in Frankfurt on the Main, 1815

Student fraternities

Johann Gottlieb Fichte

The student fraternities emerged out of the volunteer corps that had fought against Napoleon between 1812 and 1815. They adopted the colors of the Lützow Volunteers— black, red, and gold—as the "German colors." They borrowed the concepts of nationalism and liberty from Johann Gottlieb Fichte and Ernst Moritz Arndt, and they put forward demands for democratization during the Wartburg festival in 1817 and in their memorandum of 1818. In 1833, some of the members stormed the Frankfurt police station.

Students and workers storm the Frankfurt police station, 1833

| Jun 10, 1815 | Confederation Act passed | | 1819 | Carlsbad Decrees | | 1832 | Hambach Festival |
| 1817 | Wartburg Festival | | Jul 20, 1820 | Constitution of German Federation agreed | | 1833 | Storming of Frankfurt police station |

The German states prior to March 1848

German historians refer to the decades preceding the revolution of March 1848 as the "Pre-March" period, a time when radical agitation coexisted with apolitical escapism.

The suppression of revolutionaries and liberals alike took place, in accordance with the Carlsbad Resolutions, through censorship of the press and the appointment of a central investigation commission in Mainz, whose duty it was to spy on "revolutionary intrigues and demagogic associations." In addition, the universities were purged of suspect faculty members; the ❼ "Göttingen Seven," which included the Grimm brothers, were victims of this policy in 1837. The Carlsbad Decrees had been provoked by, among other instances of revolutionary fervor, the assassination of Kotzebue, the Russian State Counsellor, by a student in 1819. There followed disciplinary measures, arrests, and imprisonments, including that of the founder of the German gymnastics movement, ❻ Friedrich Ludwig Jahn. The 1830 July Revolution in France gave further impetus to liberal and nationalist groups.

The high point of the German unity and liberation movement came in May 1832 at the ❹ Hambach festival. More than 30,000 people bearing the black, red, and gold German colors marched past Neustadt to Hambach Castle and demanded the sovereignty of the people and a united republican Germany. The events at Hambach, together with the assault on

5 Biedermeier room, painting, ca. 1840

the Frankfurt Diet, represented serious challenges to the established order. The authorities responded by banning all political associations, public assemblies, and festivals and by tightening press censorship. The organizers of the festival were arrested, and the professors involved were suspended from teaching.

Contemporaneous with the radical currents of the "Pre-March" period (between the Congress of Vienna in 1815 and the March Revolution of 1848) which was supported by literary figures such as Heinrich Heine and Georg Büchner (who wrote "Peace to the cottages! War to the palaces!") was a current called *Biedermeier*. This referred to the lifestyle of the middle class, which was either apolitical or leaned toward the conservative side. Typical of Biedermeier art are the paintings of Franz Carl Spitzweg, whose gently satirical ❽ paintings of the life of the German middle class depict a harmonious world. The typical Biedermeier style expressed the notion of ❺ *Gemütlichkeit*—homely comfort—and moderation and was an intentional reaction to the opulence of the Imperial style. It can also be seen as a kind of escapism from the harsh political climate.

4 The Hambach festival, May 27–30, 1832

6 Friedrich Ludwig Jahn, politician and founder of the German gymnastics movement

Excerpt from the *Song of Hambach*:

"We want to found a fatherland,
And dedicate it to freedom:
Then in the face of tyranny
the free German will no longer bow…
If in a fight one stands for all,
and all for one, then flourishes
the people's power and majesty
and each heart glows
For a single goal, for a single good,
Let freedom burn,
for the fatherland's good."

above: Banner of the Hambach festival, 1832

7 The "Göttingen Seven": W.E. Albrecht, F. Ch. Dahlmann, H. Ewald, G.G. Gervinus, W. E. Weber, and the brothers J. and W. Grimm

8 *The Sunday Walk*, a gently ironic portrayal of a petit-bourgeois family in the countryside, typical Biedermeier style painting by Spitzweg, 1841

from 1837	"Göttingen Seven" expelled from university	**1850**	German Federation restored	**1857**	Economic crisis
March 1848	Revolutions break out	**1852**	Center Party formed	**1866**	Seven Weeks' War

■ Austria's Restoration Policy

With stifling centralism the Austrian government frustrated nationalists and radicals. Through shrewd diplomacy they were able to temporarily thwart Prussian ambitions in Germany.

1 Prince Felix zu Schwarzenberg

Metternich's successor, Prince **❶** Felix zu Schwarzenberg, established a constitutional scheme into which the various nationalities were incorporated. He saw to it that **❷** Ferdinand I was forced to abdicate after the March Revolution of 1848. **❹** Francis Joseph I, who in 1854 married Elizabeth, the daughter of Duke Maximilian of Bavaria, was crowned as his successor. The new emperor broke the promise of democratic reforms he had made prior to the bloody suppression of the 1848 revolts. The government reinforced the absolutist regime with severe police repression. In 1849 the minister of the interior, Baron von Bach, inaugurated the "Bach System," a bureaucratic measure centralizing authority in Vienna. With the New Year's Eve Decree of 1851, the liberal constitution conceded to the revolutionaries was repealed. The Catholic clergy was considerably strengthened by the Concordat of 1855. On the other hand, the support of the peasants was secured through the abolition of serfdom, and the middle classes tended to support the regime when it seemed to be threatened by radical agitation.

In foreign affairs, Austria's neutrality during the **❸** Crimean War of 1854–1856 alienated Russia without winning the support of France and Britain, leaving Austria isolated. Austria also lost many of its Italian territories, including Lombardy, in the Treaty of Zurich of 1859, while Italy's unification movement, supported by Napoleon III, resulted in grave military defeats for Austria at the battles of Magenta and Solferino.

Francis Joseph I was also forced to confront domestic challenges. Bach was relieved of his office, and a more federalist constitution was implemented. The February Patent of February 26, 1861, once again provided for stronger centralism and ensured a privileged position for the Germans in the multinational Habsburg state. This further antagonized political activists among the other nationalities.

At the same time Austria and Prussia struggled with each other for supremacy within Germany. Schwarzenberg was able to thwart the creation of a German confederation without Austria and under Prussian leadership that was supposed to be agreed upon by the "Prussian Union parliament" in Erfurt in March and April 1850. Prussia was thus frustrated and forced to delay its bid to usurp the Habsburgs' leading role among the German states.

2 Emperor Ferdinand I of Austria

"Sisi"

Empress Elizabeth, nicknamed "Sisi," was an unconventional aristocrat and did not want to submit to the ceremony of the Austrian court. She traveled extensively and maintained contact with the rebellious Hungarian aristocracy. It was at her urging that the double monarchy of Austria-Hungary was established in 1867, whereby Hungary regained its constitution. She was murdered on September 10, 1898, by an Italian anarchist. The empress was adored during her lifetime for her beauty and independence. After her death, she became an iconic figure in the empire.

above: Empress Elizabeth, painting by F.X. Winterhalter

3 The Battle of Sitistra, during the Crimean War of 1854–56

4 Emperor Francis Joseph I of Austria

■ Prussia's Rise and Austria's Decline

The Seven Weeks' War of 1866 ended Austrian influence in German politics. Thereafter the North German confederation was dominated by Prussia.

Wilhelm I, son of Frederick William III, succeeded his brother Frederick William IV as king of Prussia in 1861. He was a ruler of absolutist and autocratic ideas. When he became embroiled in a ❺ constitutional conflict in 1862, he entrusted the office of Prussian minister-president and foreign minister to Otto von Bismarck. His first action was to defy the Prussian Chamber of Deputies and push through a set of military reforms, setting the tone for his period in office. Bismarck snubbed the Habsburgs by boycotting the 1863 Frankfurt Diet of Princes, which was convened to discuss Austria's reform proposals for the German Confederation. He then turned to Russia to secure its neutrality in

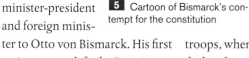

5 Cartoon of Bismarck's contempt for the constitution

any future conflict with Austria. Despite these tensions, Austria and Prussia together defeated Denmark in 1864 in a ❻ war over Schleswig and Holstein. In 1866 Bismarck reignited the dispute over supremacy by occupying Holstein. Austria secured a resolution of the Diet of the German Confederation to mobilize the neutral Confederation troops, whereupon Prussia declared war on Austria. Prussia and its 18 allied North German states defeated Austria and its 13 German Confederate state allies on July 3, 1866, at ❼ Königgrätz. The resulting Treaty of Prague, signed on August 23, dissolved the German Confederation. Prussia dominated the North German Confederation that was founded shortly afterward and was soon

joined by the South German states.

However, Bismarck had yet to achieve formal German unity under Prussian leadership. The ❽ Franco-Prussian War, which ended in France's defeat at the Battle of Sedan on September 1, 1870, provided the opportunity. On January 18, 1871, in the Hall of Mirrors at the Palace of Versailles, ❾ Wilhelm I declared himself emperor of a new unified Germany. Although Prussia had secured Germany a leading role in Europe, its arrival alarmed the other major powers. France, which lost Alsace-Lorraine after its defeat, was particularly alarmed and hostile.

6 Storming of the Danish trenches during the war over Schleswig and Holstein, 1864

7 Bismarck and General Moltke near Königgrätz

8 Prussian and French troops skirmish during the Battle of Wörth, 1870

9 King Wilhelm I of Prussia is declared German emperor in the Hall of Mirrors in the Palace of Versailles, following Prussia's crushing victory over France, 1871

Otto von Bismarck:

"Germany does not look to Prussia's liberalism, but to her power. … Not by speeches and majorities will the great questions of the day be decided—that was the mistake of 1848 and 1849—but by blood and iron."

From a speech delivered to the Prussian Chamber of Deputies, September 30, 1862

Otto von Bismarck

from 1862	Bismarck minister-president in Prussia	1864	War with Denmark over Schleswig and Holstein	Sep 1, 1870	Battle of Sedan
	1863	Frankfurt Diet of Princes	Aug 23, 1866	Treaty of Prague	Jan 18, 1871	William I proclaimed German Emperor

IMPERIAL GERMANY 1871–1914

After the founding of the Reich, Bismarck pursued an alliance policy meant to create a European balance of power while largely isolating France. Domestically he fought the power of the Catholic Church in the *Kulturkampf* ("cultural struggle"). He also sought to control the spread of socialism through the carrot-and-stick method of enacting social reforms while banning socialist organizations and literature. After Bismarck's dismissal in 1890, the German Reich found itself hemmed in on two fronts by an allignment between Russia and France as allies—exactly the situation he had always sought to avoid. The Belle Époque, in both domestic and foreign politics, was an era in which potentially explosive tensions emerged.

Berlin Congress June 13–July 13, 1878: Bismarck and the Russian deputy Earl Shuvalov

◼ European Alliance Policies

The Three Emperors' League, the Triple Alliance, and the Reinsurance Treaty temporarily protected the German Empire within the network of European great powers.

Caricature depicting the Triple Alliance of Imperial Germany, Austria, and Italy, showing Bismarck as lion tamer

The German Reich that came into existence through the constitution of April 16, 1871, comprised 22 individual states and three free cities. The constitutional monarchy was now governed by an imperial chancellor, who was appointed by the kaiser (emperor) and, as was the case with ❸ Bismarck, served as Prussian prime minister and foreign minister.

Alliances forged under Bismarck temporarily protected the German Empire within the network of European powers. In 1873 Bismarck formed the Three Emperors' League with Austria and Russia. By the time of the ❶ Berlin Congress in 1878, however, the alliance was already tot-

❸ Otto von Bismarck

tering, and Germany abandoned it in favor of a ❺ pact with Austria; this became the ❷ Triple Alliance when Italy joined in 1882.

The ❹ Balkans remained an area of contention, where the

competing interests of Austria and Russia created friction. To avoid escalation, Germany entered into the Reinsurance Treaty with Russia in 1887, which bound both to neutrality. When Great Britain allied itself to Italy and Austria—and thus indirectly with Germany—through the Mediterranean Entente in 1887, all European major powers except France were now tied with Germany through alliances. However, the Reinsurance Treaty was not renewed after Bismarck's forced dismissal in 1890. Russia instead concluded a military pact with France in 1892, thus placing Germany between the pincers of two major allied powers.

Wilhelm II, after Bismarck's dismissal

"The post of duty officer on the ship of state has fallen to me. The course stays the old one. Full steam ahead."

The captain leaves the ship; caricature about the dismissal of Bismarck by Wilhelm II

Russian-Turkish war, 1877–78

German-Austrian pact, signed on October 17, 1879

| Apr 18, 1871 | Constitution of the German Reich | 1873 | Three Emperors' League | 1878 | Berlin Congress | 1881 | Three Emperors' League renewed |
| 1873 | Viennese stock-market crash | 1878 | Anti-socialist law | 1879 | Dual Alliance |

■ Domestic Political Failures

Bismarck was as unsuccessful in his battle against the Catholic Church as he was in his struggle against the labor movement.

Bismarck's free trade policy, aided by the high reparations payments of the French, led to an economic upswing in the founding years of the German Reich marked by building activity and stock speculation, although that slackened after the ❽ Viennese stock market crash of 1873. Bismarck then introduced protective tariffs in 1879 that split the ⓫ National Liberal party, which had stood by him until then.

The National Liberals represented the hopes particularly of the upper middle class for industrial progress and of Protestant, middle-class intellectuals for a stemming of the Catholic influence that was represented in the *Reichstag* (Parliament) by the ❿ Center party; for this reason, they supported Bismarck in the ❻ *Kulturkampf*, or struggle, against the political influence of Catholicism.

Laws were enacted in the early 1870s disallowing the Catholic clergy from making political statements in office, putting their training under state control, banning the promulgation of the Jesuits, transferring the supervision

Kaiser Wilhelm II

of schools to the state, and making possible the closing of monasteries. Some of the priests who refused to recognize the laws were prosecuted. The measures, however, remained ineffective and Bismarck was forced to repeal most of them in the 1880s.

Bismarck combated the spread of socialism among the workers with a two-pronged strategy. The antisocialist law of 1878 was meant to "counter the efforts of social democracy, which is a danger to the public:" labor movement organizations and pamphleteering

were banned. This too proved unsuccessful, however. By the time the law was repealed in 1890, the Social Democratic Party had been formed and its share of voters had tripled. The gradual introduction of ❾ social security from 1883 to 1889 addressed some of the workers' concerns but was meant to preempt more far-reaching political demands.

On June 15, 1888, ❼ Wilhelm II became kaiser after the death of his father Friedrich III who had ruled for only 99 days following the death of his own father Wilhelm I in the same year. Bismarck was as little in agreement with Wilhelm's desire to conciliate workers with more social reforms as he was with the other ideas of the new kaiser. Consequently, Wilhelm dismissed the "Iron Chancellor" on March 20, 1890.

Kulturkampf 1871–89, Caricature about Bismarck and Pope Leo XIII

Viennese stock market crash on May 9, 1873

"Year of the Three Emperors"

1888 is called the "Year of the Three Emperors" in Germany. When Kaiser Wilhelm I died on March 9 at age 91, his son Frederick III was already seriously ill with cancer of the larynx and unable to speak. He was only able to breathe through a silver tube that had been inserted into his windpipe. The people had set hope in him because of his liberal political convictions, but he died that summer. His son, Wilhelm II, succeeded him.

above: Memorial coin for the "Year of the Three Emperors"

Caricature about the social laws: The unemployed demand work instead of social welfare

The leader of the Center party: Windthorst, von Mallinckrodt and Reichensperger

Rudolph von Benningsen, leader of the National Liberal party, wood engraving by A. Neumann, ca. 1880

■ The German Reich from 1890 to 1914: The "New Course"

With the dismissal of Imperial Chancellor Bismarck in 1890, two years after he had ascended to the throne, ❶ Wilhelm II rang in a new era. However, the Wilhelminian society persisted in its outdated traditions.

1
Kaiser Wilhelm II

Wilhelm II did not continue Bismarck's hard-line strategy. His "New Course" promised to end internal political stagnation. The Catholics, who had been alienated in the Kulturkampf, were given compromises; the anti-socialist law was not renewed; and the new labor law that, for example, banned child labor, showed the protective side of the monarchy. But the kaiser's social interest evaporated when the workers, even after these "gifts," could not be wooed away from the Social Democratic party.

In Count ❸ Leo von Caprivi, Wilhelm now had a less domineering imperial chancellor at his side who would not hinder him in his "personal reign." Caprivi did not remain in office for long, however. His pragmatic and conciliatory domestic politics went

2
The Social Democrat August Bebel holding a speech in the Reichstag

too far for the conservatives, and his trade policies, while making Germany a leading economic world power in the 1890s, earned him the enmity of big property owners. Caprivi was forced to resign as Prussian minister-president in 1892 and as imperial chancellor in 1894 because he had planned, as had Bismarck before him, to topple the Reichstag.

Central to the nature of Wilhelminian Era was the inner contradiction between economic modernization and the traditionalism of the elite. The ❹ aristocracy, which had set the tone socially, attempted to hold onto its leading role. This, however, had long been lost to the upper middle class, which controlled both industry and the financial market. A consequential modernization was not allowed to take place, particularly in Prussia, the most influential part of the Reich. There, the composition of the state parliament was determined up until 1918 by the three-class franchise so that it increasingly contrasted with the more progressive ❷ Reichstag. The Zabern Affair in 1913 proved what was true for the whole of the Wilhelminian Era: a parliament against an authoritarian government responsible only to the kaiser could accomplish nothing.

3
Count Leo von Caprivi

4
A ball during the Wilhelminian period, painting by Adolf von Menzel, 1878

The Zabern Affair

The Zabern Affair of 1913 made the impotence of the Reichstag clear. After German soldiers arrested protesters in Saverne (German: Zabern), Alsace, without legal grounds, Imperial Chancellor Theobald von Bethmann Hollweg, albeit reluctantly, supported the Prussian minister of war, Erich von Falkenhayn, in a cover-up together with the kaiser that denied abuse of power on the parts of the soldiers. The Reichstag passed, for the first time, a vote of no confidence in the government on December 4, 1913, and demanded the chancellor's resignation. However, there was no constitutional basis for this move, and it proved unsuccessful.

above: Theobald v. Bethmann-Hollweg, left
left: Erich von Falkenhayn

1890	Imperial Chancellor Leo Graf von Caprivi	1890	Anti-socialist law expires	1894	Franco-Russian dual Alliance
1890	Reinsurance Treaty expires	1890–91	Worker protection laws	1896	Kruger telegram

Diplomacy without a Touch of Tact

Wilhelm II proved to have little skill in foreign policy. Germany became increasingly isolated in Europe through imprudent diplomacy.

Wilhelm II began the foreign affairs segment of his New Course by abandoning Bismarck's policy of the European balance of power. Germany would now aim for an imperialistic world policy. His

5
Cartoon depicting the first Morocco crisis, 1905/06

new chancellor, Caprivi, refused Russia a renewal of the Reinsurance Treaty of 1890. France saw its chance and allied itself with Russia in 1894, which made a two-front war against Germany possible.

In spite of the theory of the inevitability of Anglo-German rivalry, Wilhelm sought close contact with Great Britain, recognizing the British protectorate over Zanzibar in exchange for Heligoland, but then antagonized the British in 1896 with his ❽ Kruger telegram—a message congratulating the president of the South African republic of Transvaal, Paul Kruger, on a victory of the Boers over the British. Furthermore, Wilhelm wanted to build up a ❾ German fleet with the help of Admiral von Tirpitz and consequently started an arms race with Great Britain in the mid-1890s that brought Germany to the limit of its financial resources. When Germany approached the Ottoman Empire in 1898 and started constructing the ❻ Berlin-to-Baghdad railroad in the Near East, the British considered it an intrusion into their sphere of influence and so allied first with France in 1904 and then also with Russia in 1907, thus creating the Triple Entente, which left Germany isolated except for Austria-Hungary.

In colonial affairs, the German Empire wanted its "place in the sun," as Foreign Minister von Bülow expressed it in 1897. Germany became politically involved in Africa, China, and the Pacific. Rebellions, such as those of the ❼ Herreros and Hottentots (Khoikhoi) in German Southwest Africa, were brutally suppressed. The conflict with France in ❺ the Morocco Crises of 1905 and 1911 soon left Germany alone in Europe, without an alliance partner other than the Austrian-Hungarian Empire, and militarily encircled. Germany decided to expand her military and naval might despite British efforts at a rapprochement. When the Austrian heir to the throne was shot in Sarajevo in 1914, World War I was unavoidable.

The "Hun Speech"

In his infamous "Hun Speech" of July 27, 1900, Kaiser Wilhelm II sent off the troops leaving for China to put down the anti-foreigner Boxer Rebellion with the words: "Pardon will not be given. Prisoners will not be taken. Whoever falls into your hands is forfeit. Once, a thousand years ago, the Huns under their King Attila made a name for themselves... May you in this way make the name German remembered in China for a thousand years so that no Chinaman will ever again dare to even squint at German!"

above: Kaiser Wilhelm II bids an expeditionary corps in Bremerhaven farewell as they leave to put down the Boxer Rebellion, June 27, 1900

6
Berlin-to-Baghdad railway, built 1903–1940

7

8
above: Kruger telegram; Wilhelm congratulates the president of the Boers, Paul Kruger, on his victory over the British
left: Herrero uprising in German South West Africa, 1904/05

9
"S.M.S Kaiserin Augusta," second-class protected cruiser

| 1898 | Beginning of the navy development program | 1905 | First Morocco crisis | 1912–13 | Balkan Wars | Jun 28, 1914 | Franz Ferdinand murdered |
| 1903 | Construction of the Berlin-Baghdad railroad | 1911 | Second Morocco crisis | 1913 | The Zabern affair | | |

AUSTRIA-HUNGARY 1867–1914

Austria, politically weakened both domestically and abroad, was forced to relinquish its leading role in Germany after its defeat by Prussia in 1866. Conservative forces sought to retain the old Habsburg glory, but the progressive industrialization had its consequences. Growing nationalism within the individual ethnic groups in the multiethnic state, especially that of the Hungarians and Slavs, consistently wrested new concessions out of Vienna, and in the process fostered Austrian xenophobia and ❶ anti-Semitism. In the midst of this powder keg—which would explode into World War I in 1914—one of the most important cultural currents of the 19th and 20th centuries developed in the form of Viennese modernism.

Karl Lueger, the anti-Semitic mayor of Vienna, at a ball

■ The Institution of the Dual Monarchy

Austria and Hungary formed a personal union in 1867. In the period of liberalization that followed, nationalist and anti-Semitic currents also became apparent.

The Hungarian parliament, which had existed briefly during the 1848 revolution, was reinstituted in 1867, and a Hungarian Ministry was created. The Austrian imperial chancellor, ❷ Count von Beust, was forced to make concessions to the Hungarian representatives, Ferenc Deak and ❹ Count Gyula

Friedrich Ferdinand Count von Beust, wood engraving

Andrassy. The union between Austria and Hungary was now merely pragmatic; they were united only by a common monarch—the Austrian emperor, who was also crowned ❺ king of Hungary—a combined army, and the ministries of foreign affairs, war, and finance.

On December 21, 1867, ❸ Kaiser Francis Joseph I proclaimed the December Constitution which remained in power until 1918 and regulated the representation in the parliaments of the two countries. These bodies, together with the monarch, now made the policies of the country. In 1868 Prince Karl Auersperg became Head of the Government. He introduced liberal figures into his Cabinet. A ten-year liberalization began, during which progressive laws were implemented. In 1868 the influence of the Catholic Church on education and family policies ended. In the succeeding year, general compulsory military ser-

vice and free compulsory education were implemented.

Count von Taaffe, as prime minister of Austria, dealt strongly with the Christian conservatives and laid the cornerstone for the Austrian social state. However, in order to obtain majorities, he had to seek support primarily from the Slavic members of the imperial council and make allowances, particularly those of the Czechs. Czech became the official language in Bohemia in 1880 and, in 1882, the language of instruction at the University of Prague. Through his "pro-Slavic" multinational policies, Taaffe nurtured the antipathy of nationalist and anti-Semitic conservatives, such as the mayor of Vienna, Karl Lueger.

Kaiser Francis Joseph I, painting, 1895

Coronation of Francis Joseph I as king of Hungary in Budapest, June 8, 1867, wood engraving, 1889

Count Gyula Andrassy, ca.1865

■ The Alliance Policies of the Danube Monarchy

The multinational policies of the multiethnic state failed. Meanwhile, the Danube monarchy sought to ally itself with Germany against Russia.

6 Signing of the Dual Alliance on Oct 17, 1879: Kaiser William I and Kaiser Francis Joseph with Bismarck and Andrassy, their ministers of foreign affairs

The imperial and royal monarchy of Austria-Hungary did not succeed in integrating the many ethnic groups under its rule. This phenomenon, paradoxically, led to a certain stability, given that no significant union was possible between so many competing nationalities. Meanwhile the civil servants remained loyal to their Habsburg paymasters.

Germans and Hungarians were favored with regard to voting rights and participation in the political process. As a result, the dual monarchy controlled its minorities with police force. The Hungarian government's Magyarization of the southern Slavic efforts at liberation from the 1870s contributed to the tension in the Balkans, which helped to precipitate World War I. These efforts led in 1914 to the assassination of the heir to the Austro-Hungarian throne, the Archduke Francis Ferdinand—nephew of the Emperor and hated by Serbs because of his strong opposition to separatist movements—by a Serbian nationalist.

In foreign affairs the Danube monarchy was forming alliances. In 1872 it formed the Three Emperors' League with Germany and Russia. In the context of the steady decline of Ottoman power in that region and given Austrian suspicions of Russian expansionism—and support of Slavic nationalists—in the Balkans, it entered the **6** Dual Alliance with Bismarck's Germany. In addition, Austro-Hungary guaranteed to come to Germany's aid if the latter were faced by a combined Russian and French attack. In 1882, the alliance was expanded into the Triple Alliance with the addition of Italy. Increasingly, the other European powers felt threatened by this concentration of power. Consequently, in 1907, Great Britain, Russia, and France formed the Triple Entente. This divided Europe into the two military blocs between which a world war would break out seven years later.

Members of the "Viennese Secession"
right: Egon Schiele, self-portrait, 1912

Exhibition hall used by the "Vienna Secession" movement, built in 1897-98 by Joseph M. Olbrich

Gustav Mahler, painting, ca. 1905

Viennese Modernism

During the two decades around the turn of the 20th century, "Young Vienna," a literary current of Jugendstil (Viennese Art Nouveau), formed around Arthur Schnitzler and Hugo von Hofmannsthal, whose play, "Everyman," captured Vienna's zeitgeist of morbid superficiality and profound decadence. Other period authors still famous today are Karl Kraus, Robert Musil, and Hermann Broch. In painting, which distanced itself from the Belle Époque's passion for grandeur, Egon Schiele and particularly Gustav Klimt, a founding member of the "Viennese Secession" movement, made names for themselves. The Late Romantic Gustav Mahler and the twelve-tone serialists Arnold Schoenberg and Alban Berg stood out as composers, Adolf Loos and Otto Wagner as architects. Schnitzler's friend Sigmund Freud developed psychoanalysis, which strongly influenced Viennese Modernism.

Sigmund Freud, father of psychoanalysis, 1909

1

FRANCE 1814–1914

After Napoleon I, France returned to the circle of European great powers. The Bourbons tried to restore their pre-revolutionary monarchy, but political suppression and social injustice led to several ❶ revolts, which increasingly gained momentum and strength. The Second Republic, which resulted from the revolution of 1848, was once again transformed into an empire through a coup d'état by President Louis-Napoleon. With time, however, the social desire for liberal policies grew again, and the conservatives found themselves under increasing pressure. The empire ended with its defeat by Germany in 1870–1871, and the Third Republic finally vanquished "Bonapartism" in the struggle between republican and conservative ideas.

Liberty Leading the People, allegory of the July Revolution depicting liberty as Marianne, icon of the French Republic, painting by Eugène Delacroix, 1830

■ The Reign of the Bourbons and the Revolution of 1830

France became a constitutional monarchy under the Bourbons, whose restoration policies resulted in the July Revolution of 1830.

On June 4, 1814—almost exactly a year before Napoleon's final defeat at the Battle of Waterloo and exile on Elba—France received the *Charte constitutionelle*, a new charter for a constitutional monarchy. It included some democratic elements such as the *Code Civil* and a two-chamber parliamentary system with a Chamber of Notables chosen by the king and an elected Chamber of Deputies. The Bourbon ❷ Louis XVIII headed a restoration regime that favored the aristocracy and property-owning bourgeoisie. This policy was continued after the intermezzo of Napoleon's

2

King Louis XVIII

Hundred Days in 1815. In 1818 the Congress of Aachen, a follow-up conference to the Congress of Vienna, resolved to recognize France once again as a European ma-

jor power. Louis's brother Charles was a leading member of the ultraroyalists, who gained great influence in domestic politics after 1820.

They succeeded in pushing through restrictions on the right to vote, reestablished press censorship, and restored to the Church its properties. When Louis died in 1824, ❸ Charles X ascended the throne and continued his reactionary policies by, for example, compensating the aristocracy that had emigrated during the French Revolution. The liberal middle-class opposition under the leadership of

Charles X, King of France

❻ Adolphe Thiers won a majority in the lower chamber in 1830, whereupon Charles dissolved it. The next day, the ❹ July Revolution began, which resulted in the ❺ abdication of Charles X and his emigration to England. King Louis-Philippe took the throne.

4

July Revolution: Street fighting in the Rue de Rohan on July 29, 1830

5

King Charles X emigrates to Great Britain following his abdication in 1830

6

Adolphe Thiers, president of the Third Republic from 1871–73, ca. 1860

| Jun 4, 1814 | *Charte constitutionelle* | from 1824 | Monarchy of Charles X | 1830 | Charles X abdicates |
| 1818 | Congress of Aachen | 1830 | July Revolution | 1830–48 | "Citizen King" Louis Philippe |

■ The Revolution of 1848 and Louis-Napoleon's Coup d'État

Social problems during the reign of Louis-Philippe culminated in the February Revolution of 1848 and a new constitution that introduced a conservative presidential system that was soon replaced by a second empire.

The workers and the middle class, who had until then been under-represented due to the census suffrage (voting only by owners of substantial property), wanted a republic. But the upper-middle-class deputies who dominated the second chamber decided to continue with the constitutional monarchy under the ❽ "Citizen King," Louis-Philippe of Orléans. In the following years, France experienced rapid industrialization, which resulted in grave social problems. Thinkers and social philosophers such as Pierre-Joseph Proudhon and ❾ Charles Fourier, who were critical of society, expressed the demands of the lower classes for improvement in their living conditions.

The criticism of the conditions first erupted in weavers' rebel-

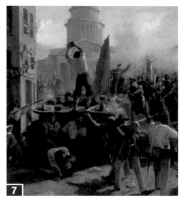

7

Barricade battle during the workers' revolt in June 1848

lions in Lyon in 1831 and 1834. Crop failures and economic crises, as well as an unbroken desire for real democracy rather than a government which was seen as ever more corrupt than the last, eventually led in 1848 to the ❿ February Revolution. The provisional government proclaimed the Second Republic, and Louis-Philippe

and Prime Minister François Guizot took their leave. After the suppression of a workers' ❼ revolt in June of the same year by the newly elected moderate government, France enacted a constitution in November 1848. In December Louis-Napoleon, a nephew of Napoleon I, was elected president by the people.

Louis-Napoleon sought support from the lower middle class, rather than from the parliamentary majority, with the aim of restoring Bonapartism. When his government's four-year term reached its end in 1851, he dissolved the parliament and had his most important opponents ❿ arrested. In January 1852, a referendum decided on a new constitution that provided for a term of office of ten years. A few months later,

8

The "Citizen King" Louis-Philippe swears upon the charter of Aug 7, 1830

Louis-Napoleon declared the end of the Second Republic, and on December 2, 1852, he ⓫ ascended the throne as Emperor Napoleon III.

9

Charles Fourier

10

Coup d'état by Louis-Napoleon on February 2, 1851, and the imprisonment of representatives of the opposition

11

From left to right: Napoleon III, his son Louis-Napoleon, Napoleon I Bonaparte, and his son Napoleon

"Enrichissez–vous!"

In response to the demand of the people to abolish census suffrage, François Guizot, the moderate liberal prime minister for Citizen King Louis Philippe, is said to have answered: "There will be no reform. Get rich, and then you can vote."

Pierre-Joseph Proudhon (1809–1865), a printer and later journalist, formulated his famous statement "Property is theft" in an 1840 pamphlet entitled "What Is Property?" As an anarchist, Proudhon rejected every form of state and dreamed of a society in which people lived and worked of their own accord, with no self-interest but rather in the interest of all. Proudhon was a member of the Constituent Assembly after 1848 and was arrested as an opponent of Louis-Napoleon in 1849. Following his release in 1852, he lived in exile in Belgium, but was able to return to France, where he hoped to be able to further the cause of social reform, after being pardoned in 1862.

Proudhon and his children, 1863, painting by Gustave Courbet

12

February Revolution of 1848: The Tri-color remains the national flag of the second Republic

■ The Second Empire

Napoleon III's reign began in an authoritarian vein, which he had to abandon in favor of liberal developments.

In Napoleon III's empire, the parliament was of little significance; the Church and the army had greater influence in the running of the state. The lower middle class accepted the authoritarian state out of fear of socialist violence. The lower class was pacified by the creation of jobs in the wake of "Haussmannization"—the renovation and modernization of Paris. Baron Georges-Eugène Haussmann, prefect of the Seine *département*, which included Paris, redesigned the city and laid out wide, corridor-like ❶ boulevards and parks such as the Bois de Boulogne. The 1889 ❹, ❺ public exhibitions held in Paris demon-

❷

Abdelkader

strated France's industrial progress.

France fought in the Crimean War from 1853 to 1856 against Russia on the side of the Ottoman Empire. Its participation in the Franco-Sardinian War against Austria in 1859—which France won primarily through its victory in the ❻ Battle of Solferino on June 24, 1859—was also profitable due to the capture of Nice and Savoy. After France annexed Algeria in 1834 and finally conquered it in 1847 in the struggle against ❷ Abdelkader, it was agriculturally exploited by the Colons, European settlers who were mostly French. France was

also able to prevail in Indochina, Syria, and Senegal. It was a different matter in Mexico, whose French-installed emperor was overthrown in 1867. The plan to absorb regions of Luxembourg and Belgium also failed.

Domestically, the liberal opposition was victorious in 1869. Napoleon III was forced to compromise with the democrats and relinquish a large part of his authoritarian regime in the *Empire libéral*. The Franco-Prussian War of 1870–1871, provoked by Prussia, resulted in the ❸ Battle of

❸

The French defeat at Sedan, September 1, 1870

Sedan on September 1, 1870, and the downfall of the Second Empire. The emperor was taken prisoner, and, in the course of the negotiations, France had to cede Alsace and Lorraine to Germany.

❶

Boulevard des Italiens in Paris

Charles Baudelaire

The poet Charles-Pierre Baudelaire (1821–1867) was arguably the most important French lyricist of the Modern Era. He became famous through his major work, a collection of poems entitled Les Fleurs du Mal *("The Flowers of Evil"), which was published in 1857 and triggered a scandal in bourgeois French society. After a trial for offend-ing the public morals, he had to withdraw six of his poems. The most important themes of his "aesthetic of the ugly" were, in contrast to Romantic literature, death and eroticism. He particularly influenced English writers such as Edgar Allan Poe. He lived in Belgium for a number of years, but died of syphilis in Paris, the city of his birth, on August 31, 1867.*

above: Charles Baudelaire, self-portrait from 1860

❹

Charles Garnier's Opera built 1871-74 in the heart of Paris.

❺

The Aquarium in the 1867 world exhibition in Paris

❻

Emperor Napoleon III during the Battle of Solferino

| 1834 | Annexation of Algeria | 1853–56 | Crimean War | Jun 26, 1859 | Battle of Solferino | 1870–71 | Franco-Prussian War |
| 1847 | Conquest of Algeria | 1859 | Franco-Sardinian War | 1869 | *Empire libéral* | | |

The Third Republic

The Second Empire was followed by the Third Republic, which was confronted by domestic political scandals. Internationally, France was able to reintegrate itself step-by-step into the community of European states.

Shortly after the capitulation of the French army under the Comte de ❼ Mac-Mahon at Sedan in the Franco-Prussian War, the Third Republic was proclaimed in Paris. In 1871, the National Assembly chose Adolphe Thiers as head of the new government.

The communists and socialists, who had joined together to run the ❾, ❿ Commune of Paris, set up a form of socialist republic that was crushed by Mac-Mahon's troops in the "Bloody Week" in May. Mac-Mahon was elected president or "placeholder for the monarchy" by the conservative majority, but he stepped down in 1879 because of the growing strength of the republicans.

The moderate republican majority under State President Jules Grévy existed until 1887 but then began to crumble due to crises and scandals. The economic crisis of 1882 had worsened the mood of the people and provided a boost for the conservatives. ❽ Georges Boulanger sought revenge against Germany following the loss of Alsace-Lorraine in the Treaty of Versailles in 1871 and united conservatives, radicals, and monarchists in an authoritarian-nationalistic movement called "Party of the Dissatisfied" that seriously threatened the Republic. The republicans' victory in the 1889 election prevented a dictatorship of the Boulangers. The Republic was shaken in the 1890s by the Panama scandal and the Dreyfus Affair, which caused political polarization. The majority coalition of republicans and left-wing radicals that existed from 1898, together with the socialists Aristide Briand and Prime Minister Georges Clemenceau, instituted the separation of church and state as well as enacting social welfare measures in 1905.

In foreign affairs, France pursued an alliance policy to preserve its colonial interests and protect itself against a possible war with Germany. In 1902, it received Italy's assurance of neutrality in case of a German attack. The alliance between France and Russia in 1894 was expanded to include Great Britain and became the Triple Entente in 1907. The anti-German mood of the French citizens, exacerbated by the Morocco Crisis, was personified from 1913 by the President ⓫ Raymond Poincaré, who aimed to regain territories lost to Prussia.

7 Eiffel Tower in Paris, inaugurated on the occasion of the 1889 world exhibition

8 Georges Boulanger, leader of the opposition nationalists' party

9 The commune of Paris builds barricades at the Place de la Concorde

10 The ruins of the town hall that was set on fire by communards in Paris on May 24, 1871

The Dreyfus Affair

Captain Alfred Dreyfus, a Jew, was wrongly accused of spying for the Germans and thus arrested and tried for treason. A military court sentenced him in 1890 to life imprisonment on Devil's Island and expelled him from the army. The Dreyfus Affair split the nation. While, for example, Émile Zola obtained a reopening of the trial with his open letter "J'accuse," anti-Semites, nationalists, and antiparliamentarianists gathered together in the opposition camp. In 1898, the principal piece of evidence, a document, was shown to be a forgery, and Dreyfus was cleared in 1906. The affair was a struggle between restorative and republican ideas, and the Republic emerged from it strengthened as liberal ideals triumphed.

Cover page of the Le Petit Journal of January 13, 1895: Degradation of Alfred Dreyfus

11 President Raymond Poincaré on the cover of Le Petit Journal of January 26, 1913, shortly after coming to power

| Mar–May 1871 | Commune of Paris revolt | | 1890–1906 | Dreyfus Affair | | 1905 | Separation of church and state |
| 1871 | Adolphe Thiers becomes head of government | | 1875 | Proclamation of the Third Republic | | 1892–93 | Panama scandal | 1907 | Triple Entente |

1

GREAT BRITAIN 1830–1914

England's economic development was almost half a century ahead of the Continent's due to its early industrialization, but the working conditions were devastating and led to impoverishment of the workers. This made worker protection laws necessary, along with the gradual extension of suffrage to ever-widening sections of the population, to alleviate the social tensions. Under ❶ Queen Victoria, whose reign began in 1837, the economy flourished at first, but social problems remained and the worker movement demanded further reforms. The British colonial empire was gradually restructured in the 19th century to become the Commonwealth of Nations.

Queen Victoria I of Great Britain and Ireland and Empress of India, portrait commemorating 50 years on the throne in 1887

■ Political Reforms of the Constitutional Monarchy

The 1830s and 1840s saw a series of successful reforms in Great Britain.

After the death of ❸ George IV, William IV, a king eager for reform, took the throne. Suffrage was modernized in the Reform Act of June 1832, and at the same time an increase in Parliament's power was passed; because the ❷ population in the cities had rapidly grown due to migration from the countryside, the division of the seats in Parliament no longer corresponded to the number of voters, and therefore the voting districts were reallocated in favor of the cities. The Municipal Corporations Act of 1835 also provided for the election of city councils. The protest against the liberal suffrage reform of 1832 was the hour of birth of the Conserva-

2

Poor quarter in London, ca. 1850

4

Cartoon about the reform laws concerning the emancipation of Catholics: "The Mountain in Labour –or much ado about nothing"

tive and Unionist party of Great Britain, which endeavored to gain the increased number of voters. But the British Conservative party split in 1846 when Prime Minister Sir Robert Peel moved toward free trade.

Reforms were also necessary in the relationship between the confessions. Compared to the members of the Anglican Church, Catholics were greatly restricted in their civil rights. It was not until April 1829 that—

3

George IV, King of Great Britain when he was still Prince of Wales, painting by Thomas Gainsborough, 1781

through the influence of, among others, ❺ Prime Minister Arthur Wellesley, the duke of Wellington— the ❹ Roman Catholic Relief Act was passed. Known as the "Catholic Emancipation," this law ended official discrimination against Catholics and allowed them to become members of Parliament.

5

Prime Minister Arthur Wellesley, Duke of Wellington, painting by Francisco Goya, 1814

The Chartists

Though the suffrage reform of 1832 meant a strengthening of the middle class, the number of voters was still very small— about four percent of the population. Consequently, in 1837 a London workers association presented the House of Commons with a "People's Charter." The Chartists demanded universal male suffrage, with elections to represent the actual proportions of the population, secret ballots, and the payment of MPs so that poorer members could afford to stand for Parliament. Parliament rejected this, despite petitions with up to three million signatures and a general strike. The leaders of the Chartists were arrested during unrest in Wales in 1839.

Friedrich Engels speaks at an assembly of the chartists in 1843

| 1802 | Factory Act passed | **Aug 16, 1819** | "Massacre of Peterloo" | 1824 | Introduction of right to strike |
| 1815 | Corn Laws | 1819 | Ban on children working in cotton mills | **Apr 1829** | Roman Catholic Relief Act passed |

■ The Social Reforms of "Manchester Capitalism"

Over time, various innovations and a series of laws implementing social reform improved the living conditions of the lower class in Britain.

6
Women work in a cork factory

On August 16, 1819, a demonstration of workers was suppressed in the "Peterloo Massacre" when the cavalry charged at a crowd that had gathered in the streets of Manchester. It was soon clear to conservatives that reforms were needed to maintain domestic peace. The first of the Factory Acts had already been passed in 1802, making night work for children punishable and limiting the workday for apprentices to twelve hours. The ❿ employment of children under nine in mills was forbidden in 1819. In 1824 workers were granted the ❼ right to strike and form coalitions.

As there was no state control, however, these laws were easy to circumvent. The first effective factory law was passed in 1833. It limited the number of hours a day ❻ women and children could work; children under age 13 were allowed to work no more than nine hours a day. A supervisory department controlled the implementation of the law. Some of the improvements in working and living conditions are attributable to ⓫ Anthony Ashley Cooper, the seventh earl of Shaftesbury. He encouraged "social housing" and provided schools for the children of the poor. He also introduced a number of social laws, including the 1842 ban on women and children working in mines and, in 1847, the regulation of the ten-hour workday for women and youths ❾ working in factories.

To maintain a high price for British grain, Parliament in 1815 passed a tariff against imports, known as the Corn Laws, but the resulting high price of bread elicited insurrections among the populace. George IV reacted by restricting civil rights, particularly the right to assemble and freedom of the press. Only after heavy pressure was applied by the

7
Impoverished worker with his family during the dockworkers strike of 1889 in London

8
Richard Cobden

Manchester School—a group of textile manufacturers led by ❽ Richard Cobden who, because of their interest in free trade, had allied with the workers—were the Corn Laws repealed in 1846. The Anti–Corn Law League founded by Cobden and John Bright in 1838 demanded general public education and suffrage reform.

Robert Owen

In 1799, at the age of 28, Robert Owen became co-owner of a cotton mill in New Lanark, Scotland. The early socialist did not allow child labor, limited the workday to ten and a half hours, and so became a supporter of early labor protection laws. His workers lived in a housing estate built for them, their children attended school, and they could buy food inexpensively at shops he subsidized. Despite these additional costs, his factories were economically successful. The Cooperative Movement, founded in 1844 in Rochdale, England, took up his ideas, which are still accepted today.

School in New Lanark, founded by Robert Owen

9
Pump station at a canal in Birmingham, with Watt's easy working pumping machine

10
Child labor in an English coal mine following the Industrial Revolution, painting, 19th century

11
Anthony Ashley Cooper, seventh Earl of Shaftesbury, painting, ca. 1870

| 1832 | Reform Bill | 1837 | "People's Charter" | 1844 | Cooperative Movement launched |
| 1835 | Municipal Corporations Act | 1838 | Founding of the Anti-Corn-Law League | 1846 | Conservative Party splits |

■ Economic Growth and the Welfare State in the Victorian Age

The economic boom in the first years of Victoria's reign slowed, and social issues once again became a focus of politics.

Crystal Palace in London Hyde Park, built for the World Exposition in 1851

Queue of people waiting outside a shelter for the poor and homeless

Queen Victoria I

Queen Victoria of England and Empress of India took the throne on June 20, 1837, and shaped a whole era of Great Britain's history during her 64-year reign. The Victorian Age was characterized by economic prosperity and the British Empire's position of leadership in the world. The Victorians also stood for a conservative lifestyle and prudery. Queen Victoria's husband, Prince Albert of Saxe-Coburg-Gotha, introduced conservative opinions to the originally more liberally inclined queen. She is the longest ruling monarch in British history.

above: Queen Victoria I celebrating her Golden Jubilee

Following a turbulent reform era, Great Britain experienced calmer decades. The Great Exhibition in 1851, featuring the famous ❶ Crystal Palace, was a symbol of the flourishing economy. Because the reform of the 1830s had established parliamentary structures, the Europe-wide revolutions of 1848 left Britain unaffected.

The boom was followed by a crisis, which exacerbated the social problems. The unions, which had organized in 1868 as the Trade Union Congress, saw an increase in membership. The strike by London dockworkers in 1889 was a sign of the unions' growing self-confidence. Many ❷ destitute workers ❸ emi-

The Irish Fight for Independence

An enormous increase in population in Ireland, along with the potato blight of 1845, resulted in a terrible famine that lasted until 1849. Prime Minister Lord John Russell largely denied state aid to alleviate the crises and instead sent soldiers to counter outbreaks of unrest. More than a million Irish died of hunger and epidemics, and about twice as many emigrated. The nationalists demanded political independence for Ireland, and secret societies such as the Fenians murdered British government representatives. It wasn't until 1921 that Ireland—with the exception of the North—became independent.

above: Starving rural population outside a poorhouse during the great famine in Ireland that lasted from 1845–1849

grated to America or Australia.

The Labour Representation Committee, founded in 1900 and renamed the Labour party in 1906, gained influence. Liberals David Lloyd George and ❹ Winston Churchill fought for the welfare of the people. Within a few years, pensions, unemployment insurance, and national health insurance had been introduced and a minimum wage agreed upon for certain groups.

William Gladstone's amendment to the reform bill of 1867 had secured suffrage for urban workers, and in 1884 farm hands were also given the vote. The House of Lords' power to veto legislation was curtailed in 1911. ❺ Suffragettes campaigned for women's right to vote.

Emigrants climb aboard an overcrowded ship

Winston Churchill in the Camberwell Labour Exchange, an employment agency, ca. 1910

Cover page of the magazine *The Suffragette* edited by Christabel Pankhurst, May 23, 1913

Jun 20, 1837	Coronation of Victoria I		1842	Opium War		1851	World Exhibition in London		1868	Trade Union Congress
		1839	Durham Report		1845–49	Famine in Ireland		1858	Sepoy Rebellion	

■ Colonial Policies and the Path to World War I

Great Britain expanded its vast colonial empire, but increasingly came into conflict with the German Empire, which wanted its own "place in the sun."

6 Crown of the Indian emperor, made for the crowning of George V as emperor of India, 1911

The long reign of Queen Victoria (1837–1902) was marked by imperial claims that continued the steady expansion of the colonial empire. When the East India Company was dissolved in 1858 in the wake of the Sepoy Rebellion, the **6** British crown took over the government of India, which was put under the rule of a British viceroy, and Victoria assumed the title of "Empress of India" in 1876. The colonies at **⓫** Hong Kong—which England had secured on a

99-year lease through the Treaty of Nanjing that ended the 1842 Opium War—and Singapore ensured Asian expansion possibilities into China and the Pacific, but also brought Great Britain into conflict with Russia.

In the "scramble for Africa," Great Britain got into disputes with France and Germany over the last colonizable regions of the world. Egypt was occupied by Britain in 1882 primarily because of the Suez Canal. In the 1890s, Britain almost came to war with France over control of Sudan, later ruled as an Anglo-Egyptian condominium in "the **7** Fashoda Incident." Both powers then allied themselves against the **9** German Empire in 1904 in the Entente Cordiale, which Russia also joined in 1907. Early on, the colonies with large populations of European immigrants demanded self-rule. The transformation of the empire into the Commonwealth of Nations of the 20th century began

with the Durham Report of 1839, which introduced the union and self-government of the **⓬** Canadian provinces. The colonies thus remained in the trusteeship of the motherland until they were released into political independence. The settlement territories joined together into large federations and adopted constitutions after the British model. Canada, Australia, New Zealand, and parts of southern Africa were defined as "dominions"—governmental regions within the British Empire that were technically autonomous—at the colonial conference of 1887. With their **8**, **⓾** entrance into World War I on the side of the motherland, the standing of the colonies and dominions changed, and they were recognized as autonomous nations of an imperial commonwealth in 1917.

A number of additions to the British Commonwealth were made after the end of the First World War, when some former

7 The Egyptian flag is flown in Fashoda, Sudan, after the retreat of the French forces in 1898

9 Caricature "The future on the water–he dares to venture onto the seas in search of power"

German and Ottoman colonies became British protectorates and mandates.

8 Advancing Indian auxiliary troops of the British army during the fights southwest of Ypres in May 1915, design for a lamp shade

10 Soldiers of the Indian auxiliary troops and British soldiers in the First World War

11 Harbor of Hong Kong, 1847

12 St. Lawrence River, Quebec, Canada, painting, ca. 1850

1

William II, King of the Netherlands

THE BENELUX COUNTRIES 1815–1914

Austria was forced to cede its territories in the southern Netherlands to France under the terms of the 1797 Treaty of Campo Formio. At the Congress of Vienna this area was joined with the united Netherlands, which were supposed to act as a buffer zone to France. However confessional, political, and cultural differences led to the separation of Belgium in 1830. At this point in time the industrialization process in the Netherlands and in Belgium began. The Belgian economy benefitted from colonial territories in Africa. The Dutch kings also ruled over Luxembourg as Grand Dukes. Differences in the laws of succession led to Luxembourg's separation from the Netherlands in 1890.

■ The Netherlands and Luxembourg

Democratic structures were gradually implemented in the Netherlands, which was ruled by the Orange-Nassau dynasty. Luxembourg became independent in the 1890s.

The Congress of Vienna in 1815 created the United Kingdom of the Netherlands, including present-day Belgium, the former Austrian Netherlands. During the course of the Revolution of 1845, King **❶** William II, son of the conservative William I, was forced to agree to a constitutional monarchy. After his death the following year, his son **❻** William III took the throne. During his reign, the parliament was able to signifi-

3 Napoleon III, French Emperor, painting by F.X. Winterhalter, 1857

cantly expand its authority. In the 1880s, the Netherlands experienced an economic boom that also promoted the development of the **❷**, **❹** workers movement, out of which the Social Democratic Workers party emerged in 1894.

Luxembourg had been granted the status of a grand duchy at the Congress of Vienna but was governed over until 1867 by the Netherlands. It was thus able to profit from the Netherlands' new liberal

constitution in 1848. In 1898 **❺** Queen Wilhelmina ascended the throne. Luxembourg law did not allow for a female monarch, however, and the country was therefore released from its union with the Netherlands.

When **❸** Napoleon III purchased the country in 1867, this created a crisis, as Prussia did not approve. The London Conference of May 11, 1867, ended the Luxembourg crisis by assuring its independence and neutrality. This agreement was disregarded by the Germans at the beginning of World War I when they occupied the country.

2

Worker at the loom, one of many paintings by Vincent van Gogh of weavers working at machines, 1884

4

Congress of the socialist Second Internationale in Amsterdam, August 14–20, 1904

5

Festivities celebrating Wilhelmina's majority on August 31, 1890

William I, steel engraving, 19th c.

William I of the Netherlands

William I of Orange-Nassau, the dynasty that governed the Netherlands, fought against the French revolutionary army between 1793 and 1795 and later lived in exile in England. He was crowned king of the Netherlands and grand duke of Luxembourg on March 16, 1815. His insensitive policies toward the Belgians resulted in that country declaring its independence in 1830. In the Netherlands, he refused any restrictions of his authority by the parliament and therefore had to abdicate in favor of his son, William II.

6

William III, King of the Netherlands and Grand Duke of Luxembourg, ca. 1865

Mar 16, 1815	William I crowned king of the Netherlands	**Sep 26, 1830**	"September Revolution" in Belgium
1797	Treaty of Campo Formio	**Aug 25, 1830** Revolt in Brussels	**Oct 4, 1830** Belgium declares independence

■ Belgium's Political and Economic Progress

Belgium had a liberal state system as early as 1830, was the most industrialized country in Europe after Great Britain, and also endeavored to gain colonies in Africa.

In 1815, the Congress of Vienna merged the Catholic region of the Austrian Netherlands with the Republic of United Netherlands situated north of it, which was reigned over by the Protestant House of Orange-Nassau. Dutch became the official language, which wounded the national pride of the French-speaking population. This and other discriminatory policies, as well as political and economic restrictions, led to a rebellion in Brussels on Au-

8
Revolution of the Belgians against the Dutch rule under William I in 1830, wood engraving, 1864

gust 25, 1830, in the wake of the Parisian July Revolution. Dutch soldiers were then chased out of Brussels during the September Revolution ❽ on September 26, and on October 4, 1830, the provisional Belgian government proclaimed the country's independence. Belgium adopted a liberal constitution on February 7, 1831, and installed a constitutional monarchy. The anglophile Leopold I of Saxe-Coburg-Saalfeld was crowned ❾ king on June 4, 1831. In 1839, Luxembourg ceded the western Walloon region to the newly independent Belgium. The Netherlands, however, did not recognize Belgium's independence until the London Protocol of April 19, 1839, but then the country's borders were fixed and its neutrality guaranteed by the Great Powers.

❼ Belgium led the Continent economically in the first half of the 19th century. Domestically, the conflict between Catholic and liberal thought over the educational policies of 1879 were resol-

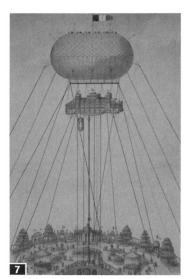

7
The "castle in the air," world exhibition in Antwerp, Belgium, 1894

ved with a liberal school law. Differences between the French-speaking Walloons in the south and the Flemish speakers in the north were not only linguistic and cultural but also represented a difference in wealth as industrialization had been more advanced in the south.

Universal male suffrage was first implemented in 1893 as a result of a ❿ general strike initiated by the Social Democrats.

Belgian Colonial Politics

King Leopold II sponsored the exploration of central Africa by, among others, Sir Henry Morton Stanley. The result of his expedition was the founding of the Congo Free State (later Zaire). The king was its personal sovereign with a neutral status at the Berlin Congo conference of 1885. When the inhuman methods he used to exploit the country and the unrest that resulted from them became known, he was forced to cede Congo to Belgian governmental control in 1908. His successor, Albert I, who was crowned the following year, restructured the organization of the colony.

9
Coronation ceremony of King Leopold I on June 4, 1831, at the Palace Royale in Brussels, painting from 1856

10
The military puts down the strike by the miners of Mons, 1893

above: The ivory stock of Congo documents the exploitation of Africa's natural resources, wood engraving, 1890
top: Sir Henry Morton Stanley and some of his African companions, wood engraving, 1890

| Feb 7, 1831 | Liberal constitution in Belgium | 1885 | Berlin Congo conference | 1890 | Wilhelmina becomes Queen of the Netherlands |
| May 11, 1867 | London Conference | 1890 | Luxembourg gains independence | | |

1

ITALY FROM THE CONGRESS OF VIENNA TO THE EVE OF WORLD WAR I 1815–1914

After the reestablishment of the Italian kingdoms and states at the Congress of Vienna, restorative and conservative policies could not prevent the emergence of a national unification movement and the creation of the Kingdom of Italy. However, political unification did not lead to a social or economic unification. The poor agricultural south had little in common with the industrialized north, and the latter dominated the politics of the new state. The government of Prime Minister Crispi, who wanted to give Italy more weight internationally, was replaced by the era of Giolitti, under whom social reforms were made and the economy blossomed.

Garibaldi monument, Rome, built in 1895

■ The Call for Freedom and the Violent Unification Movement

The restoration of the prewar kingdoms and states in Italy stood in opposition to the national unification movement.

During the Congress of Vienna, Italy was largely restored to its pre-Napoleonic condition: Naples and Sicily were reunified as the ❸ Kingdom of the Two Sicilies, the Kingdom of Sardinia was reunited with Piedmont and Savoy, and Lombardy and the Veneto became part of the Austrian Empire. In addition to the regional realignment, the *Code Civil* and the political reforms from the Napoleonic era were also revised. The absolutist policies of the Italian kingdoms caused outrage, particularly among the liberal middle classes, who demanded political representation and the national independence of Italy.

The activities of secret societies such as the ❺ Carbonari and Giovane Italia were an expression of the national unification movement known as the *Risorgimento* ("resurgence"). King Charles Albert of Sardinia-Piedmont was unsuccessful in his attempt to conquer the Italian regions of Austria in 1848–1849 and had to abdicate in favor of his son ❹ Victor Emmanuel II. In 1849, Pope Pius IX was briefly expelled from the Papal States, and a ❻ republican commune was declared in Rome by Giuseppe Mazzini and ❶, ❷ Giuseppe Garibaldi. They were hopelessly outgunned when Louis-Napoleon's French troops intervened to restore the pope, and the commune fell in July.

2 Bust of Giuseppe Garibaldi, ca. 1870

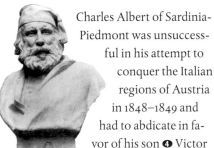

3

Ferdinand IV, King of the Two Sicilies, painting by A. R. Mengs, 1760

4

Victor Emmanuel II, King of Italy

Giuseppe Mazzini

Giuseppe Mazzini (1805–1872), who initially belonged to the Carbonari, founded the Giovane Italia ("Young Italy") secret society while in exile in 1831. He was sentenced to death in absentia for encouraging the Sardinian-Piedmontese army to mutiny. All rebellions that he instigated failed: in Piedmont in 1833, in Bologna in 1843, in Calabria in 1844, and in Rimini in 1845. Further uprisings in Mantua and Milan were equally unsuccessful. Mazzini, whose aim was the unity of Italy as a democratic republic, refused the crown after Italy unified as a monarchy. He died in Pisa in 1872.

Giuseppe Mazzini

5

Secret meeting of the Carbonari, wood engraving, 19th century

6

Crowd in front of the church of St. Maria Maggiore as the Roman republic is proclaimed, February 9, 1849, wood engraving, 19th century

| Feb 1849 | Proclamation of the Roman republic | May 1860 | "Expedition of the Thousand" under Garibaldi | 1871 | Rome becomes official capital of Italy |
| Jun 24, 1859 | Battle of Solferino | 1870 | Rome occupied by Italian troops | 1878 | "Italia Irredenta" founded |

■ The Path to Unity and International Dreams

Cavour and Garibaldi successfully fought for the unity of Italy. Internal reforms were accompanied by the attempt to turn Italy into a major European power.

After the Revolution of 1848, Sardinia-Piedmont retained its parliamentary constitution. The count of Cavour, ❿ Camillo Benso, who became prime minister of the kingdom in 1852, decided on reforms and sought an alliance partner for the unification of Italy. With French assistance, Cavour triumphed over Austria in the ❾ Battle of Solferino on June 24, 1859, which brought him Lombardy. In 1860, Emilia-Romagna, Tuscany, Modena, and Parma-Piacenza all voted to join Sardinia-Piedmont. In May 1860, Garibaldi's ❽ "Expedition of the Thousand" conquered the Kingdom of the Two Sicilies. When the Marches and Umbria acceded,

King Umberto I and crown prince Victor Emmanuel of Italy, the future King Victor Emmanuel II

almost all of Italy was united in a single state.

The Kingdom of Italy was proclaimed, with ⓫ Victor Emmanuel II as king, and the first parliamentary elections were held in 1861. Italy acquired the Veneto in a war against Austria in 1866 but decided to forego Trentino and Istria. After the occupation of the Papal States in 1870, the pope ruled over only the Vatican and Rome, which finally joined Italy as its capital in 1871. The liberals, under Prime Minister Agostino Depretis, provided for social improvements and expanded the electorate, though only to seven percent of the population. Founded in 1892, the Partito Socialista Itali-

Camillo Benso di Cavour, ca. 1855

ano became the main socialist party in Italy.

During the reign of ❼ King Umberto I after 1878, the organization "Italia Irredenta," dedicated to the incorporation of "unsaved Italian areas," was founded. Trentino and Istria stood at the center of these efforts and shaped the alliance policies of the new state until World War I. As Prime Minister, Francesco Crispi strove for a stronger and more credible Italy and also sought to acquire new colonies with the support of its two partners, Austria-Hungary and the German Empire, in the 1882 Triple Alliance. Its humiliating defeat in a war against Abyssinia in 1896, however, dashed Italian hopes of acquiring an East African empire.

After Umberto was assassinated in 1900, Victor Emmanuel III came to the throne. The left-wing prime minister Giovanni Giolitti pushed through numerous reforms in the years that followed: The right to strike and social security were introduced, and electoral suffrage was extended to almost all adult males. Internationally, Giolitti ensured continuity. In 1911, Italian forces occupied the city of Tripoli, and in a war against the Ottoman Empire, Italy seized control of the Dodecanese and the rest of Libya. At the outset of World War I Italy remained neutral but on April 26, 1915, Italy signed the "secret treaty of Lon-

Garibaldi's "Expedition of the Thousand" lands at Quarto, near Genoa, May 6, 1860

The Bersaglieri, an elite corps of the Piedmontese army, guarding Austrian prisoners captured during the 1859 war, in which Piedmont and France defeated the Austrian Empire in Northern Italy

don" with the Entente powers. The treaty offered Italy Trieste, the South Tirol, and Dalmatia in exchange for entering the war. Italy duly declared war on Austria-Hungary on May 23, 1915, and on Germany on August 28, 1916.

Pope Pius IX

Pope Pius IX, from a noble Italian family, proclaimed the infallibility of the pope in 1870 and is said to have left the Papal States with the words, "I might be infallible, but in any case I am bankrupt."

above: Pius IX, pope 1846–78

Monument to Victor Emmanuel II in Rome, built between 1885 and 1911

PORTUGAL AND SPAIN 1814–1914

Economically and politically, ❶ the Iberian Peninsula fell behind the rest of Western Europe and suffered a loss of both wealth and prestige as a result of the South American colonies' independence. Portugal was unable to industrialize during the whole of the 19th century, and democratization was achieved only after the turn of the century. In Spain, too, modernization progressed only haltingly after the restoration of the Bourbons; the power of Catholicism, the army, and the absolutist nobility was still too strong. Following the more settled 1870s and 1880s, political colonial conflicts resulted in destabilization that once more put the brakes on liberal reform.

The river Duoro, which flows from the high mountains near Soria across the Iberian Peninsula, near its mouth into the Atlantic Ocean at Porto

◼ Portugal: The Liberal Struggle and State Bankruptcy

The struggle between conservative and liberal political forces in Portugal hampered the country's modernization and made land reform impossible. In 1911 Portugal became a republic.

The Portuguese ❷ King John VI returned to Portugal from his Brazilian exile in 1821, a year after Portugal had been transformed by a liberal revolution into a constitutional monarchy. His son, as Emperor Pedro I of Brazil, proclaimed the colony independent to save it for the crown. In Portugal, the queen and her son Miguel attempted a coup against John VI in 1824, which was thwarted with the aid of the English.

When John VI died in 1826, Pedro— still in Brazil—took the Portuguese throne as King Pedro IV and strengthened the rights of the king through a new constitution. He then granted a constitutional charter and abdicated in favor of his daughter, Maria da Glória, but the Holy Alliance forced him to make his brother Miguel regent in 1827. The regent then had himself proclaimed King Miguel I in 1828 and reintroduced absolutism. Again the English came to Portugal's aid, and Pedro was able to restore his daughter to the throne in 1834 as Queen ❹ Maria II. In the ensuing years, the liberal Septembrists and the conservative Cartists struggled against each other; in 1836 a revolution restored the 1832 Constitution and a people's rebellion in 1846–1847 was suppressed. The governments of kings Pedro V and ❻ Louis I were marked by internal political turmoil in which foreign powers sometimes intervened. By 1892 the

Manuel II flees Portugal in 1911

country was also bankrupt.

Under Louis's successor, the weak ❺ Charles I, Prime Minister João Franco abolished the *Cortes*—the parliament— in 1907 and set up a dictatorship. In the next year, Charles and his eldest son Louis Philip were both assassinated. Thereupon the 19-year-old Manuel II ascended the throne. Despite coalition governments, amnesties and liberal legislation, the inexperienced king of Portugal was driven into ❸ exile in Great Britain following a republican coup d'état. On August 31, 1911, a new democratic constitution was proclaimed. In 1916, Portugal entered World War I against Germany. The Portuguese forces suffered heavy losses, but as a victor Portugal obtained some minor colonial territories from the dismantled German Empire in the final peace settlement.

John VI, king of Portugal

Maria II da Glória, queen of Portugal

Louis I, king of Portugal

Charles I, king of Portugal, with his wife, Amelie, and their firstborn child, Louis Philip, 1888

| 1822 | Independence of Brazil | 1834 | Maria II da Glória becomes queen | 1847–74 | Carlist Wars | 1892 | Bankruptcy of Portugal |
| 1828 | Independence of Uruguay | 1846/47 | People's rebellion | 1876 | New constitution in Spain |

■ Spain: Family Feuds and Sluggish Modernization

Carlist wars and rebellions obstructed Spain's progress in the 19th century. The flourishing period that began just after 1876 was already over by the turn of the century.

❼, ❾ King Ferdinand VII of Spain, even more than most other European monarchs after the end of the Napoleonic wars, pursued a restoration policy of extreme reaction. After he returned from France in 1814, he restored the Inquisition and then repealed the

9
Ferdinand VII, king of Spain

12
Isabella II, queen of Spain

13
Alfonso XII, king of Spain

1812 constitution that had given the word "liberal" to the world. A popular revolution in 1820 was crushed with French help, and Ferdinand's absolute authority was restored. In 1831 he designated his newborn daughter **❷** Isabella as the new queen rather than his brother Don Carlos. This triggered the turmoil of the Carlist wars that lasted more than 40 years, at the end of which Isabella's son **❸** Alfonso XII took the throne after the very brief First Republic.

Alfonso XII did away with absolutism in the constitution of 1876, which prohibited both the king and the army from interfering in politics. The next two decades were marked by stability and growing prosperity. **❽** Carlist revolts were suppressed, as was **⓫** the Cuban revolt of 1878, although it flared up again in 1895. The United States then **⓾**

7 Silver coin worth eight *real*, depicting King Ferdinand VII and the royal Spanish coat of arms, minted in 1822

intervened in Cuba, sparking the Spanish-American War of 1898, in the course of which Spain lost Cuba, Puerto Rico, the Philippines, and Guam to the United States.

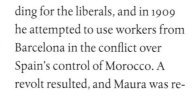

10
Spanish cartoon questioning the motives behind US support for the 1895 anti-Spanish revolt on Cuba: "I've had my eye on that morsel for a long time, guess I'll have to take it in!"

The Spanish defeat produced domestic instability. Anarchist and socialist factions gained in strength, and regionalist movements sought autonomy. The conservative head of government from 1907, Antonio Maura, demonstrated little understanding for the liberals, and in 1909 he attempted to use workers from Barcelona in the conflict over Spain's control of Morocco. A revolt resulted, and Maura was re-

8
Zumala-Carregui, commander of the forces of the royal pretender Don Carlos, conquers Bilbao in June 1835, during the Carlist Wars

11
Cubans burn down the sugar refinery at Los Ingenios, near Trinidad de Cuba, during the 1878 revolt

placed by the more liberal José Canalejas y Méndez; however, his promising reforms were cut short when he was murdered in 1912. Spain remained neutral during World War I, which allowed it to profit from record exports.

The Carlist Wars

The Carlist wars stemmed from the disputed succession of Ferdinand VII, who had designated his daughter Isabella II as heir to the throne. The Carlists, who wished to bring Ferdinand's brother Charles to the throne, waged war against the followers of Isabella's mother, María Cristina. The Carlists, whose strength was in rural northern Spain, fought against the more urbanized south. In 1839, the Carlists were defeated, but Isabella's coronation in 1843 triggered a second Carlist war. Isabella remained in power until the "glorious" revolution of 1868. In 1870 Amadeo, the son of the Italian king, came to the throne, but was forced to step down in 1873. After the First Republic, a military coup in 1874 placed Isabella's son, Alfonso XII, on the throne and brought an end to the Carlist wars in 1876.

Revolt against Queen Isabella II, Madrid, 1868

SCANDINAVIA ca. 1800–1917

The Scandinavian countries of Denmark, Norway, and ❶ Sweden gradually developed into modern democracies over the course of the 19th century. At the turn of the 20th century, they began developing into the social welfare state models that have typified Scandinavia ever since. At the same time, Denmark suffered territorial losses and economic problems, while Finland remained largely dependent on Russia, even after its political independence. Sweden experienced economic growth, but its union with Norway was not of long duration as Norway strove successfully for national autonomy.

Moon rising over Valdres, painting by Eugene, Prince of Sweden, 1890

■ Descent of Denmark and Finland into Dependency

Denmark lost Norway to Sweden, following which it also experienced a severe economic crisis. Finland was able to win independence from Russia in 1917.

above: Nyhavn in Copenhagen, part of the original harbor
left: Bust of the Russion tsar Nicholas I, marble, Christian Daniel Rauch

In 1801 and 1807, ❸ the British Royal Navy destroyed the Danish fortifications and fleet in ❷ Copenhagen, which was resisting the British blockade of Western

Bombardment and occupation of Copenhagen by British Navy in 1807

Europe. Denmark was then forced to ally with Napoleon, but as a result lost control of Heligoland and Norway to Sweden in the Treaty of Kiel in 1814. This loss of many markets led to inflation,

great poverty and eventually the bankruptcy of the state in an economic crisis that lasted until 1828. The country became a constitutional monarchy with universal suffrage and universal education in 1849.

A year earlier, Denmark had fought with Germany over ❻ Schleswig and Holstein, and in ❺ 1864 a second German-Danish war erupted, in which Denmark lost both duchies along with Lauenburg. After that, it maintained neutrality, even during World War I. A parliamentary constitution and the socialist legislation under Minister-President Jacob Estrup in the 1890s

won Denmark a reputation as a "model social state." Russia's plan to annex all of Finland was implemented following the Treaty of Tilsit in 1807. Finnish nationalist efforts following Napoleon's defeat were unsuccessful under the restoration policies of the Russian tsar ❹ Nicholas I. Liberal reforms by Alexander II—including equality for the Finnish language, reinstatement of the Finnish state parliament in 1869, and the creation of a conscript army in 1878—were repealed by Alexander III. In 1899, Finland lost its autonomous status through the February manifesto of Nicholas II, although it was reinstated for a time after the revolution of 1905 in Russia. On December 31, 1917, Vladimir Lenin confirmed Finland's independence.

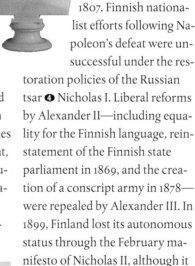

Danes flee Flensburg ahead of Prussian troops, 1848

Storming of the trenches of Düppel near Sonderburg, Denmark, by Prussian troops on Apr 18, 1864

Søren Aabye Kierkegaard

Denmark produced one of the greatest philosophers of the 19th century during its period of crisis. Søren Aabye Kierkegaard was born in 1813 in Copenhagen. After finishing his studies, he published—over a period of only ten years beginning in 1843—the philosophical papers that set the foundation for existentialism as one of the most significant philosophical movements of the 19th and 20th centuries. Kierkegaard died in Copenhagen in 1855.

above: Søren Kierkegaard

Sweden's Modernization and the Union with Norway

Sweden became a modern democracy in the 19th century. It united with Norway, which then chose independence at the turn of the century.

A coup in 1809 forced the ❽ abdication of the Swedish king Gustav IV Adolph in favor of his uncle Charles XIII, who in turn was forced to cede significant Finnish territories and the Åland Islands to Russia. In 1814, Sweden gained

8
An officers' coup forces the abdication of the Swedish king Gustav IV Adolph, March 13, 1809

Norway from Denmark, but also yielded its Pomeranian region, the last of its German territories.

Charles adopted the French marshal ❿ Jean-Baptiste Bernadotte as the heir to his throne in order to gain support from France. Under the name Charles XIV

John, Bernadotte became the king of Sweden and Norway in 1818, both of which flourished both economically and ⓫ culturally. His son ❼ Oscar I (1844–1859) supported liberal reforms and the pan-Scandinavian movement, which had the goal of uniting the Scandinavian nations. Oscar's son, Charles XV, continued these reforms and turned Sweden into a modern constitutional state. His brother ❾ Oscar II continued to improve social legislation. During the reign of ⓬ Gustav V, Sweden established universal suffrage and wise measures of social welfare.

The Swedish-Norwegian Union of 1815 had granted Norway its own administration, legislation, and army but all under the Swedish king. The Norwegian parliament abolished the *Storting*, or higher nobility, in 1821. The European revolutions of 1848 resulted in an increased national enthusiasm and consequently a desire for autono-

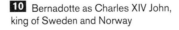

10 Bernadotte as Charles XIV John, king of Sweden and Norway

my. Universal suffrage was introduced in 1898, and in 1905 the Norwegians voted to sever their ties with Sweden. In November 1905 ⓭ Prince Charles of Denmark was crowned Haakon VII, king of Norway. Norway carried out exemplary social legislation and remained neutral in World War I, as did all the other Scandinavian nations.

Considerable numbers of emigrants left Sweden and Norway in the second half of the 19th century—about 1.5 million people from Sweden and another 100,000 from Norway—particularly to North America.

Swedish socialism was aided by the growth of industry, though it was successful mostly in the rural parts of the country which were attracted by theories of cooperation and social security.

7
Oscar I, king of Sweden and Norway, champion of a united Scandinavia

9
Oscar II, last king of Sweden and Norway before separation of the thrones

The Two Norwegian Languages

Under the banner of patriotic nationalism, the Norwegians wanted their "own" national language. Until this point, a Norwegian dialect of Danish, Riksmål ("national language"), had been the official written language in government and literature. The philologist Ivar Aasen then created Landsmål ("country language"), based on old rural Norwegian dialects, mid-century. Today, both languages—now named Bokmål ("book language") and Nynorsk ("new Norwegian")—are equally supported by the government and are both taught in schools.

11
The Norwegian composer Edvard Grieg, painting by Lenbach

12
Gustav V, king of Sweden, with his wife Victoria von Baden

13
Haakon VII, King of Norway and formerly Prince Charles of Denmark

---

1899 February Manifesto	**1909** Universal suffrage in Sweden	
1898 Universal suffrage in Norway	**1905** Norway cuts ties to Sweden	**Dec 31, 1917** Finland gains independence

1

Czars' residence: Winter Palace, St. Petersburg

RUSSIA FROM THE TREATY OF TILSIT TO THE ABDICATION OF THE LAST CZAR 1807–1917

Russia remained isolated from many of the political and economic developments that transformed Western Europe in the 19th century. Domestically autocratic and with an economy long based on a semi-feudal agricultural system, Russia faced a growing gulf between the vast majority of the population and the high nobility. Although Russia conquered large territories, its failures in foreign affairs weakened ❶ czarism. Tentative reform initiatives were always followed by periods of extreme reaction, which forced moderate liberals toward radicalism. With the onset of industrialization urban workers joined radical intellectuals in the Revolution.

■ Expansionism, Poland, and the Decembrist Rebellion

Russia was able to expand its vast territory, and Poland fought unsuccessfully to regain its independence. Young liberal army officers sought to bring about reform in a failed revolt.

The pact with Napoleon in the Treaty of Tilsit in 1807 gave the Russian Czar ❷ Alexander I the opportunity to expand his own empire. Russia gained the Åland

3

Soldiers and citizens prepare for the defense of the Polish capital, Warsaw, against Russian attack in 1830

4

The Polish Prometheus as personification of the rebels, in the talons of the eagle, heraldic symbol of czarist Russia

Islands and Finland from Sweden in 1809 and Bessarabia after the Russo-Turkish War of 1806–1812. In 1813 it seized Dagestan in a war with Persia; Czar Paul I had already occupied neighboring Georgia in 1801. After Napoleon had been defeated in his Russian campaign and definitively eliminated at the Battle of Waterloo, the 1815 Congress of Vienna also awarded Russia the major part of the Grand Duchy of Warsaw.

Poland was not prepared to accept the foreign rule of the Russians. Although it initially remained an independent kingdom, resistance—particularly the ❸ November 1830 insurrection—was suppressed, and Poland lost its autonomy. A further Polish uprising in 1863 was ❹ crushed, and Russia completely dissolved the kingdom five years later.

Domestically, Alexander I initially introduced some liberal reforms, such as the reorganization of the government and education system. The Holy Alliance that Russia formed with Austria at the Congress of Vienna in 1815 for the

purpose of preserving the monarchical order in Europe led to the czar's post-1820 restoration policy. In effect Russia became a bulwark against political radicalism in Europe, intervening to support regimes threatened by popular unrest. Within the Russian Empire, Alexander increased censorship and police powers.

2

Czar Alexander I Pavlovitch, portrait by François Gérard, 1814

Decembrists

Many Russian intellectuals were influenced by Western reform ideas and opposed an autocratic Russia. Some formed secret societies. Shortly after the death of Alexander I, a group of young liberal officers who wished to establish a constitutional monarchy organized a revolt in December 1825 in St. Petersburg. Though their demands were moderate Nicholas was deeply alarmed by the events. The extreme reaction and harshness of his reign is often linked to the effect of this revolt on the young czar. Six hundred of the Decembrists were subsequently condemned, five executed, and more than 100 exiled.

Execution of Decembrists on board the Russian warship *Grand Duke Vladimir*

Medallion with the leaders of the Decembrist revolt: Pestel, Ruilejev, Bestuchev, Muravjev, Kachovski

Territorial Gains and the Crimean War

Nicholas I intensified repressive policies and led his country to war in the Crimea.

❻ Nicholas I, brother and successor to Alexander I, increased repression through a clampdown on liberal universities and the arrest of dissidents. Following the European revolutions of 1848, he tightened these measures further and sent Russian troops into Austria to fight the Hungarian revolt there. Furthermore, he planned to Russianize the non-Russians in his empire in language and religion to make them loyal subjects.

Externally he continued an expansionist course. In 1828, Persia was forced to cede territories in Armenia. The sixth Russo-Turkish War secured sovereignty for Russia in the Caucasus and a "protectorate" over ❼ Walachia and Moldavia in the Treaty of Adrianople on September 14, 1829. Nicholas I occupied these territories militarily in 1853 with the aim of taking control of the Dardanelles, thereby fulfilling a long held ambition to gain naval access to the Mediterranean. This alarmed other major powers and drove his country into the calamitous Crimean War.

The Ottoman Empire allied itself with France, Great Britain, and the Kingdom of Sardinia against Russia. The Russians were able to annihilate ❾ the Ottoman fleet on November 30, 1853, but when the coalition declared war on Russia in 1854 Austria failed to enter the war on the side of its longtime ally, Russia. The Habsburgs's neutrality ended up alienating both sides. In September, the Allies then launched an attack in the Crimea against the main port of the Russian Black Sea fleet, ❺ Sevastopol. After an 11-month siege of the city, the Russians surrendered on September 9, 1855. Under the terms of the subsequent ❽ Treaty of Paris of

5

The capture of Fort Malakoff in Sevastopol by the French General Mac-Mahon, September 8, 1855

March 30, 1856, Russia lost Armenia and southern Bessarabia, as well as its protectorate over the Danubian principalities. The Black Sea was declared a neutral demilitarized zone, which represented a major setback to Russian ambitions in the region.

6   Czar Nicholas I Pavlovitch

7
Villagers in Walachia

8
Paris Congress from January to March 1856

The Crimean War

The significance of the Crimean War lay less in the conflict over a particular region. Rather, it was a turning point in the 19th century that sealed the end of the European balance of power that had been in place since the Congress of Vienna. For the first time in four decades the Great Powers engaged in a major war and the Holy Alliance of Austria and Russia was torn apart. The modest success of the British and French forces also helped to preserve the weak Ottoman Empire from Russian expansionism. Russia's role in continental affairs, developed under czars Alexander I and Nicholas I, was significantly weakened by the Crimean War.

9
Destruction of a part of the Ottoman fleet by the Russians in the port of Sinope, November 10, 1853

Russia under Alexander II

Czar Alexander II expanded the empire to the Pacific Ocean. Cautious reforms did not satisfy the reform movement, and the czar was assassinated by radical militants in 1881.

1 Construction of a bridge over the river Jenisseij, part of the Trans-Siberian railroad, built between1891 and 1904

2 Office of Czar Alexander II in the Winter Palace in St. Petersburg

3 Alexander II, Czar of Russia and Grand Duke of Finland, in military uniform

2, **3** Alexander II, who succeeded his father in 1855, ended the Crimean War. Following this fiasco in the south, Russia turned to focus its expansionist plans on the east. In 1856, Russia annexed portions of Sakhalin Island and in 1858 seized all the territory up to the Pacific coast, where **6** Vladivostok was founded in 1860. The czar sold Alaska to the United States in 1867.

In 1891 the **1** construction of the Trans-Siberian Railroad began, connecting the empire's far-flung provinces. Russia seized further territories in the southeast during the 1860s and 1870s so that the borders of the empire

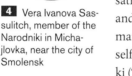

4 Vera Ivanova Sassulitch, member of the Narodniki in Michajlovka, near the city of Smolensk

extended almost as far as India.

Alexander II complied with the desires for reform in Russia by abolishing serfdom in 1861, followed three years later by the introduction of *zemstvos*—elected institutions of local government—and compulsory military service. But these measures did not satisfy the opposition and secret societies remained active. The self-styled **4** Narodniki ("Friends of the People") group was active primarily in rural areas.

A rebellion by Serbs and Montenegrins against Turkish rule in 1876 presented Russia with another opportunity to realize its ambitions in the Dardanelles. Russia took the side of the rebels,

igniting the Eighth Russo-Turkish War in January 1877, which further **5** weakened the Ottoman Empire. In the Treaty of San Stefano, on March 3, 1878, Russia gained large areas of Ottoman dominions and consequently gained hegemony over the Black Sea region. The Great Powers substantially revised this settlement at the Berlin Congress—under the Treaty of Berlin of July 13, 1878, which cut back

Russia's influence—but they did not resolve the "Eastern Question" of the disintegrating Ottoman Empire or prevent the looming crisis in the Balkans.

5 Capitulation of Turkish fortress Plevna, in present-day Bulgaria, December 10, 1877: The wounded Osman Pasha is presented to Czar Alexander II

Peter Kropotkin

In 1862, at the age of 20, Peter Alekseyevich Kropotkin joined the army. During his period of service he worked as a geographer in Siberia. In the 1870s he traveled to Western Europe for the Russian Geographical Society where he became acquainted with revolutionary social theories, and became a convinced anarchist. After returning to St. Petersburg in 1874, he was arrested for agitating against the czar but was able to escape to Western Europe two years later. He was put under house arrest for four years in France in the 1880s and then lived in exile in England until 1917. There he wrote a number of papers, notably his famous blueprint of an anarchist utopia, Mutual Aid *(1902). Disillusioned with the statism of Lenin's Bolshevism after his return to Russia, he gradually removed himself from political life.*

above: Prince Peter Alexseyevich Kropotkin

6 The port of Vladivostok on the Pacific coast, founded in 1860

| 1860 | Founding of Vladivostok | 1864 | Introduction of compulsory military service | 1876 | Serbs and Montenegrins revolt | Mar 3, 1878 | Treaty of San Stefano |
| 1861 | Serfdom abolished | 1867 | Alaska sold to USA | 1877 | Eighth Russo-Turkish War | Jul 13, 1878 | Treaty of Berlin |

■ The Russo-Japanese War and the First Revolution

The war against Japan was lost, which indirectly triggered the revolution of 1905, but the czar was once more able to regain control.

7 Assassination of Czar Alexander II by radical militants, March 13, 1881, in St. Petersburg

Czar Nicholas II Alexandrovich

11 Pogrom against the Jews in Russia in the second half of the 19th century

12 Cossack infantry in the Russo-Japanese War, 1904–1905

❼ Alexander II was assassinated with a bomb in 1881 by members of the terrorist group Narodnaya Volya ("People's Will"). His son and successor, **❾** Alexander III, repealed many of his liberal reforms. The authority of the zemstvos was truncated, censorship was increased, and the political police force was strengthened. Nationalist policies were also pursued in earnest: **⓫** discrimination against the Jews increased, and the Russianization of ethnic minorities was pushed further. All of these measures provided a boost to the anti-czarist resistance. Although Russia was still far from industrialized—economic measures were implemented in the 1880s in order to increase factory production—socialist ideas were slowly spreading among the workers. The organizations that formed were often led by exiles.

In international affairs, Russia allied with France against the Central Powers in 1890, thus establishing the constellation of the warring factions in World War I. The last czar, **❽** Nicholas II, who was crowned in 1894, continued to pursue an expansionist policy in the east. This brought Russia into conflict with the emerging power of Japan, which was also seeking to establish an empire on the Asian continent. A quarrel developed over Manchuria and the **⓬** Russo-Japanese War began with a Japanese attack on the Russian harbor of Port Arthur. Despite its numerical superiority

Russia suffered defeats on both land and at sea, climaxing in a naval battle in the Strait of Tsushima in May 1905. Russia was forced to admit defeat in the Treaty of Portsmouth in 1905.

Russia's humiliation in the war revealed the weaknesses of the czarist government, and this inspired a **❿** revolution in 1905. The result was a new census suffrage law that provided a conservative majority in the third Duma, the legislative assembly, which convened until 1912 but accomplished nothing. The need for change was highlighted in World War I. The October Revolution (in November by the western calendar) of 1917 resulted in the abdication of the last czar. Shortly afterwards, Nicholas II and his family were murdered in 1918.

9 Czar Alexander III Alexandrovich, who repealed his father's reforms, portrait by Ivan Nikolajewitsch Kramskoj

10 Lenin with revolutionaries during the revolt, December 1905

The "Bloody Sunday"

A meeting of the zemstvos in St. Petersburg demanded democratic changes from the czar. A rally on January 22, 1905 was attended by almost 200,000 people. Hundreds were killed when soldiers opened fire on the orders of the czar's uncle. This "Bloody Sunday" provoked outrage nationwide. Despite Nicholas II's October manifesto, uprisings occurred everywhere. The government ended the revolution at the beginning of 1906 with the aid of the military. The Duma that had been promised was dissolved following its protests against the new antidemocratic "fundamental law of the empire" of May 6, 1905.

above left: "Bloody Sunday" in St. Petersburg, January 22, 1905
above right: Caricature of Nicholas II, 1905

from 1891	Construction of the Trans-Siberian Railroad	**1905**	First Russian Revolution	**May 1905**	Battle of Tsushima
1904–1905	Russo-Japanese War	**Jan 22, 1905**	"Bloody Sunday"	**Nov 7, 1917**	Second Russian Revolution

THE BALKANS 1821–1914

Until the middle of the 19th century, the Balkans were almost completely in the hands of the Ottoman Empire, but it was in a process of decline, and by the outbreak of World War I in Europe its control had shriveled to a narrow strip of land. The Greeks were the first to rebel ❶ against the Turks in their war of independence in the 1820s. They were followed by other nationalities, who were supported by Russia, which saw itself as the patron of the Slavic nationalist movement. But the Balkan countries also fought among themselves over territory, which created an explosive political situation that was partly responsible for the start of World War I.

1 Colonel Favier leads the Greeks in the battle against the Turks, decorative wallpaper, 1827/28

■ Liberty in Greece

Greece's successful war of independence made it the first country on the Balkan Peninsula to free itself from Ottoman rule.

Patriotic nationalism in Greece increased at the end of the 18th century and led the Greeks to liberate themselves from Ottoman control. Though the rebellion of

2 Ypsilantis   **3** Lord Byron

❷ Alexander Ypsilantis, the leader of the Hetairia Philikon secret society, failed in 1821, the Peloponnesus region also rose up, led by ❺ Bishop Germanos of Patras.

Europe supported the Greeks: money and, above all, volunteer fighters such as ❸ Lord Byron, came to Greece to join the ❺ fight for independence. Many of these were romantics, motivated by the idea of liberating a country descended from Ancient Greece.

The long struggle was accompanied on both sides by ❼ massacres of the civilian population. The Peloponnesus was almost completely retaken by the Turks, but the sultan, Mahmud II, had to

4 George I, King of Greece

ask the Egyptian viceroy, Muhammad Ali, for help. The Egyptians reconquered the southern Peloponnesus in 1826. Russia, Great Britain, and France then sent a fleet to Greece that annihilated the Turkish fleet at Navarino in 1827. Russia was also victorious in the Russo-Turkish war in 1829, and Greece—which at first consisted mainly of the Peloponnesus—was granted the status of an independent kingdom at the London Conference on February 3, 1830.

The first king of the Hellenes was Otto of Bavaria, who was crowned in 1832. With little success, he struggled with internal uprisings that led to his abdication in 1862. His successor in 1863 was Prince William George of Denmark as ❹ George I, who ruled for 50 years before he was assassinated in 1913 in Salonika. Over time, the Greeks were able to significantly expand their territory through wars against the disintegrating Ottoman Empire and in the Balkan Wars of 1912–13.

5 Hellas with her "children" Kapodistrias, Ypsilatni, Lord Byron and the bishop Germanos and others, painting by Theodoros Vryzakis

Count Ioánnis Antónios Kapodistrias

Count Ioánnis Antónios Kapodistrias was foreign minister of Russia and a negotiator for Czar Alexander I at the Congress of Vienna in 1815. He quit the Russian service when a dispute developed between

him and the czar over the fate of Greece. Kapodistrias then participated in the Greek war of independence and was elected president of an independent Greece in 1827. He was assassinated on October 9, 1831, in Nauplia.

above: Ioánnis Antónios Kapodistrias

6 Bishop Germanos of Patras blesses the flag of an independent Greece, painting by Theodoros Vryzakis

7 *The Massacre of Chios*, retaliatory strike of the Ottomans in April 1822, painting by Delacroix, 1824

The Balkan Powder Keg

The Balkan nations were able to liberate themselves and gain independence from the Ottoman Empire but fought among themselves over land.

Bulgaria, Romania—created in 1861 out of the unification of Walachia and Moldavia—Montenegro, and Serbia became autonomous under the Treaty of San Stefano following the Russo-Turkish War of 1877–78. Bulgaria became a principality obligated to pay tribute to the sultan. Serbia had dreams of a greater Serbian Empire, however, and in 1885 ❾ King Milan I Obrenovic waged a war against Bulgaria over Macedonia; Austria-Hungary made sure that Serbia gained only a small western region. Prince Alexander I of Bulgaria lost his throne in a coup to ❿ Ferdinand I of the House of Saxe-Coburg-Gotha, who made himself tsar of Bulgaria in 1908 and proclaimed the country independent. Bosnia and Herzegovina were occupied in the same year by Austria-Hungary, creating an ⓫ annexation crisis that almost led to war with Serbia, which saw its dreams of a great Serbian Empire as destroyed.

Serbia, Montenegro, Greece, and Bulgaria formed the Balkan League and declared war on the Ottoman Empire in October 1912 and in short order captured almost all of its European territories and reduced it to its present territories. The Treaty of London on May 30, 1913, left the Turks

8
The inhabitants of Melknik burn their city before they flee

with only a small piece of territory in Europe, but did not resolve the problem of control over Macedonia, contested between Bulgaria and Serbia. Consequently, Serbia and Greece began the ❽ Second Balkan War against Bulgaria on June 29, 1913. By July, Romania, the Ottoman Empire, and Montenegro had joined in against Bulgaria. The Treaty of

Bucharest of August 10, 1913, stated that Bulgaria was to cede territory to Romania; Macedonia was absorbed for the most part by Serbia and Romania; and Albania became independent.

Unfortunately, that still did not eliminate the tension in the Balkans. Serbia had become significantly stronger, which the multinational state of Austria-Hungary, with its strong and vocal slavic population, regarded with distrust. When the heir to the Austro-Hungarian throne, Archduke Franz Ferdinand, was ⓬ shot on June 28, 1914, in Sarajevo by Gavrilo Princip, a Serbian nationalist, it led to the July Crisis during which Serbia was unable to fulfil an Austo-Hungarian ultimatum and Vienna declared war on Serbia. This escalated when the other European nations intervened and it ultimately led to World War I.

9
King Milan I Obrenovic

10
Ferdinand I

The Congress of Berlin

From June 13 to July 13, 1878, the Great Powers—Austria-Hungary, Great Britain, France, Italy, Russia, and the German and Ottoman empires—sat down together in an attempt to defuse the Balkan situation. The other powers were particularly interested in halting Russia's advance on the Black Sea in the direction of the Dardanelles, which would put it in a position of dominance. Among other things, the north of Bulgaria was declared independent and Eastern Rumelia in the south was made an autonomous province.

The Congress of Berlin, painting by Anton von Werner, 1881

11
Analogy of the Annexation Crisis: The peal bell can not ring because each nation pulls it in a different direction

12
Assasination of the Austro-Hungarian heir to the throne, Franz Ferdinand, by Gavrilo Princip

THE OTTOMAN EMPIRE CA. 1800–1914

The ❶ Ottoman Empire, which at its height stretched from the Mediterranean to Persia, experienced political and economic decline during the 19th century. From the late 1700s, the Ottoman government had instituted reforms from above, but these were not supported by the old elite and, later, did not go far enough to please the increasingly strong and liberal reform-minded younger generation. The period of reforms was accompanied by a great loss of territory that was the start of the breakup of the great empire.

The palace Dolmabahçe Sarayi near Istanbul, capital of the Ottoman Empire, completed in 1843

■ Territorial Losses and Internal Reforms

The Ottoman Empire suffered territorial losses at the end of the 19th century primarily in the Balkans. Domestically, the sultan prepared reforms.

Decree signed by Sultan Mahmud II

The French Revolution and the Wars of Liberation against Napoleon also awoke thoughts of freedom and nationalistic feelings in the European territories dominated by the Turks. ❷ Greece revolted and finally gained its independence in 1829, while the rest of the Balkans was in rebellion during the whole of the 19th century. The European great powers, above all Russia, increasingly intervened,

Memorial to Count von Moltke, military instructor for the restructuring of the army of Mahmud II, Istanbul

and they supported the independence of Bulgaria, Romania, Serbia, and Montenegro at the Congress of Berlin in 1878.

In North Africa, Egypt, too, sought independence from the Ottoman Empire. Despite initial support of the Turks by an alliance of Austria, Prussia, and Great Britain, the Egyptians succeeded in 1841. The Maghreb states increasingly came under the influence of Europe. In 1830, France occupied and then colonized Algeria, and in 1881 it made Tunisia a French protectorate.

Domestically, the Ottoman sultans had to contend with a weakening of their central power. The first so-called reform sultan was Selim III, who ascended the throne in 1789 and reorganized the state, its financial administration, and the army according to Western European models. He was not able to withstand the resistance of the traditional elite, however—particularly the military Janissaries, who finally murdered him. His plans were later carried out by ❸ Mahmud II, who destroyed the Janissaries after a ❹ revolt in 1826 and replaced them with a conscription army

controlled by the central government. He also fostered the sciences by establishing state schools in which he advocated a general secularization. The Tanzimat reform era, a new phase of reforms, was instituted under Sultan Abdülmecid I. Along with a new

Suppression of the Janissary revolt of 1826

Railway viaduct at the narrow pass of Ushak

Attacking Janissaries engage Greek fighters during the Greek war of independence from the Ottomans, painting by Eugéne Delacroix, 1827

❺ restructuring of the army, the administration was reorganized in line with the French model and the legal standardization of all of the empire's subjects was carried out. New roads, ❻ railroads, and a telegraph system were constructed. For this purpose, foreign loans were drawn, but the government was unable to pay the interest on them after 1875. This, together with corruption and the enormous luxury in which the sultans lived—Abdülmecid had just had a huge new ❼ palace built on the shores of the Bosporus—finally led to the financial ruin of the Ottoman Empire.

Stairwell in the Dolmabahçe Sarayi palace

1826 | Janissaries climinated

1830 | France occupies Algeria

1875 | State bankruptcy

1829 | Greece gains independence

1841 | Egypt gains independence

1877 | Parliament created

■ End of the Reforms and Rise of the Young Turks

The Young Turks wanted the political and economic modernization of their country, but failed with their policies.

After the death of ❽ Sultan Abdülmecid I, his brother Abdülaziz ascended the throne in 1861, but he was forced to abdicate in 1876 and was replaced by Abdülhamid II. He put a constitution in force, guaranteed freedom of religion and the press, and installed a ⓫ parliament in 1877—which he then dissolved again when the empire had to defend itself against the pressure of the Europeans. Russia declared war on the Ottoman Empire. By the Treaty of San Stefano of 1878, Turkey surrendered

8 Sultan Abdülmecid

Bessarabia. The Congress of Berlin (1878) marked a further loss of Ottoman territory. Abdülhamid's reign soon became a dictatorial and centralized one. The ❿ mass murder of 200,000 Armenians in 1896 occurred during his reign. Although the sultan was able to improve the economic situation, his autocratic regime stirred up resistance from liberals, who organized in the Young Turk movement. A revolt took place in 1909 with the support of General ❾ Enver Pasha.

The Young Turks assumed power, restored the constitution and parliament, and ruled for ten years under the nominal regency of ⓬ Mehmed V. They attempted to modernize the country by curtailing the influence of religion in schools and the legal system while seeking to kick-start industrialization. But even this couldn't save the "sick man of Europe."

The two ⓭ Balkan Wars of 1912–1913 further weakened the declining empire and left it only a small piece of land—Eastern Thrace—in Europe. The Turkish government tried to remain neutral during World War I, but was pulled in on the side of the Central Powers by a promise of German support and funding and the need for allies against Russia.

9 Enver Pasha

10 Massacre of the Armenians in the Turkish part of Armenia, 1896

11 The first Turkish parliament meets in the year 1877

12 Prince Reshad is proclaimed Sultan Mehmed V

13 The Turks flee from the conquered areas of the Balkan states

The Young Turks

This movement had been formed by Midhat Pasha in 1868, with the aim of reforming Turkish institutions. Around the 1880s, many officers, officials, and intellectuals, mostly young, who were not in agreement with the autocratic running of the Turkish state and sought a revitalization of the country, began uniting. The Young Turks advocated a strategy of liberalization, with the goal of establishing a constitutional monarchy, but were still forced at first to act from abroad. Various groups joined together and were able to depose Sultan Abdülhamid II and install Mehmed V on the throne. The Young Turks were not able to put the Ottoman Empire back on its feet, however, and were forced to hand over the government in October 1918.

Sailors loyal to the Sultan shoot their Young Turk commander, who wanted them to attack the sultan's palace

1

EGYPT 1798–1914

Since being conquered by Sultan Selim I in 1517, Egypt had been administered by governors from the Mameluke dynasty. This regency ended with the success of Napoleon's campaign. After the expulsion of the French, the Ottoman officer ❶ Muhammad Ali Pasha ruled Egypt autonomously and with his policies laid the foundation for the modern Egyptian state. To accomplish this, the country borrowed heavily, which strained the treasury but was profitable for European powers—especially Great Britain, which occupied Egypt at the end of the 19th century.

Muhammad Ali, governor of Egypt

■ Egypt under Muhammad Ali

Muhammad Ali extended Egypt's borders and began modernization.

Napoleon landed at Alexandria in 1798 and began the conquest of Egypt, which was accompanied by ❸ the research and plundering of Egypt's archaeological treasures. The French defeated the ❷ Mamelukes near the ❹ pyramids, presenting a challenge to Great Britain, which had its own interests in North Africa and the Ottoman Empire. When the Ottomans expelled the French in 1803, Egypt became autonomous, although it formally still belonged to the Ottoman Empire.

❺ Muhammad Ali Pasha, an Albanian who had fought against Napoleon as a Turkish officer, became the Ottoman governor of Egypt in 1805. He used the weaknesses of the Mameluke upper

The Suez Canal

A route between the Mediterranean and the Red Sea has existed sporadically since antiquity. Spurred by the investigations of Napoleon's scientists, Egypt granted the Frenchman Ferdinand de Lesseps permission to build a canal in 1854. The construction took ten years. After the opening of the canal in 1869, a majority of the stock of the company owning the concession came into French possession, while the rest was Egyptian. The Suez Canal was of particular interest to the British because it shortened the sea journey to India. Consequently they bought the bankrupt Egyptians' share of stocks in 1875 and then militarily occupied the canal in 1882.

above: Viscount Ferdinand de Lesseps

class to strengthen his power and destroyed them in 1811. In the following years, he invested in developing industry and agriculture. To gain control of the trade routes, he extended the country's borders to the east and south. Muhammad Ali's son Ibrahim Pasha defeated the Wahhabis living in the Arabian Peninsula in battle in 1819 and conducted further campaigns in 1820–1822 in the Sudan and in 1833 in Syria.

Only a few years earlier, the Egyptian fleet had helped Sultan Mahmud II against the Greeks. Now the Egyptians attacked the Ottoman Empire. The advance of the Egyptians was halted only by the intervention of Prussia, Austria, Great Britain, and Russia—who had an interest in saving Constantinople from being conquered. Ibrahim Pasha's fleet was defeated in the ❻ naval Battle of Navarino in 1827. The Egyptians still had control of Syria but lost it when they attacked the Ottoman Empire for a second time in 1839. Egypt then became a viceroyalty and Muhammad Ali was awarded hereditary rule over Egypt.

2

Mameluke warrior

3

Scientists measure the Sphinx in Giza as part of the Egyptian expedition

4

Napoleon defeats the Mamelukes in the battle at the pyramids

5

Muhammad Ali, accompanied by his son Ibrahim Pasha

6

Naval battle at Navarino on October 20, 1827

The Internal Development of the State and Growing Influence of the European Powers

The building of the Suez Canal and the development of its infrastructure led Egypt to financial ruin while it fought against the revolt in Sudan. Great Britain occupied the Suez Canal and later controlled the entire country.

7 The ships of the sovereigns cross the Suez Canal for the first time on November 17, 1869

Muhammad Ali died in 1849 and his successors continued with the modernization of the country but came increasingly under the influence of European powers. Muhammad Ali's fourth son

9 Ismail Pasha

11 Cartoon of the relationship between Abbas II Hilmi and the occupying British power

8 Said Pasha incurred huge debts abroad, which increased again as a result of the development projects of his successor **9** Ismail Pasha. The building of factories, the development of roads and the postal system, and particularly the construction of the **7** Suez Canal—commissioned by Said Pasha in 1854—overburdened the state treasury. The growing debt forced the Egyptians to accept French and British ministers in their cabinet in exchange for finances. Ismail Pasha, who had once so victoriously fought in the south of the land and extended Egyptian hegemony to the borders of Ethiopia, was deposed and replaced by his son Tawfiq Pasha, who restructured the country's public finances.

Meanwhile, Great Britain was working on securing **10** control over the Suez Canal. After the British acquired the Egyptian allocation of stock in 1875, a rebellion of Egyptian officers under War Minister Arabi Pasha broke out against Tawfiq very conveniently in 1881. In 1882 the Christians of Alexandria were massacred, which led to British intervention. The British crushed the rebellion and then in 1882 took full control of the country with a powerful garrison. Egypt had became an Anglo-Egyptian condominium to which Sudan was added between 1895 and 1899. The dynasty of Muhammad Ali remained on the throne with Abbas II Hilmi Pasha, but the **11** British governor-general ruled

the land. Abbas, who supported Egyptian efforts to regain self-government, was replaced by his uncle Hussein Kamil in 1914. In order to prevent Egypt from supporting the Central Powers in World War I, as the Ottoman Empire had done, it was declared a British protectorate.

8 Said Pasha

10 The occupation of the Suez Canal by British troops

The Mahdi Rebellion

After Muhammad Ali, the Egyptians continued the conquest of Sudan in 1874, which from 1877 was placed under the administration of British governors. In 1881 a rebellion led by Muhammad Ahmad broke out against the occupation. As the self-proclaimed Mahdi, "the (divinely)

Grave monument of Muhammad al-Mahdi in the Great Mosque of Omdurman, Sudan

guided one"—the messianic deliverer expected by Muslims—he supported a war against Egypt, conquering Kordofan in 1883 and, two years later, Khartoum after his victory over the English. He was then recognized as ruler of East Sudan, though he died the same year in Omdurman. The Mahdi State existed only until the invasion of the Egyptians and British, who defeated the Mahdists in 1898 at Omdurman. From 1899, Sudan was also an Anglo-Egyptian condominium.

| **1854** | Commission to build Suez Canal | **1881** | Mahdi revolt | **1914** | Egypt becomes British protectorate |
| **1881** | Putsch by Arabi Pasha | | **1882** | British occupy Canal Zone | |

PERSIA AND AFGHANISTAN CA. 1800–1914

Competition between Great Britain and ❶ Russia over control of the "Asian hub" heavily influenced the history of Afghanistan and Persia in the 19th century. Russian plans for expansion in southern Asia presented a threat to India, the "crown jewel" of the British Empire. The European powers were threatening Persia and Afghanistan externally and striving for influence internally, destabilizing regimes in both countries. The discovery of oil in Persia in 1908 raised the stakes, but Afghanistan managed to secure a degree of autonomy as a buffer state between the Russian Empire and British India.

Reception in the Russian embassy in Teheran in the 1830s

■ Persia: Dependency on the British and Russians

Two great powers, Great Britain and Russia, vied for control of Persia, and this was reflected in the increasing influence of these two on Persia's internal politics.

Fath Ali, the shah of Persia, suffered numerous defeats at the hands of the Russians during his reign. In the treaties of Golstan in 1813 and Turkmanchay in 1828, the Persians lost all their possessions in the Caucasus. In the 1870s and 1880s, the Russians again put further pressure on the country, occupying the Persian territories east of the Caspian Sea and south of the Aral Sea, and in 1884 the area around Merv.

The internal strains grew as well. ❷ Shah Nasir ad-Din, who had traveled throughout Europe, pursued a cautious reform policy during his 1848–1896 reign, which introduced a measure of European liberal thought into his country. Great Britain had a particularly strong interest in and influence over the Persian economy. As a result, the shah was forced to contend with powerful pro-British merchants who opposed the autocratic system and demanded a hand in decision making, while any concessions to reform were met with accusations of Europeanization from the influential Shiite clerics.

Since the 1840s, the shah had been fighting the Bab movement, which later gave rise to the ❸ Baha'i faith. He used harsh measures against this Islamic offshoot group and almost completely eradicated its followers after an attempted assassination in 1852.

Shah Nasir ad-Din

Internal tension grew with every concession the shah made to the British, who, for example, demanded permission to build a railroad and industrialize the country. The granting of the tobacco trade monopoly to Britain provoked widespread protest. In October 1906, the shah was forced to summon a national assembly and establish a constitution, turning Persia into a constitutional monarchy. Shah Muhammad Ali, who came to power the following year, attempted to reverse these changes, but ❹ unrest and rebellions forced him to abdicate. When Russia and Britain signed the Anglo-Russian Entente of 1907 in St. Petersburg, they divided Persia into respective zones of influence which they proceeded to occupy in 1909.

Oilfields in Persia

Oil field in Baku

Oil reserves were first discovered in Persia in 1908, and within a year the first processing refinery had been built. The Anglo-Persian Oil Company developed oilfields in the southwestern province of Khuzestan on the Persian Gulf, which today is thought to have more than 10 percent of the world's known oil reserves. The British government secured a controlling interest in the company and occupied the region on the pretext of securing its commercial interests, which had previously been designated as "neutral territory" in an agreement with Russia. However, the British attempt to gain complete control of the country and the oil in the following decades failed, partly due to the hostility of the Persian population to foreign occupation.

Abdu'l-Baha, son of the founder of the religion of the Baha'i, preaching the Baha'i faith in Constantinople

Rebel fighters during the unrest that led to Muhammad Ali's abdication in 1907

■ Afghanistan: Precarious Independence

The Russians and British effectively neutralized each other in their struggle for strategic hegemony in Central Asia, thus permitting Afghanistan a precarious independence.

Ahmad Shah Durrani, who ascended to the throne in 1747, founded what is today known as Afghanistan. He expanded it in all directions, particularly into northern India. However, the empire had collapsed completely by 1818 due to internal divisions. In 1826, Dost Muhammad Khan captured Kabul and established a new emirate, which soon presented a threat to the interests of the British and Russians.

After Dost Muhammad opened ❺ negotiations with the Rus-

6 Shir Ali Khan gives instructions to his men during the Second Anglo-Afghan War of 1878–1879

8 Fortress occupied by British troops on the frontier with the Russian empire

sians, the British took the initiative and marched in. During the First Anglo-Afghan War of 1838–1842, the British seized Kandahar and Ghazni. Shah Shuja, a grandson of Ahmad Shah Durrani, was installed as a sovereign acceptable to the British. A counterattack by Akbar Khan, son of Dost Muhammad, proved successful, and the British troops were forced to withdraw. Dost Muhammad once again took over his emirate, and the conflict ended peacefully with the Treaty of Peshawar in 1855.

When ❻ Shir Ali Khan decided to resume dialogue with Russia in 1878 and refused to accept British representation in Kabul, the British army once again invaded Afghanistan. This time, there was no reaction from the Afghans to the conquest of ❾ Kabul during the ❽ Second Anglo-Afghan War of 1878–1879. In the ❿ Treaty of Gandamak that ended the war, Yaqub Khan permanently conceded the ❼ Khyber Pass and other territories to Great Britain; the British made guarantees of protection from foreign aggression but retained the right to import British products and control Afghan foreign affairs. In 1893,

5 An Afghan diplomatic envoy with his entourage, Russia, 1830s

the Durand Treaty fixed the frontiers of Afghanistan with British India, which forms the present Afghan-Pakistan border.

In 1907 Afghanistan became independent indirectly, when Russia and Great Britain reached an agreement to abandon territorial claims there. Afghanistan effectively became a buffer state between the two major powers, and despite the Anglo-Russian alliance, Kabul remained neutral during the First World War. Britain, however, retained its influence in the country, and especially Afghan foreign policy, until 1919, when the heir to the throne was assassinated due to resentment of the pro-British stance of the monarchy.

7 Summit of Mount Hindukush

9 Conquest of Kabul by British forces in 1879

10 Signing of the Treaty of Gandamak, May, 1879

| 1878–79 | Second Anglo-Afghan War | 1906 | National Assembly called | 1909 | First oil refinery |
| 1893 | Durand Agreement | 1907 | Treaty of St. Petersburg | 1909 | Persia occupied by Russia and England |

INDIA CA. 1800–1914

The imperial rule of extensive areas of India by the British required a large administration and the co-option of local elites. Ironically the forced unification of the vast fragmented subcontinent served to raise awareness of common history, ❺ culture, and ❶ religion. This led in the course of the 19th century to concrete demands, first for participation in government, and eventually for self-determination. The Indian National Congress was the organ of the Liberal Nationalists, which began the struggle for independence in the 20th century.

The goddess Durga fights the demon Mahishasura

■ Expansion of British-ruled Territories in India and the outbreak of the Sepoy Rebellion

The East India Company pushed further into the country. The introduction of a Western-style administration and education system led to the emergence of an Indian intellectual class that soon began to demand democratic rights.

The city of Delhi ca. 1850

India was a patchwork of 500 separately governed territories that the British appropriated piece by piece during the wars against the Maratha Confederation in 1775–1782, 1803–1805, and 1817–1818. The conquered territories were either administered directly by the British or left under the rule of ❹ Indian vassal princes. Only the Sikhs and the Gurkhas were truly independent of British rule.

The development of the administration system and infrastructure was given priority—the construction of an enormous ❸ railroad network, which opened in 1853, to open up the interior of the country, better roads, and a reliable postal system. A unified, national legal system and a single currency were also introduced.

At the beginning of the 19th century the need for qualified Indian workers led to the introduction of Western educational insti-

Platform of an Indian railway station on the network that opened in 1853

tutions where Indians qualified as officials, lawyers, and teachers. In 1857 universities opened in Madras, Bombay, and Calcutta, and a wealthy few came to Britain to study. A small class of Indians with Western education thus emerged, and some came to express anger over the conquests and annexations of the British. Political organizations were soon composing petitions that demanded democratic rights and access to things. These critical voices were all but ignored by the British at first, but this changed with the Sepoy Rebellion

of 1857 in ❷ Delhi which, though limited to northern and central India, affected the whole of the country. The mutiny was provoked by the use of cartridge grease which, containing both pork and beef, defiled both Hindus and Muslims.

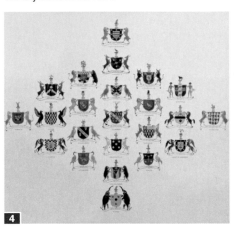

Emblem of the Indian Rajas

❺ Indian astrolabe

The uprising of the Sepoys

The Sepoys were Indian soldiers primarily from the Punjab region, which had been annexed in 1849. In 1857 the Sepoy Rebellion (or Indian Mutiny) erupted. Resentment of the gulf between the British officer class and the common soldiers was one of the main causes, as was the fear of Christian missionary efforts sparked by insensitivities to religious practices. The Sepoys liberated imprisoned soldiers in Meerut, near Delhi, killing British citizens in the process. This mutiny ignited the rebellion of the recently disempowered upper class in Oudh, and princes, lords of manors, and peasants fought side by side. Delhi was seized and the last Mogul, Bahadur Shah II, was proclaimed emperor of India. Delhi and the encircled British seat in Lucknow were retaken by the British in 1857.

Execution of Indian soldiers following the mutiny's suppression

■ The Awakening of the Indian Nation

The Indian educated class organized itself into political movements and demanded a voice in the running of British India.

Following the Sepoy Rebellion of 1857, the last Mogul, Bahadur Shah II, was banished, and the British crown took direct control of India. The East India Company was dissolved in 1858 and

6

Victoria, Queen of Great Britain and Ireland, Empress of India

7

Hindi begging the British for food, ca. 1873

8

Indian military units revolt against the British occupying forces

❻ Queen Victoria assumed the title of "Empress of India" in 1876; from this time until Indian independence, the British monarch was simultaneously the **❾** Emperor of India. The governor-general, formerly the head of the East India Company, was then appointed viceroy. In addition to India, his domain included the

present-day states of Sri Lanka, Pakistan, Bangladesh, and Myanmar.

In the second half of the century, the British continued the development of the administration and infrastructure. Revenues gained from property taxes, the opium monopoly, and a salt tax were sent to London, while the Indian people suffered under the ruthless exploitation of their country. Millions lost their lives in **❼** famines.

The new generation of Indian intellectuals increasingly absorbed ideas of democracy and

nationalism; the latter began to develop strongly in the 1870s. On the one hand there was the desire for recognition by the West; on the other there was **❿** cultural and religious pride. These contradictory desires shaped the nationalists' debates into the 20th century. The government of the liberal viceroy Lord Ripon gave the nationalists further impetus. In 1885 the Indian National Congress was founded, which would lead first to negotiations with the British and later an independent India. In 1906, Indian Muslims formed their own party, the Muslim League, which better represented them as a minority.

When the British wanted to divide the Bengal region to form a province with a Muslim majority, there were attacks against the British, boycotts, and a **❽** revolt. The British were forced to abandon the division. Because the rebellious Bengals had become a danger for the viceroy, the seat of government was moved from Calcutta to Delhi in 1911.

Sir Rabindranath Tagore

In 1913, Rabindranath Tagore became the first Asian to win the Nobel Prize for literature. This increased the Indian sense of nationalism, as the Indian culture was now in some respects recognized by the West as an equal. Tagore did what he could for the farmers in the villages of Bengal. Among other things, he established a cooperative grain silo and had roads and hospitals built. He criticized the English school system and the neglect of the mother tongue that it caused. He founded a school after the ancient Indian model called Ashram in Shantiniketan, West Bengal, where a university still operates today.

above: Rabindranath Tagore

9

George V, king of Great Britain and Ireland, is crowned Emperor of India during a lavish ceremony held in Delhi, in 1911

10

Sitar player, miniature from Dhubela, Rajasthan, ca. 1800

CHINA TO THE LAST OF THE EMPERORS

CA. 1840–1912

The high point of the Manchu Dynasty (1644–1912) had passed. China was increasingly losing political and economic power to the British, who had prevailed in two Opium Wars. The British, Russians, and French were claiming more and more Chinese territory for themselves. Internally, the Manchus had to contend with secret societies and religious movements, as well as the widespread opium use within the country. Weakened in this way, the Manchu state broke apart after hesitant reforms and was replaced in 912 by a republic.

1 Chinese poster against increasing European influence in the country

■ The Opium Trade and European Treaty Ports

The Opium Wars forced ❶ European economic and cultural influence upon China.

Ever since the British had begun importing opium from India into China, China's trade balance had significantly worsened. The import of opium into China was banned under Chinese law, as the country was able to manufacture enough for medicinal purposes domestically. The use of opium was banned in 1810. When the imperial Chinese government in Canton confiscated large amounts of opium, it led to the ❷ First Opium War in 1840, because the

4
Hung Hsiu

British refused to relinquish the drug trade. An expeditionary force with warships militarily enforced the continuation of the trade. The weakened Chinese were forced to agree to the first

"unequal treaty," which was signed in Nanjing on August 29, 1842. It stipulated the payment of war reparations by the Chinese, the cession of Hong Kong to the British, and the opening up of five further ports to British trade. But the new conditions still did not go far enough for the British because they did not coincide with their concept of free trade.

The Europeans also won the Second Opium War, or Lorcha War (1856–1860). In the ❸ Treaty of Tientsin in 1858, they secured ten more "treaty ports." When the Chinese resisted and mishandled British prisoners, 20,000 British and French soldiers destroyed the ❺ emperor's summer palace. The Treaty of Beijing in 1860 legalized the opium trade. In addition, cheaper European products flooded into China after the import duty was lowered, destroying the Chinese economy and its chances of modernization.

Internally, the *Taiping* (Great Peace) movement—a synthesis of traditional religious and Christian views demanding an egalitarian social system—became a serious opponent of the Manchus. Its followers revolted against the impe-

rial government under the leadership of ❹ Hung Hsiu in 1851 in the Taiping Rebellion and erected their own state, which encompassed a large portion of southern and southeastern China with Nanjing as its capital. The rebellion was ended in 1864 by the Manchus with British and French aid and cost the lives of 20 million people. After that, Muslim uprisings shook the province of Yunnan between 1864 and 1878. In Sinkiang, on the western rim of the Chinese Empire, Yakub Beg established a Muslim Turkish empire from 1865 to 1877 as khan of Kashgar.

2
The English force the Chinese to buy British opium from India

Treaty of Tientsin between England and China, June 26, 1858

5
The emperor's summer palace in Beijing

1840	First Opium War		1851	Taiping Rebellion		1858	Treaty of Tientsin		1864–78	Muslim revolts in Yunnan
		Aug 29, 1842	Treaty of Nanjing		1856–60	Second Opium War		1860	Treaty of Beijing	

■ The End of the Empire

China's influence in Asia diminished. The Boxer Rebellion demonstrated the weaknesses of the Manchu government, and it was soon replaced by a republic.

After China had already lost its northern territories to Russia in 1860, it lost Vietnam to France in the Sino-French war of 1884–1885 and Burma to Great Britain in 1886. The intervention of Japan and China in a revolt in Korea in 1894 then triggered the ❼ Sino-Japanese War. Despite China's superiority in troops, the war—especially after the lost naval battle in the estuary of the Yalu River—ended with defeat and a large loss of territory. Influence in Korea, which then became independent, had to be given up.

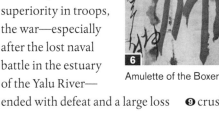
6
Amulette of the Boxer

Toward the end of the 19th century, the voices that demanded ever more reform, after the Japanese model, finally reached Emperor Te Tsung. He was willing to transform China into a constitutional monarchy with further modernizations. But a coup d'état by the powerful dowager empress Tz'u-hsi and her conservative followers put an early end to the reforms phase. In 1899 she recognized the ❻ secret society of the Boxers, which then gained ground. The Boxers denounced the exploitation of the country by the Europeans and strove for a restoration of China's former greatness. To this end, they ❽ attacked foreign installations and murdered Europeans. The ❿ Boxer Rebellion of 1900, which was ❾ crushed by the Japanese, Europeans, and Americans, led to even greater restrictions on China's sovereign rights.

Only after the Russians and Japanese had divided Manchuria into spheres of influence in 1904–1905 was the Chinese court ready for reforms. A constitution and the formation of a parliament were planned, but only hesitantly enacted. In 1911 there was a military revolt in Wuchang that spread through the empire and finally forced the last emperor, P'u-i, to abdicate. P'u-i had ascended the throne as an infant in 1908, after having been designated the successor to the throne by dowager empress Tz'u-hsi as she lay dying. The republic that was proclaimed at the end of the year by the revolutionaries around ⓫ Sun Yat-sen was governed by General Yuan Shikai from 1912. Under an agreement signed with the new Chinese leadership, P'u-i retained his imperial title. It also stipulated that he was to be treated with the same official protocol as a foreign leader.

7
Battle during the Sino-Japanese War, 1894–1895

8
Group of armed Boxers

9
European troops defeat the Boxers and carry out punitive expeditions

10
Boxer Rebellion in Beijing

11
Sun Yat-Sen

The murder of the German ambassador, Baron von Ketteler, on June 20, 1900

The Boxer Rebellion

The Boxer Rebellion was triggered by the murder of the German ambassador, Baron von Ketteler, in Beijing in June 1900, and the siege of the foreign embassy quarter by the secret society of the Boxers. It was finally crushed by an international expeditionary force including Japanese, European, and American troops which occupied Beijing on August 14, 1900, and made several bloody punitive expeditions under a German general, Field Marshal Count von Waldersee, against the insurgents.

The Boxer protocol of September 1901 ended the conflict and committed China to, among other things, large reparations payments and the toleration of foreign military bases.

JAPAN 1854–1912

Japan had been almost wholly isolated from the West since the 17th century under the shoguns of the Tokugawa. Japan was ruled by a noble upper class with the shogun at the top. Though it gave the empire a long, peaceful period of ❶ cultural flourishing, it also prevented access to Western modernization in the areas of technology and politics. Under internal political pressure, the last shogun was forced to step down in 1868 in favor of the emperor, who pushed ahead with modernization. During the Meiji period, Japan quickly came to lead Asian industrialization and was also successful in foreign affairs.

The Great Wave, colored wood engraving by Hokusai, 1830

■ The End of Seclusion and Domestic Changes

The Western states contributed to the development of Japan as a market and trading center. The resulting domestic crisis brought the end of the shogunate.

During the early 19th century, the Tokugawa shoguns tried to keep Japan sealed off from the Western world. However, the United States demanded the opening of Japan and forced the ❷ 1854 Kanagawa Treaty, which ensured the Americans the use of two ports for trade. ❸ European states then made similar treaties, and in 1860 Japanese envoys traveled to Europe to initiate trade with the West. Many of the treaties made were disadvantageous to the Japanese, often guaranteeing the foreigners significant privileges.

This opening of the country had domestic consequences. The foreigners were considered enemy intruders by the Japanese people. When several nationalistic-minded ❹ samurai attacked foreign merchants, European warships shelled Kagoshima in 1863 and Shimonoseki in 1864.

An influential group that demanded political reorganization and the restoration to the emperor (*tenno*) formed in Japan. The Japanese modernizers, as well as the armed foreign powers, highlighted the Tokugawa shogunate's shortcomings. The shoguns recognized that Japan had to adapt its policies to the new conditions. They were anticipated by the military leaders of the Satsuma, Choshu, and Tosa provinces, who seized the emperor's palace in ❺ Kyoto on January 3, 1868. Tokugawa Yoshinobu then restored to the tenno the power of government that had been in the hands of the shoguns for over 250 years. Edo was declared the capital in 1868 and renamed Tokyo, and Tenno Mutsuhito (Meiji) moved there in 1869.

Commercial treaty between the United States and Japan, March 31, 1854

European and American ships at Yokohama

Ukiyo-e: Pictures of the Floating World

Originating in the 17th century, in the form of hand-colored woodblock prints with subjects taken from Bohemian society, the art of the Ukiyo-e school showed actors and demimondaines. Later, nature and city scenes featured. In the 19th century, Ando Hiroshige and Hokusai were the outstanding artists of Ukiyo-e, which declined in the Meiji period.

Moon rising over a landscape with a river, colored wood engraving by Ando Hiroshige

Samurai in armor

The emperor's palace in Kyoto, ca. 1900

Modernization and Territorial Gains

The reforms of the Meiji Restoration brought Japan into the Modern Era and made it the leading political and military power in East Asia.

The Boshin War, a short civil war against the last followers of the Tokugawa, led directly to the Meiji Restoration. ❻ Tenno Mutsuhito, named Meiji ("the Enlightened"), had set as his goal Japan's modernization through comprehensive reforms. This was accomplished above all with the aid of his powerful ministers Kido Takayoshi, Saigo Takamori, and Okubo Toshimichi. With one decree in 1871, they abolished the traditional feudal structure and installed governors to replace the previous system of local self-government. European military advisors and engineers restructured the army, industry, and ❽ transport. Laws and educational institutes were renewed in the Western mold. The rapid pace of these changes, however, also incited resistance. When in 1877 the warrior class of the samurai was disbanded, War Minister Yamagata Aritomo—who, following the Prussian example, had introduced compulsory military service—was forced to put down the Satsuma Uprising.

The Prussia state served as the model when drafting the new constitution of 1889 that formally made Japan a constitutional monarchy. A parliament with an upper and lower house was created as of 1890, although the tenno was still able to intervene in politics through decrees or by dissolving the lower house. The military also had a right of veto in the appointments of minister posts.

Industrialization demanded an expansion of the country's territories primarily to tap raw materials and markets abroad. In the 1870s, Japan came to an agreement with Russia about the Kurile Islands north of Japan and occupied the Chinese Ryukyu Islands in the south. The Japanese used a revolt in Korea to seize additional Chinese territories. They won the ❼ Sino-Japanese War of 1894–1895, and in the Treaty of Shimonoseki took Taiwan and the Pescadores. Japan was also victorious in the ❾ Russo-Japanese War of 1904–1905, which was fought over Manchuria and Korea; in a treaty negotiated at Portsmouth, New Hampshire, in 1905, Japan gained the southern half of Sakhalin Island and the lease of the Liaodong Peninsula, among other things. Japan annexed Korea in 1910.

❿ Tenno Mutsuhito died in 1912 in Tokyo. During his reign, Japan had become the most progressively industrialized country in Asia and a major political and military power.

6
Emperor Mutsuhito ("the Enlightened") with his family

8
Railway station between Ueno and Nakasendo

7
Japanese attack upon the Chinese defenders

9
Official declaration of war by Japan on Russia from February 10, 1904

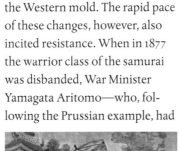

10
The death of Tenno Mutsuhito, color print, 1912

Saigo Takamori

General Saigo Takamori was a commander of the troops in the Boshin War and led over 50,000 samurai. Along with Kido Takayoshi and Okubo Toshimichi, he was one of the "Three Heroes" of the Meiji government. He soon withdrew from public life and founded a school for samurai who had resigned their offices. Saigo led the 1877 uprising in Satsuma of samurai who felt dishonored by their loss of privileges. Seriously injured in battle, he asked his comrades to behead him to avoid capture and further dishonor.

Samurai in attack stance

| 1877 | Satsuma revolt | 1904–05 | Russo-Japanese War | 1912 | Tenno Mutsuhito dies in Tokyo |
| 1877 | Samurai dissolved | 1895 | Treaty of Shimonoseki | 1910 | Japan annexes Korea |

SOUTHEAST ASIA UNTIL 1914

Apart from Siam—present-day ❶ Thailand—nearly all of Southeast Asia came under the colonial rule of European powers during the 19th and early 20th centuries. In addition to the British, who had been expanding their Indian empire eastward by annexing ever more colonial territory to it, Holland—with control of Indonesia—and France were the most significant colonial powers in Southeast Asia. Trapped between British-occupied Burma and French-ruled Indochina, Siam was able to escape colonization only through the wise politics of kings Mongkut and. Chulalongkorn. These kings opened up the country to Western notions of modernization and industrialization.

1 Guard figure at the Wat Phra Kaeo (Temple of the Emerald Buddha) in Bangkok, 19th century

■ The French and British Conquest of Southeast Asia

Indochina and Burma fell victim to the expansionist ambitions of France and Great Britain.

In 1802 the French ended the local power struggles in Vietnam by helping Nguyen Anh defeat the ruling Tay Son dynasty. Nguyen centralized administration, following the Chinese model, and significantly expanded his dominion. He claimed the title of Emperor from 1806 on and made efforts to win landowners over to his side against the rebelling peasants, but his successor Minh Mang was no longer able to prevent the uprisings. The ❸ persecution of Christian missionaries under Minh offered the French and the Spanish the opportunity to attack Vietnam. The Spanish withdrew, but the French com-

mander stayed on, governing with the help of his officers, and thus established the beginning of the French empire in the Far East. By 1867 they had conquered Cochin China, the southern part of Vietnam; Annam and ❷ Tonkin, the middle and northern parts of Vietnam, became ❹ protectorates in 1883–1884.

In the first half of the 19th century, Cambodia was besieged by Siam and Vietnam. In 1845, the two powers finally agreed on joint administration of the old

2 French-Chinese war over the province of Tonkin, the Battle of Nam Dinh, 1883, contemporary lithograph

3 Execution of the French missionary Pierre Borie, 1838

Khmer Empire. On the request of the Khmer king Norodom, the French—primarily interested in rice and rubber—established a ❺ protectorate. They supported the monarchy and acted as its advisors. A national administrative elite was trained and the infrastructure of the country was modernized. The ❻ "Union of Indochina," combining Vietnam and Cambodia, was the largest French colonial possession apart from its African territories.

Meanwhile, Burma—now known as Myanmar—came into Britain's range of vision. When the Burmese occupied large parts of Siam, the East India Company used the opportunity for an expansion of its sphere

of influence. In the First Anglo-Burmese War in 1824, which began with the conquest of the capital Rangoon, the British made only small territorial gains. In the Second Anglo-Burmese War, Great Britain was able to annex the south with its fertile rice plains and as a result of this became the most important Asian exporter of rice. After the Third Anglo-Burmese War in 1885, all of Burma was a British colonial territory.

INDO-CHINE
LES HOMMES D'ACTION

4 Establishing the French protectorate over Annam, 1883

5 Cambodia as French protectorate, painting, 1885

6 Captives of the French in Indochina

| 1802 | Deposition of Tay Son dynasty | 1824 | First Anglo-Burmese war | 1855 | Bowring Treaty |
| 1806 | Emperor Nguyen Anh | | | 1863 | France "protective rule" in Cambodia |

Modernization and Independence in Siam

Kings Mongkut and Chulalongkorn opened Siam up to Western influences, and in this way the country was able to avoid colonization.

8
Chakri Maha Prasat (Grand Palace) in Bangkok, built under Rama V

The ruling dynasty of Siam, the ❽ Chakri, was confronted with the expansion designs of the British. Therefore, in 1826, Siam entered into a trade agreement that increased the position of power of the British—whose merchants had been present since the early 17th century—but prevented total colonization. This strategy remained that of future Siamese kings: making conces-

sions to Western modernization ideas to the point where they could use their advantages and simultaneously defend against the occupation of their country.

With Vietnam coming under French rule, Siam was threatened by both the French in the east and the British in Burma. Having little choice, the Siamese king Mongkut (Rama IV) made the Bowring Treaty with Britain in 1855, which granted concessions such as a British consulate in Bangkok and gave the British advantages along the lines of the "unequal treaties" of the Europeans with China. Mongkut, a former monk who had unearthed the records of King Rama Kamheng of the 13th century that are important for Thailand's identity, had intensively investigated the European world of ideas. After his accession to power in 1851, he gave up the previous policy of isolation. Advised by Europeans,

he improved the infrastructure of the country with new streets and canals, modernized agriculture, and created a military after the European example. Mongkut's son ❼ Chulalongkorn (Rama V) continued his father's direction during his long ❾ reign from 1868 to 1910. The administration was reformed and organized along more strictly centralized lines, and a modern justice system, based on the ideas of a European constitutional state and respect for human rights, was implemented. Chulalongkorn did away with slavery. Hospitals were constructed, the postal system built up, road works continued, and the construction of a railway network begun. Franco-British negotiations concerning the frontiers of their colonies with Siam took place in 1895.

In the course of the creation of French Indochina, ❿ Siam lost Laos and regions in Cambodia and Siam itself. But the Siamese heartland was preserved from colonization and kept its independence.

7
Chulalongkorn (Rama V), King of Siam, with his family, photography, ca.1905

Chulalongkorn

Rama V, better known as Chulalongkorn, was crowned king of Siam in 1868. He shared the opinion of his father, King Mongkut, that his country had to modernize following European models. As the first Siamese king since Rama Kamheng to leave his country, Chulalongkorn traveled to India, Burma, Java, and Singapore in 1871 and visited Europe in 1907. He was able to fend off many attempted coups, but as a result was only able to carry out cautious reforms. The "Beloved Great King," as the Thai people called him, died on October 23, 1910; October 23 is now honored as a Thai national holiday.

9
Visit of Chulalongkorn (Rama V), King of Siam, to Otto von Bismarck in Friedrichsruh, 1898

10
French gunboats make the claim to Laos in Siam, contemporary newspaper

Funeral procession for the Siamese king Chulalongkorn

| 1867 | French conquest of Cochin China | 1885 | Burma becomes a British colony | 1907 | Loss of Battambang and Siam Reap |
| 1868–1910 | Rule Chulalongkorn (Rama V) in Thailand | 1885 | Loss of the eastern Mekong-Area | | |

1

AFRICAN STATE BUILDING AND COLONIZATION 1814–1914

At the turn of the 19th century, Africa was hardly colonized at all, apart from the coasts. The European outposts became unprofitable after the ❶ slave trade was banned at the Congress of Vienna in 1814–1815; African states on the west coast and the East African sultanate of Zanzibar, however, lived off the slave trade until well into the 19th century. The states formed in Africa were often kept under the "protective rule" of European countries. However, many independent African states were able to assert themselves until the Europeans pushed into the interior and divided Africa among themselves at the Berlin Conference of 1884–1885.

British soldiers deliver the message to the African people that the slave trade has ❶ been abolished, colored etching, 19th century

■ State Building in the 19th Century

In both West and East Africa, which were shaped by the slave trade of the preceding centuries, states were founded that outlasted the colonial period.

During the Vienna Congress of 1814–1815, the European colonial outlawed the ❹ slave trade, though not the ownership of slaves, which had been a source of great wealth for West African states such as Ashanti, Dahomey, and regions of present-day Ghana, as well as the East African sultanate of ❺ Zanzibar. In the course of the 19th century, numerous African states were newly reestablished or expanded. In 1822, freed slaves from the United States founded the set-

3
Emblem of Liberia: Sun, sailing boat, dove with a letter in its beak, palm leaves, and a plow

tlement of ❸ Liberia, which became an independent republic in 1847. An Arabic trading empire in the eastern Congo region was founded by Mohammed bin Hamad (Tippu Tib) in 1870 for purely economic reasons.

In Abyssinia (Ethiopia), Ras Kassa reunited the empire in 1853 after the governors of the provinces had strongly curtailed the power of the emperor in the 18th century. He ruled as Emperor Tewodros II until 1868 and was repla-

ced by John IV, who was helped by the British. During his reign, John successfully repelled attacks by Egyptian military units. His successor ❷ Menelik II allied with Italy, which exercised its influence over Abyssinia. When the Abyssinian empire terminated this alliance, the Italians declared war. In the Battle of Aduwa, ❻ Menelik's troops triumphed, and in the peace of Addis Ababa in 1896, the independence of the country was secured.

In West Africa at the beginning of the 19th century, Usman dan Fodio called for a jihad or holy war against the Muslims of the

2
Menelik II, Emperor of Abyssinia

4
Slave hunters attack a village to capture villagers, wood engraving, 1884

Hausa city-states in present-day northern Nigeria. With his forces' victory, dan Fodio began to set up a great Islamic empire. A few years later, his son Mohammad Bello created a caliphate that was divided up into emirates. With conquests as far as the land of the Yoruba and victory over Adamawa (present-day northern Cameroon), he ruled from Sokoto over the Fulani Empire. Even as a British protectorate, the emirs did not lose their power, and the empire outlasted the colonial era.

5
American and British trading ships in the harbor of Zanzibar

6
Menelik II in the battle of Aduwa

■ South Africa between the Boers and the British

In South Africa, the warrior state of the Zulus emerged and soon came into conflict with the Boers. Great Britain, despite great resistance, conquered the Boer Republic.

In South Africa, ❼ Shaka founded the state of the ⓫ Zulu, which he ruled as king until his murder in 1828. He practically became master of South Africa from the Cape Colony to the Zambesi River. He supported his power within the empire on a strict organization and administration of the nation. His military reforms, the introduction of a new battle order, and the deployment of a new throwing spear for close combat provided the success of the Zulus in their campaigns. Through the conquest of large territories, the Zulus put the Bantu people, particularly the Herero and the Matabele, to flight. Shaka's half-brother and successor continued his policies, yet soon came into conflict with the Boers, the descendents of Dutch settlers

in the Cape Colony. In 1806 the Boers had come under British rule. Due to internal tensions, particularly resulting from the banning of the slave trade, which, following the teachings of the Dutch Reformed Church, the Boers believed was biblically ordained, around 5000 Boers set off from the Cape Colony in 1837 on a "Great Trek" into the interior of the country, where they came upon the Zulus. The Zulus killed Piet Retief, the leader of the Boers, but in the ensuing battle in 1838 under Andries Pretorius, the Boers killed more than 3000 Zulus. After the victory, the Boers founded the Republic of Natal in 1839, but this too was annexed by the British in 1843.

In the 1850s Britain recognized the independence of the South

9 Cecil Rhodes

African Republic (Transvaal) and the Orange Free State—Boer republics founded shortly after Natal. However, when diamonds were found in the border regions between the Cape Colony and the Boer areas and gold was found near Johannesburg, the British once again increased the pressure on the Boers. After the annexa-

8 Caricature of "Ohm" Kruger and King Edward VII of England: "Mr. Kruger's new ashtray"

tion of Transvaal in 1877, the Boers rose up and defeated the British. In the following years, ❾ Cecil Rhodes, prime minister of the Cape Colony from 1890, encircled the Boer republics with the conquest of Rhodesia and Bechuanaland. With the deployment of troops, the British provoked the president of Transvaal, ❽ Paul Kruger, to declare war in 1899. In the Boer War, the British lost initial battles against generals ⓬ Smuts, Botha, and Hertzog in Natal and the Cape Colony. However, in 1900 British troops captured the capital of the Orange Free State, Bloemfontein; Johannesburg fell in May and Pretoria, the capital of Transvaal, in June.

Kruger fled to Europe, but the Boers began a guerrilla war. For two years they resisted the British attacks, until Lord Kitchener defeated them. He allowed the destruction of Boer farms and the internment of women and chil-

7 Monument for the Zulu king, King Shaka, erected at the site of his murder in Stanger, Kwadukuza, his former place of residence

dren in ❿ concentration camps. In 1902 Transvaal and the Orange Free State were declared British colonies with administrative autonomy. The Boer states were integrated in the Union of South Africa in 1910 and became dominions of the British Empire.

10 British concentration camp where the Boer were interned from May 1900

12 Jan Christiaan Smuts, later Prime Minister of South Africa, 1910

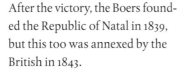

11 Zulu women dancing at a wedding, 1970

Africa: The Apportionment of the Continent by the Europeans

With Henry Morton Stanley's expedition, the push into inner Africa began. In order to avoid war, the colonial powers agreed among themselves on the division of the continent at the Berlin Conference.

In the wake of discussions originating from the new philosophies that emerged from the Enlightenment, the ❸ slave trade caused widespread human rights protests, and a general ban on slave trading was incorporated into the documents of the Congress of Vienna in 1815. The British Navy played a significant part in sup-

3 Shell money made of cowry, used as method of payment in the slave trade in Africa

pressing the slave trade. The African bases of European trading companies thus lost their main source of income and much of their economic value, which was subsequently diminished further as a result of the opening up of the Suez Canal in 1869, signifi-

Berlin Conference of 1884–85

At the Berlin Conference of 1884–85, the colonial powers sought to agree on and define their interests in Africa. Following their signing of the general act in February 1885, the result for Africa was disastrous. The agreement allowed whichever European country that explored an African territory and claimed possession of it to keep the land as long as it informed the other signatory powers of this. As this gave the territorial rights to whoever was there first, a final stage of the "scramble for Africa" began. Similar rules held for the settlement of the coasts: The borders of coastal colonies could be pushed as far into the interior as desired, until they reached the territory of another power. Borders were drawn arbitrarily and ignored African cultural boundaries. The legacy of this agreement has been numerous wars between African states and peoples up to the present time.

above: The Berlin Conference, November 15, 1884–February 26, 1885

1 Stanley's expedition transports a boat through the jungle

2 Henry M. Stanley and his officers, wood engraving, ca. 1890

cantly shortening the sea trade routes to India. ❷ Henry Morton Stanley's ❶ exploration of the Congo region gave the Europeans the opportunity to force their way into the interior of the continent. In 1878, Stanley joined the Belgian ❹ king Leopold II and helped him to establish his rule over the "Free State of Congo," which he established under his personal control. Not long after, the leading world powers divided up the continent definitively at the ❺ Berlin Conference of 1884–1885.

In the 1880s, the economic value of the colonies began to increase again as the raw material needs of the expanding Industrial Revolution once again made them economically profitable; some of the colonies even brought the European colonial powers enormous wealth. In addition, through the belief in their own civilizing superiority, the European nations wanted to carry their ideals out into the world, with little regard for the existing culture of the colonized lands.

4 Leopold II, the Belgian king

5 Bismarck carves up the African cake, caricature, 1885

■ The Great Colonial Powers

France's and Great Britain's zones for expansion overlapped south of Egypt and the Fashoda Crisis almost led to war.

Under ❼ Prime Minister Benjamin Disraeli, the British had aggressively worked to set up a world empire since the 1870s. The intention was to acquire as much land, and thereby economic power, as possible. Raw materials, labor, markets, and—last but not least—soldiers from the colonies made Great Britain a world power.

A decade later, at the height of the power of the Third Republic, the French pushed toward the same goal. In the same way as the British conquered ❻ Egypt in 1882, France capitalized on Tunisia's poor economic situation and violently established ❽ "protective rule" in 1881. France, from its coastal bases in Senegal, the Ivory Coast, Dahomey, and the Congo, established a colonial network that stretched over West Africa and was connected to the northern French colonies of Tunisia and Morocco by the Sahara.

The French conquests soon led to conflict with Great Britain, which planned the so-called

7
Queen Victoria and Prime Minister Benjamin Disraeli

Capeto-Cairo Road, a contiguous chain of colonies from the Cape of Good Hope to the Mediterranean Sea together with an accompanying railway. The ❾ Fashoda Crisis of 1898 nearly caused a war between France and Britain, which was avoided only by the restraint of the middle-ranking officers who were in command of the military forces that faced each other.

While those two colonial powers had divided the majority of Africa between them, Germany

and Italy also endeavored to acquire regions in Africa. The Germans had engaged themselves—first as private trading colonies, then subordinated to the German empire in 1891—in Togo and Cameroon as well as in German East Africa (Tanganyika) and German Southwest Africa (Namibia), where in 1904 and 1905–1907 they put down with ❿ great brutality uprisings of the Herero and the Maji-Maji. Italy's dream of an East African colonial empire burst when the Italians, after the obliterating defeat in the Battle of Aduwa,

6
Disraeli at the Suez Canal, the shortest route to India: "Oh, why does this passage to my home not belong to me?", caricature, lithograph

were expelled by the Abyssinians in 1896. Until 1936, when Italy took control of most of Abyssinia, Italian possessions were limited to Eritrea and Italian Somaliland.

8
Uprising by the native population of Tunisia following France's occupation of the country, colored lithograph, ca. 1910

The Fashoda Crisis of 1898

After Lord Kitchener had destroyed the Sudanese "Empire of the Mahdi," he marched south, where he met French troops under Jean-Baptiste Marchand in Fashoda and forced them to retreat. Great Britain saw the Sudan as a part of British Egypt, but the French saw it as a free area that could be occupied. French foreign minister Théophile Delcassé proffered a compromise. In 1899 it was decided that the British would have sovereignty over the Upper Nile region, while France would control the area of Darfur to Lake Chad—the so-called Equatorial Africa.

above: The French major Jean-Baptiste Marchand meets the envoy of the British, General Kitchener, in Fashoda, drawing, 1898

9
The conflict between the colonial powers England and France: France is depicted as Little Red Riding Hood, England as the wolf, caricature, 1898

10
Skulls of Hereros who were executed or died in action are packed and sent to the Pathological Institute in Berlin, 1905

THE UNITED STATES: BEGINNINGS AND RISE TO WORLD POWER 1789–1917

The ❶ United States, spiritually still strongly rooted in the European tradition, strove to develop its own identity. A foreign policy of isolationism, manifested in the Monroe Doctrine, was implemented. During the 19th century, the territory of the United States increased through the purchase and annexation of land. After 1828 the differences between the Southern and Northern states became increasingly apparent, particularly over the issue of slave ownership. The Civil War from 1861 to 1865 traumatized the young country. Nevertheless, the Union was preserved with the North's victory. After the Civil War, the country's economic and technological ascent began. The entry of the United States into World War I in 1917 signaled the abandonment of isolationism.

The Statue of Liberty in New York, unveiled on October 28, 1886

■ Founding Years

In the early years, there was intense debate over the sociopolitical orientation of the young republic. The unfortunate involvement of the United States in European disputes led to the isolationist policy of the Monroe Doctrine, which was formulated in 1823.

After the 13 original states ratified the US constitution in 1787, two years after it had been drafted in Philadelphia, George Washington was elected the first president, with John Adams as vice president, serving a term from 1789 until 1797. The political options open to the young nation were explored during the first years. Two positions developed: a course toward a strong national government that would promote industry and commerce, advocated by Alexander Hamilton and others and later adopted by the Federalist party; or an agriculturally oriented America with strong individual states, an idea endorsed by the Democratic party headed by Thomas Jefferson. In 1794 farmers were forced to accept a federal excise tax on whisky.

Thomas Jefferson

While Washington had promoted a policy of noninterference, the question of whether to ally with France or England arose during the presidency of John

Farmers and settlers trek to Black Hills

Adams (1797–1801). The question was whether to tolerate the Royal Navy stopping and searching United States ships and pressing American seamen into the Navy. In 1803, ❷ Thomas Jefferson (1801–1809) bought the vast stretch of land between the Mississippi River and the Rocky Mountains—the Louisiana Purchase—from France, doubling the territory of the United States. In foreign affairs, the United States became embroiled in the war between Napoleon and Great Britain, leading to war against the British under President Madison. The experience led to James Monroe's (1817–1825) declaration of the Monroe Doctrine on December 2, 1823, stating that the United States would neither interfere in European conflicts nor tolerate colonization attempts by European powers in the Americas.

With the economic upswing after the War of 1812 came the de-

George Washington, 1793

"'Tis our true policy to steer clear of permanent alliances with any portion of the foreign world."

above: George Washington

velopment of the Midwestern territories by ❸ farmers searching for new land. This precipitated continuing conflicts with the Indian tribes, which had been driven north or settled in reservations.

An Indian reservation, photo, 1906

The Supreme Court

The young United States endeavored to follow the separation of powers advocated by the French philosopher Montesquieu. John Marshall, who served as Chief Justice of the Supreme Court from 1801 to 1835, repeatedly restricted the presumption of authority of presidents Jefferson and Madison. In the case of Marbury v. Madison in 1803, he succeeded in establishing the right of the Supreme Court to review the constitutionality of federal laws and, when necessary, to nullify them.

1787 | Ratification of the Constitution   1797 | John Adams becomes 2nd president   1803 | "Louisiana Purchase"   Dec 2, 1823 | "Monroe Doctrine"

Feb 4, 1789 | George Washington becomes 1st president   1801 | Thomas Jefferson becomes 3rd president   Jun 18, 1812 | US declares war on England

■ Political Reorientation and Expansion

Under President Jackson, popular democracy and party dominance began to shape the political system of the United States. President Polk annexed areas in the West, further expanding the territories of the nation, pushing its borders ever farther toward the Pacific.

5

Geronimo, the last Apache chief

6

Sioux and General William T. Sherman signing the Treaty of Fort Laramie, 1868, which granted the Sioux an unclaimed territory

Starting in 1830 Jackson implemented a ruthless Indian policy. ❺ Indian tribes were forced west to ❻ unclaimed territories or were settled in ❹ reservations that were constantly encroached upon by the relentless expansion.

Texas declared its independence from Mexico in 1836. Mexico then sent military forces to reestablish its authority. After a series of defeats, including the massacre of American settlers by Mexican troops at the Alamo in San Antonio in March 1836, the Texans finally crushed the Mexican army at San Jacinto.

A period of US weakness ended with the presidency of ❽ James K. Polk (1845–1849). Polk proclaimed that it was the "manifest destiny" of US citizens to inhabit the whole continent, and he pushed the admittance of Texas as a state through Congress in March 1845. With this, he knowingly provoked a ❿ war with Mexico, which began in June 1846. The US troops were victorious. In February 1848, Mexico was forced to sue for peace, and California and New Mexico were annexed. Furthermore, the government had signed the Oregon Treaty with Great Britain, securing the territory between the Rocky Mountains and the Pacific for the United States. The US-Canadian border was set at the 49th parallel.

By 1848, the territory of the United States had doubled once

more and gold mines were discovered in California. The ❾ Gold Rush began. In the Western towns, it was the "law of the gun" that reigned.

The economic crises of the 1820s, after which many farmers found themselves in debt to the banks, was followed by a political U-turn. ❼ Andrew Jackson (1829–1837) was the first president who was not from the Eastern elite. He pursued a "policy of the common man." In 1832–1836, he destroyed the Second Bank of the United States and developed an aid program for farmers and settlers. His style of "Jacksonian democracy" marked US politics until 1860. It involved the domination of the middle class over the economic elite, the development of the party system, and political dominance of the west and south over the northeast.

Protective tariff laws that had been passed in 1828, over the vehement objection of the Southern states and their spokesman John Calhoun, led to the Nullification Crisis, a controversy over the right of states to negate federal laws. Jackson threatened the South with military intervention and in this way saved the Union.

7

Andrew Jackson

8

James K. Polk

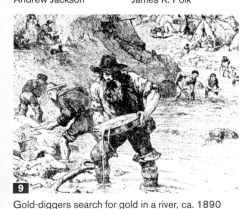

9

Gold-diggers search for gold in a river, ca. 1890

The Nullification Crisis

In November 1832, the state of South Carolina under John Calhoun's leadership threatened secession from the Union—a threat later made good in 1860. President Jackson spoke of treason and made preparations for military intervention, but escalation was averted. The conflict, which smoldered until the Civil War, began at a presidential dinner in April 1830. Jackson proposed a toast: "Our federal Union— it must and shall be preserved," whereupon Calhoun countered: "Our Union—next to our liberties, most dear."

10

Capture of the capital of Mexico by US troops under General W. Scott, September 14, 1847

■ The Start of the Civil War

In protest over the election of antislavery candidate Abraham Lincoln as president of the United States in 1860, eleven Southern states seceded from the Union. In consequence a bloody civil war began in 1861.

Slaves on a cotton farm in the southern states, wood engraving, 1885

The unresolved issue of ❶ slave ownership created a deep chasm between the overwhelmingly middle-class, commerce-oriented Northern states and the patriarchal, agrarian South. Slavery had already been abolished in all states north of Maryland by the end of the 18th century, but the South, with its extensive plantation economy, could not survive without the slave labor that constituted the work force.

The dispute heated up again following the war against Mexico in 1848 when newly acquired territories—California, New Mexico, and Texas—were to be incorporated into the Union as states. The North wanted to ban slavery in all of them; the South wanted it to be the prerogative of the individual

Defeat of the Union troops in the battle of Bull Run, July 21, 1861

Attack at Fort Sumter in Charleston, 1861

The Republican Party

The Republican party was formed in 1854 by the unification of antislavery factions from the Democratic and Whig parties. Its foremost goal initially was to engineer the repeal of the Kansas-Nebraska Act of 1854, which allowed the western territories to implement slavery. The Republicans were represented and supported chiefly in the northern and western states.

Abraham Lincoln

states to decide. Internal disagreement over the slavery issue weakened the leading Democratic party, while diverse antislavery factions gathered in the new Republican party. In 1860, for the first time, a Republican candidate, Abraham Lincoln, won the presidential election (1861–1865). Thereupon, South Carolina seceded, declaring its independence from the Union in protest. Another ten states (Mississippi, Florida, Alabama, Georgia, Louisiana, Texas, Virginia, Arkansas, Tennessee, and North Carolina) joined in seceding, and in February 1861 they formed the Confederate States of America with its own constitution and president, ❸ Jefferson Davis.

On April 12, 1861, troops from South Carolina fired upon the Union troops stationed in ❹ Fort Sumter in Charleston, and the ❷ American Civil War began. After initial Confederate successes, the momentum changed in favor of the Union in 1863.

❸ Jefferson Davis

Abraham Lincoln, Gettysburg Address, November 19, 1863

"It is rather for us to be here dedicated to the great task remaining before us—that from these honored dead we take increased devotion to that cause for which they gave the last full measure of devotion—that we here highly resolve that these dead shall not have died in vain—that this nation, under God, shall have a new birth of freedom—and that government of the people, by the people, for the people, shall not perish from the earth."

| Nov 6, 1860 | Abraham Lincoln elected president | Feb 18, 1861 | Jefferson Davis President of "Confederate States of America" | Apr 9, 1865 | End of Civil War |
| Dec 24, 1860 | South Carolina secedes | Apr 12, 1861 | American Civil War begins | Jul 1–3, 1863 | Battle at Gettysburg |

■ The Union's Victory and Reconstruction

From the victory of the Union in 1865 until 1877, American politics were dominated by disputes over the reconstruction of the ruined South in the wake of the Civil War. The construction of the transcontinental railroad brought with it economic growth .

5
Celebratory procession following the abolition of slavery, 1865

At the beginning of 1864, Lincoln appointed General ❼ Ulysses S. Grant as supreme commander of the Union forces. Grant forced the Confederacy's leading general, ❽ Robert E. Lee, to surrender on April 9, 1865, at Appomattox, Virginia, in effect ending the war. Five days later, Lincoln was shot and killed by a fanatic Southerner in Washington, DC. On December 18, 1865, slaves were ❺ liberated through the 13th Amendment to the Constitution.

Like Lincoln, his successor, Andrew Johnson (1865–1869), advocated a Reconstruction policy of reconciliation with the South, which was so devastated that its agricultural production would not reach even half its 1860 level until 1870. The majority of the radical Republicans in Congress, however, insisted on a thorough dismantling of governmental and social structures, and they installed military administrations to control the Southern states.

The Freedman's Bureau, which was set up in 1867 for the protection of the freed slaves, was overwhelmed by the more than three million liberated slaves—almost half of the Southern states' total population. Social attitudes in the South were slow to change, especially in relation to civil rights for former slaves. A racist movement that encompassed numerous secret societies, the largest being the ❻ Ku Klux Klan, terrorized the freed slaves. Fundamental reform of Southern society

stalled in its initial stages under Grant, who was less successful as president (1869–1877) than he had been as a general. His second term in office was overshadowed by corruption scandals.

Following the withdrawal of Union troops from the South in 1870 and the official end of Reconstruction, the old systems of white supremacy soon crept back again onto the plantations, if not as open slavery. At the end of the 19th century, strict racial segregation was introduced, affecting schools, public transportation, and restaurants.

After the Civil War, the North experienced a strong economic upswing, particularly through the construction of the ❾ transcontinental railroad. By 1893, five rail lines had been completed, opening up the thinly settled West.

7
Ulysses Grant, commander of Union forces

8
Robert Lee, commander of Confederate forces

6
Procession of the Ku Klux Klan

Indian Uprisings

The opening of the West by settlers, gold miners, and the railroad was carried out at the expense

Sitting Bull

of the Native Americans. Their land was ruthlessly expropriated, they were resettled in reservations, and tribes that defended their territory were dealt with harshly, even annihilated. Among the largest conflicts was the Battle of the Little Bighorn in 1876, where the Sioux led by Chief Sitting Bull overwhelmed an attacking expedition led by George Armstrong Custer. When a new uprising threatened in 1890, an attempt was made to arrest Sitting Bull, during which he was killed. Two weeks later, on December 29, 1890, the US Cavalry massacred 200 Sioux at Wounded Knee in South Dakota.

The Battle of Little Bighorn

9
Atlantic Pacific Railway, 1868

■ Economic Rise

The rapid growth of US cities between 1877 and 1897, swelled by immigrant labor and industrial workers, was accompanied by social and economic problems.

"Haymarket Riots," Chicago, 1886

The rise of the United States as a world power began with its rapid economic progress. Following the construction of railroads, the discovery of ❹ oil led to further economic expansion and wealth as well as capital for further economic investment. John D. Rockefeller founded the Standard Oil Company in 1870, creating the first "trust" in the United States; by 1911, it controlled about 90 percent of the oil business. In 1873, Andrew Carnegie began building up the steel industry.

The rapid growth of the ❷ cities and the steady rise in the number of predominantly destitute ❸ immigrants from Europe and Asia led to the development of ethnic neighborhoods in the big cities and a huge rise in number of industrial workers. There were no binding regulations covering labor conditions. Wildcat strikes and acts of violence were the order of the day, and unions were organized only locally.

The ❶ "Haymarket Riots" in May 1886 demonstrated the urgent need for social solutions. Two days after police shot six strikers during a mass demonstration, twelve people, including several police, were killed in a bomb attack. Four "anarchists" were hanged as a result, although there was no proof of their guilt. The Haymarket affair directly inspired the celebration of May 1st as International Workers' Day.

State Street, Chicago, 1903

While the unions were consolidating their organization, the economic middle class demanded that politics finally be brought into line with the expansive economic development of the country. An explosive issue was protective tariffs, which favored the sale of American over foreign goods within the United States, but also hurt those sectors that were dependent on imported commodities. President Grover Cleveland (1885–1889 and 1893–1897), an opponent of prohibitively high tariffs, was unable to prevent his successors from placing record tariffs on dutiable goods in 1890 (the "McKinley Tariff") and 1897 (the "Dingley Tariff"). By 1909, protective tariffs were set at 57 percent.

In 1893, a collapse of the foreign markets and risky speculation by the trusts resulted in a serious economic crisis in the United States.

Medical examination of immigrants, Ellis Island, New York, 1900

The Trusts

A trust (short for "trusteeship") is an amalgamation of formerly independent companies into a single joint-stock company with the goal of controlling the market, that is, creating a monopoly in a specific industrial sector. In contrast

"Standard Oil" share

J. D. Rockefeller, 1936

to a cartel, a trust is a tightly organized unit of administration and capital. Since trusts were first created, the US government has been trying to abolish them to ensure free competition, though often with only moderate success. Important US antitrust laws include the Sherman Act (1890), the Elkins Act (1903), and the Federal Trade Commission and Clayton Act (1914).

Oil field in California, 1925

| 1870 | Foundation of "Standard Oil Company" | May 1–4, 1886 | "Haymarket-Riots" | Apr 25, 1898 | Declaration of war on Spain |
| since 1873 | Development of the steel industry | 1890–97 | Setting of the protective tariffs at over 50% | Sep 6, 1901 | McKinley assassinated |

■ The Policy of Imperialism

In 1897–1898, McKinley and Roosevelt intensified US imperialistic expansion into Latin America and the Caribbean regions. President Wilson concentrated on domestic and internal policies after 1913, but the political situation in the world forced him to enter World War I on the side of the Allies in 1917.

Republican William McKinley was the first "modern" president of the United States (1897–1901). He strengthened the personal authority of the president, raised protective tariffs, introduced the gold standard for the dollar, and built up the confidence of commerce, industry, and the labor unions in the government. In 1898, McKinley intervened in Cuba's fight for liberation from Spain. The interest of the government directed itself toward the new markets and sources of raw materials of Latin American and the Pacific region all the way to the Far East. Cuba became a republic in the Treaty of Paris, and the Philippines, Guam, and Puerto Rico were ceded by Spain to American possession, which led in 1899 to the formation of a critical anti-imperialism league in Democratic circles.

Following McKinley's assassination in September 1901, his successor Theodore Roosevelt (1901–1909) stepped up the expansion policy. Domestically, he brought about more effective

5
Opening journey on the Panama Canal 1914

control of the trusts and actively settled labor disputes. Reelected in 1904, he intervened in several Central American countries and mediated the Russo-Japanese War of 1904–1905, for which in 1906 he became the first American awarded the Nobel Peace Prize. After installing a US-dependent government in Panama in 1903, Roosevelt acquired control of the Canal Zone for the United States and had the ❺ Panama Canal built (dedicated 1914), connecting the Atlantic and Pacific oceans. In 1913, ❻ Woodrow Wilson

brought the Democrats to power again (1913–1921). Wilson curbed the expansion policy and concentrated more intensely on domestic issues. His "New Freedom" program aimed at social reform. Wilson followed a liberal cultural policy and promised to respect the rights of other nations.

Wilson responded to the outbreak of World War I with a declaration of neutrality. His course was controversial, but his promise of noninterference secured him reelection in 1916. However, he was pushed into action particularly by Republicans, especially since unrestricted submarine warfare was affecting US shipping. With the approval of Congress, Wilson declared ❼ war on Germany on April 6, 1917.

President McKinley on the Monroe Doctrine

"Isolation is no longer possible or desirable. The period of exclusiveness is past. The expansion of our trade and commerce is the…problem. Commercial wars are unprofitable. A policy of good-will and friendly trade relations will prevent reprisals."
above: William McKinley

6
President Woodrow Wilson

The Roosevelt Corollary

On December 6, 1904, President Theodore Roosevelt amended the Monroe Doctrine with his own "Roosevelt Corollary." He proclaimed an American right to intervene in the Western Hemisphere (Latin America and the Pacific region) and justified the entitlement of the United States to exercise international police powers in Latin America. The role of the United States as a "world policeman"—which remains controversial to this day—began with him.

Theodore Roosevelt

7
American soldiers set sail for Europe, 1917

Sep 14, 1901 | Theodore Roosevelt becomes president   **1913** | Woodrow Wilson becomes president   **1916** | Reelection of Wilson

Dec 6, 1904 | Proclamation of the "Roosevelt Corollary"   **Aug 15, 1914** | Panama Canal opens   **Apr 6, 1917** | US declares war on Germany

LATIN AMERICA 1810–1914

When Napoleon occupied the Iberian Peninsula, the Spanish and Portuguese colonies in Latin America saw the defeat of the European metropoles as an opportunity for self-determination. In the next two decades, most of the South American states were able to gain independence under the leadership of the native Creoles—the descendents of Spanish colonists. Brazil was the only country to free itself from its motherland without military battles, however. Civil wars and internal political struggles shaped events in most of the states of Latin America for a long time after independence. The political organization of the states alternated between ❶ monarchies, dictatorships, and republics.

1 Emperor's palace in Petropolis near Rio de Janeiro, Brazil, built in 1845

■ The South American Wars of Independence

Simón Bolívar fought for the independence of Venezuela and Colombia, while José de San Martín liberated Chile. Together the two commanded forces that expelled the Spaniards from Peru and the rest of the continent.

❷, Simón Bolívar (1783-1830), one of the leaders of the Wars of Independence, was born into an aristocratic family of Spanish descent in Caracas, Venezuela. After his mother's death when he was nine years old, he spent several years in Spain, where he formed a poor impression of the Court of Charles IV. After two years in revolutionary France, he returned to ❸ Venezuela but was again in Paris for the coronation of Napoleon Bonaparte

2 Simón Bolívar

as Emperor. Together with ❹ Francisco de Miranda, the "Father of South American Independence," he helped free Venezuela from Spain in 1811–1812, although Spain was later able to reestablish its rule. From New Granada (which included present-day Colombia), he resumed his battle, and Venezuela was again freed in 1817. In 1819 Bolívar announced the unification of Venezuela with New Granada to create Gran Colombia, of which he became the first president. Panama joined Gran Colombia in 1821 and Ecuador was added in 1822.

To the south, local elites in Río de La Plata province had used the weakness of the central government in Napoleonic Spain to dislodge the viceroy in 1810. In 1816 a congress in Tucamán proclaimed

4 Francisco de Miranda

the independence of the United Provinces of Rio de La Plata (present-day Argentina, Uruguay, Paraguay, and Bolivia). Once the local Spanish forces had been expelled from the northwest of the region in a series of pitched battles, an Argentine army under ❺ José de San Martín set off to free Chile and Peru.

Along with the Chilean revolutionary Bernardo O'Higgins, San Martín crossed the Andes mountains. The rebel army beat the Spanish in 1817 at Chacabuco, and he was able to proclaim the independence of Chile in 1818. When San Martín marched on to Peru and

3 The "Libertador" Simón Bolívar entering Caracas, Venezuela, in 1813

reached ❻ Lima, the Spanish had already abandoned the town and Peru declared itself independent in 1821. San Martín became president and joined the army of Simón Bolívar, who had marched down to Peru from the north. The battles at Junín and Ayacucho in Peru in 1824 marked the end of metropolitan Spain's dominion over South America.

5 Unveiling of the memorial for José de San Martín, 1909

6 The city of Lima, ca. 1850

| 1816 | United Provinces of Rio de La Plata | 1817 | Independence of Venezuela | 1819 | Gran Colombia established | 1824 | Battles at Junín and Ayacucho |
| 1817 | Battle of Chacabuco | 1818 | Independence of Chile | 1821 | Independence of Peru | 1828 | Santa Cruz takes power |

■ Development after Independence

Once independence had been achieved, many of the new South American states experienced political turbulence and military dictatorships.

When Peru and Venezuela seceded from Gran Colombia in 1830, ❽ Bolívar resigned and the country broke up into New Granada—after 1861, Colombia—Bolivia, and Ecuador. During a civil war in Bolivia in 1828, the Peruvian general Andrés Santa Cruz took power and forced the unification of Bolivia with Peru in 1836. However, before long Argentina and Chile dissolved this confederation and deposed Santa Cruz.

In the following decades General Ramón Castilla was able to bring stability to Peru. The country experienced an economic revival, and the raw materials guano and niter brought wealth. In Bolivia, however, internal sta-

❽ Simón Bolívar

bility continued to prove elusive. Bloody civil wars shook the country. Similar struggles took place in many of the other newly independent Southern American countries: At the center of these conflicts lay disagreements over the political structure of the state.

In Argentina, the policies of General Juan Manuel de Rosas, who sought national unity through authoritarian means, brought stability to the country for a long time. In 1852, ❼ General Justo Urquiza toppled the dictatorship and, once the federal constitution came into effect, became president of the Republic of Argentina. The province of ⓫ Buenos Aires, which had been forced to accept the constitution during the civil war, rose up un-

der General Bartolomé Mitre in 1861 and established his presidency. The 1879–1880 "conquest of the desert," led by Julio Argentino Roca against the Indians, brought the country huge areas of agricultural land in the ❾ pampas. With Chile he agreed on the division of Tierra del Fuego. The United States acted as adjudicator for a dispute in which Argentina seized regions of Brazil in 1895, and in 1902, through the mediation of Great Britain —which had conquered the Falkland Islands in 1833—it gained ❿ Patagonia from Chile.

Chile only managed to expel the last Spanish troops in 1826. The restorative constitution of General Joaquín Prieto was opposed by the liberals until 1859, but to no avail. Prieto's and the succeeding governments worked toward a stable internal political situation, which helped to bring about an economic and cultural

7 General José de Urquiza is killed on April 11, 1870, in San José

9 Ostrich hunting on horseback in the Argentinian pampas

resurgence. The mining of copper, silver, and niter, the opening-up of markets for agricultural products, the development of ship and rail transport networks, and the improvement of education, were the cornerstones of this boom. In 1891, acting president José Manuel Fernández was toppled, and the ensuing civil war ended with the storming of the capital, Santiago, at the cost of more than 10,000 lives.

Nitrate War 1879–1883

In 1879, a Chilean nitrate company in Antofagasta, then part of Bolivia, objected to a tax increase. Chile then occupied the port and conquered the provinces of Tacna and Arica in Peru, an ally of Bolivia. Bolivia gave up the fight, and Chile occupied Lima, Peru, in 1881. Under the Treaty of Ancón, signed on October 20, 1883, Peru lost Tacna, Arica, and Tarapacá to Chile. With the loss from Antofagasta and the province of Atacama, the Bolivian state no longer had access to the sea.

above: Nitrate is quarried in Chile

10 Ushuaia, world's southernmost city, founded in 1868 on the Beagle channel, Tierra del Fuego Island, Argentina.

11 Buenos Aires, capital of an independent Argentina and its largest port city, in the 1840s

---

| 1830 | Decline of Gran Colombia | 1852 | Fall of de Rosas' dictatorship in Argentina | 1881 | Chilenian occupation of Lima | Oct 20, 1883 | Peace of Ancón |
| 1831 | Government of Prietos in Chile | 1879–80 | "Conquest of the Desert" | 1879–1883 | Nitrate War | | |

■ Mexico in the 19th Century

Mexico won its fight for independence. Under alternating monarchies and republics, the gradual liberalization and development of the economy took place.

1

Antonio López de Santa Anna

2

Porfirio Diaz, Mexican president

3

General Agustín de Itúrbide signs the Mexican declaration of independence

In New Spain (Mexico), the demand for independence and self-determination grew as it did in the rest of Spanish America. In 1810 a village priest, Miguel Hidalgo y Costilla, called upon the people to fight the Spaniards. The declaration of independence was proclaimed in 1813 and a republican constitution decreed. The country did not officially become independent, however, until the military leader of the Creoles, ❸ Agustín de Itúrbide, allied with the leader of the rebellion, Vicente Guerrero, and proclaimed a monarchy in 1821. The Creole upper class and the higher clergy had joined with Guerrero to prevent the acceptance of a liberal Spanish constitution. Itúrbide reigned for a short period as Emperor Agustín I of Mexico, until he was toppled by ❶ Antonio López de Santa Anna in 1823.

A republican and federal constitution was adopted in 1824, and Guadalupe Victoria was elected president. The young republic was divided by conflicts between the proponents of a centralized state and those of a federalist system. Victoria was ousted by Santa Anna in 1833, who long maintained influence over politics in the country. The United States of Central America, which included most of the present Central American countries, seceded from the republic of Mexico in 1838–1839.

After a war against the US, Mexico was forced to cede its territory north of the Rio Grande in 1848. The US also intervened in its internal politics, supporting the liberal Benito Juárez against conservatives. As president, Juárez had plans to develop the country and sought to default on interest payments to foreign lenders. Upon hearing this, the countries concerned—Great Britain, Spain, and France—invaded Mexico City in 1863 and appointed the Austrian archduke Maximilian as emperor. However, Juárez reconquered the country and had ❹ Maxmilian shot in 1867 under martial law.

Through a coup d'ètat, the liberal General ❷ Porfirio Diaz came to power in 1876 and furthered internal peace and economic development. Under his government, the resentment of the landless peasants exploded in the ❺ Mexican Revolution of 1910 under the leadership of Emiliano Zapata, Francisco Villa, and Venustiano Carranza. Following the revolution's success, Carranza became president of Mexico and adopted a liberal constitution in 1917.

4

Execution of the Emperor Maximilian, painting by Édouard Manet, 1868–69

5

Supporters of the revolutionary Emiliano Zapata marching during the Mexican Revolution

The Mexican Revolution

After the reelection of Diaz, a revolution led by politicians broke out in 1910. Before long, however, this developed into an uprising of the peasants (campesinos) who had lost property due to Diaz's policies. In the south they fought under Zapata for the recovery of their lands; in the north under Villa, they fought for the independence of small agricultural undertakings. After a number of conflicts among the leaders, Carranza defeated the others and installed himself as president. In office he enacted agrarian reforms.

Zapata, portrait in a leaflet distributed in the Mexican revolution

Brazil in the 19th Century

Brazil was the only country of Latin America to gain its independence peacefully, separating from Portugal in 1822.

At the beginning of the 19th century, Brazil was the place of refuge for the Portuguese king John VI, under British naval escort, after he had been expelled by Napoleon. He made ❻ Rio de Janeiro the capital of the Portuguese kingdom. Rio was opened to international trade. Ministries and many other organs of government were established. Rio saw the construction of hospitals, theaters, libraries, naval and military academies, and a school of medicine. After the Congress of Vienna, John returned to Europe in 1821 to rule in Lisbon, while his son ❼ Pedro remained behind as regent. However, Pedro resisted the plans of Portugal's parliament to turn Brazil into a colony once again and put himself at the head of the Brazilian independence movement. This was influenced by autonomist movements and liberal ideas from all over the Continent. On September 7, 1822, he declared independence on the banks of the River Iparanga in Sao Paulo and in the same year was ❿ crowned Pedro I, emperor of Brazil. He was a constitutional monarch. After a campaign against Portuguese forces, in which a British admiral, Lord Cochrane, commanded the newly formed Brazilian fleet, the Portuguese were forced to evacuate Bahia and in 1825 Portugal recognized Brazil's independence.

After a war with Argentina between 1825 and 1827, Brazil lost the province north of Río de La Plata—later Uruguay—in the Peace of Montevideo in 1828. This external failure, as well as conflicts with the parliament and the leading social classes, forced Pedro I to abdicate in 1831.

Under the liberal government of ❽ Pedro II after 1840, the country stabilized. The economy developed well, with a high rate of European immigration and the growth of ❾ coffee farming, particularly in the south of Brazil. The biggest internal problem was ⓫ slavery. When an influential group of opponents demanded its abolition, Pedro II outlawed it in 1888, but without compensating the slave owners. He thereby drove this powerful group into the republican camp. After an uprising by the garrison of Rio de Janeiro in 1889, under General Manuel Deodora da Fonseca in 1889, Brazil became a republic. Fonseca ensured he was the first president.

In 1891, an assembly decided on a new constitution for the United States of Brazil. Fonseca was deposed the same year by Floriano Peixotos, and a series of dictators followed. Up until the First World War, the territory of Brazil expanded due to treaties made with neighboring states. During the course of the war, industrialization began as new markets opened and the country's infrastructure was strengthened.

6 Copacabana district in Rio de Janeiro, ca. 1915

8 Pedro II, Emperor of Brazil, ca. 1870

7 Pedro I, Emperor of Brazil

9 Coffee farming in Brazil

10 Acclamation of Pedro I in Rio de Janeiro, 1822

11 A slave being whipped in Brazil

Feb 2, 1848	Treaty of Guadalupe Hidalgo	1867	Maximilian executed	1888	Slavery abolished in Brazil	1910	Mexican Revolution
1864	Maximilian crowned emperor	1876	Coup d'ètat by Porfirio Díaz	1889	Brazil becomes a republic		

The World Wars and Interwar Period

1914–1945

The first half of the 20th century saw the world entangled in two global wars, conducted with an unprecedented brutality. The First World War developed from a purely European affair into a conflict involving the colonies and the United States. It altered Europe's political landscape and shifted the power balance worldwide. In World War II, the nations of Europe, Asia, the Americas, and Africa werc drawn into the conflict through the aggressive policies of an ambitious Nazi Germany. The war was conducted with the most up-to-date weapons technology and cost the lives of more than 55 million people. The Holocaust, the systematic annihilation of the European Jews, represented an unparalleled moral catastrophe for modern civilization.

The re-integration of war veterans was problematic to the societies of all nations who had participated in the World Wars; maimed war veterans often ended up begging on the streets

1 The end of the European monarchs, caricature, 1918

2 British geographers change the map of Europe

3 Parade in the Red Square, Moscow, 1927

THE AGE OF WORLD WARS

Rampant nationalism and an international arms race made European politics potentially explosive at the beginning of the 20th century. It took only the assassination of the Austro-Hungarian heir apparent in July 1914 to ignite a world war that tore apart the ❶ old state structures. Totalitarian political forces emerged, strengthened by the social and economic crises of the postwar period. In 1939, German Nazism plunged the world into the most devastating war in history. At the war's end in 1945, Europe lay in ruins.

Consequences of World War I: Reorganization of States

The First World War, waged with all the resources then available, shifted worldwide power relationships and redrew the ❷ map of Europe. Even the militarily victorious nations Great Britain and France were economically weakened by the war. The United States profited most from the war, replacing Great Britain as the dominant world power, and it sought to bring peace to Europe based on the principle of the right to national self-determination. The postwar order created in Paris by the victorious powers was contradictory, however. It became the source of new conflicts and thereby set the stage for the next war. The military losers bristled at being assigned sole responsibility for the war and saw the reparations that they had been saddled with as greatly unjust. Germany in particular, which was forced to cede its colonies and large parts of its empire, sought revisions in the treaty from the start. The breakup of the multicultural empires of Austria-Hungary and the Ottomans created unstable nation-states in Eastern and Central Europe with strong ethnic minorities. In the ❺ Near East, the victorious powers broke their promise to grant national independence. The former territories of the Ottoman Empire were divided into British, French, and in-ternational mandates. Great Britain's inconsistent posture toward Jewish immigration into Palestine set the groundwork for the Arab-Israeli conflict that would erupt after 1945.

Totalitarianism: Communism and Fascism

World War I mobilized and politicized whole nations for the first time. It shook up the established social order in many countries and led to revolts and revolutions. Centuries-old monarchies collapsed in Russia, Germany, Austria, and Hungary. Parliamentary democracies were established, with mixed success, in many places. The most momentous development proved to be the ❸ Bolsheviks' victory in Russia in 1917. The founding of the Soviet Union in 1922 influenced the internal development of the whole of Europe. The Soviet goal of a communist world revolution stirred up fears of left-wing communist uprisings by broad sections of the populace in the unstable European democracies of the ❹ postwar period. In response, new right-wing fascist factions gained strength everywhere. Although these varied greatly from country to country, they all had a militarily nationalist, radical antidemocratic and

4 Paying out unemployment money, 1930

anticommunist position in common. These movements gained the upper hand in Germany and Italy against the backdrop of the worldwide economic depression. In Spain a fascist regime was established only after a bloody civil war. Authoritarian systems also established themselves in South America, and a nationalist military leadership in Japan sought to establish a colonial empire in Asia. In China, the most populous nation of the world, nationalist and communist factions fought for control. Among the leading powers, only France, the United States, and Great Britain retained their liberal democratic systems despite economic crises.

5 Jews demonstrate for the right of free immigration to Palestine, New York, 1920s

Jul 28, 1914 | Start of World War I

1917 | Balfour Declaration

1922 | Founding of the Soviet Union

1915 | Einstein's *General Theory of Relativity* published

1919 | Treaty of Versailles

6 Destroyed German city after a bombardment, 1944

7 Alexander Fleming, the discoverer of penicillin, 1940

8 Assembly of cars on a production line, US, ca. 1940

Terror and Total War

An aggressive fascist movement gained power in Germany in the form of Hitler's National Socialist party. The German Reich started ❻ World War II in 1939 with the goal of reorganizing Europe according to Nazi racial theory. An extermination campaign was begun against entire ethnic groups in Eastern Europe, which culminated in the mass murder of millions of European Jews. The United States, Great Britain, and the Soviet Union formed an alliance that finally put an end to the Nazis' rule of terror and occupied Germany in 1945. Germany's ally Japan surrendered only after the first atomic bombs had been dropped. World War II, which was waged with highly developed technology and an enormous numbers of soldiers, cost the lives of more than 55 million people. The carpet bombing by the air forces claimed appalling numbers of victims and destroyed complete cities. As a result of the war, the Soviet Union and the United States rose to become the two world superpowers. After 1945, the differences between them, however, led to the ideological division of both Europe and the entire world.

The Dawning of Modern Mass Culture

The development of science and technology in the industrialized nations between the wars fundamentally altered daily life. In 1915, physicist ❾ Albert Einstein published his *General Theory of Relativity* and revolutionized the concept of time and space. In 1929, bacteriologist Sir Alexander Fleming discovered the medical use of ❼ penicillin. Thanks to the ❽ assembly line, the car became the means of transport for the masses. Life in the cities became more hectic and dynamic, as new and more efficient technology led to an increase in the pace of everyday life. Communication over further distances and within a shorter amount of time was made possible, and increasing numbers of people began to move farther

9 Albert Einstein, ca. 1930

11 The dancer Josephine Baker, star of the interwar period, ca. 1930

away from their place of origin in the search of work and happiness, aided by the new mobility given them by the car. New technology also revolutionized the entertainment industry: Radio and ❿ film sprung up as the dominant entertainment media. A consumer and leisure-oriented culture that set new fashions developed. Daily newspapers, made possible through cost-efficient technology that facilitated the mass production of the printed word, courted the favor of a growing number of readers. Neon advertising and oversize billboards established a new aspect of consumer-orientated commercialization on the streets. The entertainment industry with its nightclubs and dance halls came to define a lifestyle associated with the mystique of the "Roaring Twenties."

Access to consumer goods and the spread of lifestyles through the media began to blur the lines between the middle class and the working class. The roles of the sexes began to change. The feminist movement achieved political emancipation; women's rights to vote and run for office were introduced in most of the industrial nations after 1918. Women also increasingly ⓬ entered paid employment, although they often remained blocked from positions of responsibility for a long time to come. These changes took place primarily in the industrialized United States and Europe. Much of the rest of the world took little part in this revolution, sometimes even countering the modern Western lifestyle with more traditional cultural beliefs and practices.

10 Myrna Loy and William Powell, film stars of the thirties

12 Geography students survey land, United States, 1920

1929 | Discovery of penicillin   Sep 1, 1939 | Start of World War II

from 1929 | World economic crisis   Jan 30, 1933 | Hitler comes to power in Germany   Aug 8, 1945 | First atomic bomb dropped

WORLD WAR I 1914–1918

World War I is considered the "first calamity of the 20th century." Stemming from the imperialist policies of the European powers and the entwined alliances that resulted, the "Great War" claimed a total of around 10 million dead and 13 million wounded. The mobilization of whole nations and the previously unknown ❶ brutality of trench warfare triggered social upheavals, whose political and social consequences shaped the twentieth century.

Soldiers and mule wearing gas masks, 1916

■ The Outbreak of World War I

The immediate cause of the war was the assassination of the heir to the Austrian throne in June 1914. The "July Crisis" soon escalated as the alliance system saw the European powers mobilize one after another for war.

Following the ❸ assassination of Archduke Franz Ferdinand and his wife Sophie by Serbian nationalist Gavrilo Princip on June 28, 1914, in Sarajevo, Austria-Hungary wished to effect a quick retaliatory strike to restore its political influence over Serbia. As Russia supported Serbia and the German Reich supported Austria through their respective alliances, an escalating crisis threatened the peace of Europe.

The Great Powers stood behind their alliance commitments in the following month of frenzied diplomatic activity, known as the July Crisis. Austria's Emperor Franz Josef I delivered a highly provocative ❺ ultimatum to Serbia, after making sure of Germany's support; he was reassured by Kaiser Wilhelm II of his unconditional support—the so-called "blank check" conveyed

Assassination of Franz Ferdinand in Sarajevo, June 28, 1914

on July 5–6, 1914. British attempts to mediate failed, and so Austria-Hungary declared war on Serbia on July 28, 1914.

Czar Nicholas II's Russia reacted with a ❷ general mobilization on July 30 that continued even after a German ultimatum demanded it end. The German Reich then declared war on Russia on August 1. Because France, an ally of Russia and a potential party to the war, was itself mobilizing troops, Germany felt threatened from both sides and two days later declared war on France as well. The extent to which German military planners engineered the war is still disputed by historians, but in the circum-

Czar Nicholas II meets Russian soldiers before they enter battle, August 1914

German troops march into Antwerp, August 1914

stances the best chance for a German victory in a two-front war lay in taking advantage of Russia's slow mobilization process by rapidly defeating France. The long prepared Schlieffen plan involved a rapid attack on France via Belgium. This inevitably drew Great Britain into the war since German troops thereby ❹ violated Belgium's neutrality. The British had long felt challenged by the aggressive ❻ navy-building policies of the German Kaiser, and British policy was not to allow a hostile power to gain control of the Flemish coast. Through the auto-

The Austrian envoy hands over the ultimatum to the Serbian government, July 1914

matic inclusion of the British dominions Canada, Australia, New Zealand, and South Africa in the war, the conflict quickly became a global war. In Europe, as British foreign minister Edward Grey put it, "the lights went out."

Kaiser Wilhelm II talks to members of the navy, 1915

> **The Opponents in World War I:**
> **The "Central Powers"**
> *Austria-Hungary, Bulgaria, Germany, Turkey*
>
> **The "Entente Powers"**
> *Belgium, France, Italy (1915), Japan, Russia, Serbia, the United Kingdom and US (1917).*

The flags of the Central Powers

Jul 1914	July Crisis	Jul 30, 1914	General mobilization in Russia	Aug 3, 1914	Germany declares war on France
Jun 28, 1914	Assassination in Sarajevo	Jul 28, 1914	Austria-Hungary declares war on Serbia	Aug 1, 1914	Germany declares war on Russia

The Course of the War 1914–1916

The German westward advance was halted just 25 miles (40 km) from Paris, and the Western Front then stagnated into trench warfare. The Central Powers gained territory in the east and southeast of Europe, but without decisively weakening the Entente powers.

Both the Germans and the French went to war on a wave of ❾ popular enthusiasm in August 1914. The first battles were actually fought on Belgian territory, however, because the French generals knew of the German plan to march into France through Belgium and met the advance. The swift march to Paris that had been hoped for by the Germans was stopped just short of Paris by a counteroffensive of the Entente powers. The Germans were forced to retreat by the "Miracle of the Marne." The Western Front then stagnated over a length of nearly 500 miles (805 km), and the years of ❼ trench warfare's deadly attrition began.

From the start, both sides employed poison gas as a weapon of mass destruction. Following France's use of non-lethal tear gas in 1914, the Germans employed deadly chlorine gas for the first time in 1915 near Ypres in Flanders. Although expressly forbidden in the rules for land wars laid down by the 1907 Hague Conference, ❿ gas warfare was waged on all fronts.

On the Eastern Front, the Russian army marched into East Prussia in the middle of August 1914, but was defeated in the battles of Tannenberg and the Masurian Lakes and by February 1915 had retreated. The German army, led by Supreme Commander Paul von Hindenburg, then seized Russian Poland, Kurzeme, and Lithuania, after which the offensive became stuck in East Galicia. Attacks from both sides followed without significant gains, until the Russian Revolution of 1917 decisively changed the situation on the Eastern Front.

The Balkan region, where the conflict had begun with Austria-Hungary's declaration of war, became a second arena of conflict. ❽ Serbia was defeated by Central Powers troops in October 1915 to secure the land routes to the Ottoman Empire. The Entente allies

7

French soldiers biding their time in the trenches, 1915

8

Schoolhouse in Soldau, Serbia, destroyed during the Winter Battle of Masuria, 1915–16

Romania and Montenegro were also occupied at the end of 1916. Entente troops were forced back, taking a stand in Saloniki, and in 1917 forced Greece, which had been neutral up until then, into the war. But no major breakthroughs occurred on the boundaries of the Southeastern Front.

9

German volunteers on a train to France, August 1914

10

Soldiers blinded by poison gas, 1918

Fritz Haber

Fritz Haber

The German chemist and Nobel prizewinner Fritz Haber gained dubious fame through his role in the arms race to produce chemical weapons. After the outbreak of war, he put his research institute at the disposal of the German military, and he personally supervised the first gas attacks on the front. He was also the scientist who developed the gas Zyklon B, which the Nazis later used to exterminate the Jews in their death camps. Haber himself had to flee Germany after 1933 because of his Jewish ancestry.

Aug 4, 1914	Great Britain declares war	**Sep 6–15, 1914**	Battle of the Masurian Lakes	**1916**	Capture of Bucharest
Aug 4, 1914	German troops march into Belgium	**Aug 26–30, 1914**	Battle of Tannenberg	**1915**	Battle of Amselfeld	**1917**	Russian Revolution

The War of Attrition on the Western Front

On the Western Front, the two sides ground each other down in the *Materialschlacht* ("battle of materials"). The entry of the US into the war tipped the balance in favor of the Entente Powers.

At the beginning of 1916, the German military leadership was determined to break the ❺ stalemate on the Western Front by any means. Without any real prospects of territorial gains, the aim of the subsequent war of attrition was to bleed the enemy into defeat. The months-long battle for ❷ Verdun became a fight for each foot of ground and resulted in 700,000 dead and wounded on

each side. During the unsuccessful British-French counterattack on the ❸ Somme, 57,000 British soldiers died within the first hours; in total, more than a million died on both sides. Both of the battles demonstrated the pointless ❻ mass death of technological war and the serious effects on the psyche and morale of the soldiers. It had become impossible to launch a successful attack on deeply dug-in defensive positions without huge losses. Germany and France weakened each other with no prospect of a victory by either side. Due to these failings, the military leadership on both the French and German sides changed; Robert Nivelle took over from Joseph Joffre in France, and in Germany Erich von Falkenhayn was replaced by Hindenburg, who ultimately ended the attack on Verdun.

At sea, the superiority of the Entente powers—thanks primarily to the British war fleet—had been overwhelming from the beginning. Consequently, ignoring international law, Germany used its ❹ submarines to destroy merchant ships of both warring and neutral nations beginning in 1915. After the sinking of the ❶ *Lusitania*, a

passenger steamer used to transport munitions on which 100 Americans also lost their lives, the United States broke its neutrality with vehement protests, causing Germany to terminate its unrestricted submarine warfare. However, after the Battle of Jutland at the end of May 1916, which caused heavy losses for the British, the German Reich decided to resume its unrestricted submarine warfare on February 1, 1917. The United States then declared war on Germany, and later on Austria-Hungary as well. With the ❼ entry of the United States

The sinking of the torpedoed *Lusitania*, carrying American civilians, 1915

into the war on the side of the Entente powers, the course of the war finally turned against the Central Powers. From then on, the Central Powers were at a hopeless material disadvantage.

German navy poster: "Submarines out!," 1914

French artillery with British guns on the Somme, 1917

French propaganda poster with the exhortation to hold the fortress of Verdun, 1916

Improvised graves on the Western Front, 1916

English military cemetery on the Somme, drawing by Louis Étienne Dauphin, 1916

I am telling you
On June 28th I expect you to enlist in the army of war savers to back up my army of fighters.
W. S. S. Enlistment

US poster for the recruitment of volunteers, 1917

Psychology

World War I provided an endless stream of test subjects for the fledgling science of psychology. Many soldiers on the Western Front suffered from severe traumatic and hysterical disorders. In the face of bloody slaughters and confinement in the trenches, the soldiers turned into neurotic palsy victims and psychosomatic paralytics. Their example disproved the widely prevailing belief of the time that hysteria was nothing more than a "woman's illness."

Dec 8, 1914 | Naval battle of the Falkland Islands   **May 7, 1915** | Sinking of the *Lusitania*   **May 31–Jun 1, 1916** | Naval battle of Skagerrak

Feb 22, 1915 | Beginning of unrestricted submarine warfare   **Feb 21–Jul 21, 1916** | Battle of Verdun   **Jun 24–Nov 26, 1916** | Battle of the Somme

■ Secondary Theaters of War and the First Resistance Movements

The colonial possessions of the European powers meant that the theaters of war were spread throughout the world. Due to the enormous material and human sacrifice, the first mutinies occurred in 1917 on all sides.

The European colonial powers fought each other on the high seas worldwide. German cruisers fought under the flag of their Turkish allies in the Black Sea against Russia; they also destroyed a British cruiser squadron at Coronel, Chile. The British destroyed German warships at the Falkland Islands off the coast of Argentina. Japan joined the naval war of the Entente Powers as the first independent overseas ally in 1914 because Germany had been unwilling to relinquish its Chinese territorial holding of ❾ Kiaochow.

The Entente Powers fought in Africa for the German colonial

8
Soldiers of the Ottoman army, part of the Axis alliance, 1916

possessions. Togo, Cameroon, and German Southwest Africa were conquered in the first years of the war. The Germans were able to hold onto German East Africa until the end of the war in 1918, but only with the help of

the ⓫ Askari and other native soldiers.

In the Near East, the ❽ Ottoman Empire joined the Central Powers early on, but despite much support, it was unable to wage a multi-front war. Though successful against the British and Australians in the Gallipoli Peninsula in 1915, the Turks collapsed in Sinai and Palestine. The defeat of the Central Powers in 1918 resulted in the complete dismantling of the empire. Like Austria-Hungary, it was reduced to its core country, Turkey.

In order to keep the worldwide machinery of war running, the domestic economies in the warring nations were adjusted to the needs of the ⓰, ⓬ war industry. As the war went on hunger and malnutrition fostered resistance to the war—especially in Germany which was losing the war and suffering under a blockade. Discontent also spread to the front. In August 1917, German sailors refused orders because of the bad supply situation. The first civilian revolts took place in January 1918 when workers in German cities went on strike for a swift peace settlement, but the German military leaders continued fighting. Some resistance was seen in other countries as well. Mutinies of French soldiers on the Western Front occurred after battles involving heavy losses, and a group of Russian soldiers deserted after a failed offensive against the German army in May 1917, avowing friendship and brotherhood with the enemy.

9
German war postcard referring to the fight for Kiaochow, 1914

10
US poster with an appeal for the conservation of food supplies for the soldiers fighting in Europe, 1918

The Aerial Warfare

For the first time, war was also waged in the air. The Germans employed the rather sluggish Zeppelin airship, while the British performed reconnaissance with small, maneuverable airplanes. Grenades were thrown by hand, and pilots fought dogfights over the front lines.

British plane hit by the German Luftwaffe, artist's impression

11
Askari troops in German East Africa, 1915

12
Women working in the French war industry, 1915

■ The Collapse of the Central Powers and the Armistice 1918

Although the Entente had the advantage in every area after the United States entered the war, the Central Powers were unshakably set on a military victory.

After his electoral victory in 1916 ❶ US president Woodrow Wilson sympathized with the Allies and provided financial support to them. Under the slogan "Peace without victory" he supported the idea of a balancing peace, whereas France and Great Britain aimed for the complete defeat of the German Reich. On April 6th, 1917, the United States declared war on Germany because the latter insisted on maintaining its policy of unrestricted sinking of neutral merchant shipping by submarines, which could not rescue survivors. By June 1917, the first US troops had landed in France. On January 8, 1918, Wilson gave a speech proposing 14 points, which formed the basis of the later peace treaties, though significantly modified.

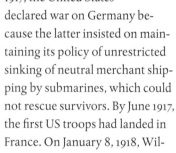

US President Thomas Woodrow Wilson

The most important provisions were the evacuation of all territories seized by the Central Powers, the ❷ return of Alsace-Lorraine to France, international disarmament, the right of all peoples to national self-determination, and the general joining together of all nations for the mutual guarantee of political independence and territorial integrity.

The German Reich, however, continued to pursue the goal of a "victorious peace," particularly given that there had been a permanent cease-fire on the Eastern Front since December 1917 after the revolutionary developments in Russia. This had allowed substantial numbers of German troops to be switched to the Western Front. In the Treaty of ❸ Brest-Litovsk on March 3, 1918, the Central Powers coerced the Soviets to relinquish Poland and Kurzeme, Ukraine, and later the newly founded Baltic states, would also become formally independent but remained under German control. Portions of Georgia and Armenia fell to the Ottoman Empire.

The Germans' hopes for a military victory in the West after the end of the conflict in the East quickly proved to be illusory. After the Entente Powers' successful counter-offensive in the summer of 1918, German troops were pushed back all the way to the borders of the Reich. When, at the end of October, Germany's main allies, Austria and the Ottoman Empire, collapsed and made peace on their own, the German Reich was finally defeated. To avoid a bitter peace, the German government accepted the "14 Points" as the conditions for peace negotiations.

Marshal Pétain rides triumphant through a conquered Metz, 1918

Peace of Brest-Litovsk: Trotsky (right) and other Russian deputies on their way to the negotiation, 1918

The events in Germany came thick and fast. German sailors' refusal to put to sea for a naval battle on October 28, 1918, was the prelude to the ❺ November Revolution that ended in the overthrow of the monarchy. On November 9, the kaiser ❻ abdicated and a German republic was proclaimed in Berlin. Two days later, Matthias Erzberger, as representative of the German Reich, signed the ❹ Armistice of Compiègne. The war was ❼ over.

Signing of the Armistice of Compiègne, November 11, 1918

German mutineers, November 1918

Wilhelm II leaves Berlin on November 9 for exile

Soldiers heading home

■ The Peace Settlements

After a power struggle among themselves, the victorious powers agreed upon harsh peace terms for Germany in the Treaty of Versailles. The Germans were forced to take sole responsibility for the war and pay heavy reparations to the countries they invaded.

The victorious Allied powers met in January 1919 in Paris to discuss a new postwar order. The negotiations of the more than 100 delegates lasted into June. The peace discussions were dominated by the U.S. president

8 David Lloyd George

❸ Woodrow Wilson, British prime minister ❽ David Lloyd George, French prime minister ❾ Georges Clemenceau, and to a lesser extent Italian prime minister Vittorio Emanuele Orlando. Neither defeated Germany nor Bolshevik Russia were invited.

The goals of the victorious powers were widely divergent. Wilson wanted to secure a permanent peace and create a corresponding organization with the formation of a League of Nations. Great Britain wanted to spare Germany—mostly out of fear that the defeated Central Power might embrace Bolshevism. France, on the other hand, wanted to fundamentally weaken its powerful neighbor. In the final Treaty of ❿ Versailles, a compromise prevailed, with harsh terms but no dismantling of Germany, and the US desire to establish a League of Nations.

9 Georges Clemenceau

and Germany lost territory to Poland, Czechoslovakia, and Lithuania. The left bank of the Rhine was to be ⓫ demilitarized and occupied by the Allies; the German army was to be reduced to 100,000 men without a General Staff. The reparations had not yet been fixed in the treaty, but it was clear that the amount would be large; the German Reich ended up paying 53 billion marks in gold by 1932. The "War Guilt clause" that held Germany fully responsible for the war was particularly resented.

Separate peace treaties were signed with the other Central

Graf Ulrich von Brockdorff-Rantzau, foreign minister of the Weimar Republic, in the peace negotiations at Versailles:

"We know the force of the hate that confronts us here. It is asked of us that we confess ourselves to be solely responsible for the war. Such an admission coming from my mouth would be a lie."

Graf Ulrich von Brockdorff-Rantzau

10 Conference room in Versailles, 1919

11 Decommissioning a German tank, 1920

12 Treaty of Versailles, 1919

13 US President Wilson in Paris, 1918

tions. The German National Assembly at Weimar voted to accept the terms by 237 against 138. Germany ⓬ signed the peace terms on June 28, 1919, though with no real alternative.

Germany lost about 13 percent of its pre-war territory. Alsace-Lorraine was returned to France

Powers. At St. Germain on September 10, 1919, the Austro-Hungarian Empire was dismantled. Austria (forbidden from uniting with Germany) and Hungary became two small states and had to recognize the independence of Czechoslovakia and Poland, as well as the loss of all other impe-

rial territories. In the peace treaty of Sèvres of August 10, 1920, the Ottoman Empire was carved up in accordance with a prior agreement between the Allies: The Bosporus, the Dardanelles, and the city of Constantinople were placed under French and British control.

| Nov 1918 | November Revolution | Nov 11, 1918 | Armistice of Compiègne | Jun 28, 1919 | Signing of Treaty of Versailles |
| Nov 9, 1918 | Proclamation of the Republic | Jan 18, 1919 | Paris Peace Conference | Sep 10, 1919 | Treaty of St.-Germain |

1 马列主义毛泽东思想万岁！

IDEOLOGIES OF THE 20TH CENTURY

After the social and moral upheavals of World War I, the proponents of two opposing totalitarian political models for the restructuring of society came to power. With National Socialism, inhuman fascism triumphed over the democratic movement that had established the unstable and weak Weimar Republic in Germany. The other ideology that came to influence world politics was ❶ Communism. Both models saw themselves as a radical counterpoint to the "Western" model of a liberal democracy.

Communists Marx, Engels, Lenin, Stalin and Mao, Chinese poster

Democracy: Self-Determination of the Citizens

Abraham Lincoln described democratic rule, which is based on the principle of sovereignty of the people and the equality of all, as a "government of the people, by the people, for the people." The ❻ United States under President ❹ Woodrow Wilson justified its entry into World War I ideologically, stating that its aim was "to make the world safe for democracy."

After the war, demands for greater self-determination by groups sharing a cultural or national heritage led to electoral reforms in almost all countries of Europe. Initially the predominant form of democracy was that which

2 Polling station in Spain, 1936

relied on nonviolent party competition, guaranteed individual rights and minority rights, and let each citizen participate in elections according to the ❷ rule of the majority. In the face of the social crises of the postwar societies, however, many democratic governments were crushed between the radical right and radical left-wing parties. Of the major powers, only the traditional democracies of Great Britain and the United States proved immune to totalitarian promises of utopias for world happiness.

After World War II, liberal democracies reasserted themselves in Western Europe. Since the collapse of the Soviet Empire in 1989–1991, almost all of Eastern Europe and many other parts of the world have committed to democratic principles, although many struggle to establish a true democratic form of rule.

4 Woodrow Wilson

6 Stamp with the New York Statue of Liberty

Communism: Deliverance Claims and Paternal Dictatorship

With their 1848 *Communist Manifesto*, Karl Marx and Friedrich Engels conceptualized a new historic-philosophical theory that was used as the ideological foundation of the revolutionary workers' movements of the 20th century. The manifesto instructed the workers that their historical duty was to free all of mankind from repression and injustice ("Proletarians of the world,

3 DOMJU LATVIJA MŪŽOS LAI DZĪVO.

Soviet propaganda poster, 1945

5 РАБОЧИМ НЕЧЕГО ТЕРЯТЬ, КРОМЕ СВОИХ ЦЕПЕЙ, А ПРИОБРЕТУТ ОНИ ЦЕЛЫЙ МИР.

1 МАЯ

Call for the class struggle, 1919

unite") inherent in society as it was in the early 20th century.

Marx and Engels interpreted history as a series of ❺ class struggles between rulers and the ruled. Only with the historically necessary victory of the proletariat over the bourgeoisie would the free self-development of every

human be possible. The middle-class capitalist society had to be overcome and the means of production converted to common property—only this would free humankind from all pressures. In the name of communism, the October Revolution led by Vladimir Lenin in 1918 triumphed in Russia, but the ❸ Union of Socialist Soviet Republics remained the only socialist country until 1945. There, a socialist "dictatorship of the proletariat" through a revolutionary party cadre was supposed to create the conditions for a future true communist "classless society." With their self-conception as the historical vanguard of a communist world revolution, the Soviet Communists under Lenin legitimized their absolute claim to leadership of all other Communist parties. Under Josef Stalin, the Soviet Union became a totalitarian dictatorship and systematically eliminated its political opponents.

Only after the central role of the Soviet Union in World War II in the victory and the spread of Communism throughout the world did certain states seek their own, national

Victory Parade of the fascist Falange in Spain, 1939

form of communism. During the Cold War after 1945, a particular movement referred to as "Euro-communism" emerged in many countries of the West. It evolved into socialism, represented throughout Europe by socialist parties within the democratic system. With the upheaval in Eastern Europe in 1989 and the collapse of the Soviet Union in 1991, Communism lost its power base. As the only major Communist power remaining, China ostensibly bases its authority on the state teachings of Marx and Engels.

Fascism: Violence and the Cult of the Leader

The right-wing Italian nationalists around **9** Benito Mussolini called themselves fascists, after the old Roman power symbol, the *fasces*—rods bundled around an ax. When he came to power in Italy in 1920, Mussolini set up a new type of dictatorship that was

Adolf Hitler, NS painting, 1935

the forerunner and example—though never a totally emulated model—for fascist movements throughout the world.

In some European states, diverse authoritarian groupings

Benito Mussolini, 1935

with fascist traits won control over the state apparatus. After the **7** civil war in Spain in 1939, General Francisco Franco set up a dictatorship. In Portugal, António de Oliveira Salazar created the "Estado Novo" ("New State"), while in Austria a particular form of Austro-fascism developed. In South America there were also authoritarian regimes with fascist characteristics. Notable similarities among these fascist movements included hierarchical organizational structures, the cult around a socially integrative leader figure, suggestive symbolism, and total mass mobilization that left hardly

any rights to the individual. The state controlled all areas of life with its political police force.

Ideologically, the fascist state increasingly followed an "anti" ideology: antidemocratic and antiliberal, anticommunist and anticapitalist, antimodern, yet extremely nationalistic and prone to use violence as the decisive measure of politics. Racism, however, was not a central element of fascism. After World War II, fascism lost practically all significance.

National Socialism: Anti-Semitism and Ideology

German National Socialism or Nazism, with its leader (*Führer*) **11** Adolf Hitler, was in its state structure a particular variety of fascism. However, due to the central significance of anti-Semitism, race ideology, and the doctrine of **8** *Lebensraum* ("living space"), in its political ideology, it had an unprecedentedly all-encompassing worldview. Nazism defined history as the battle between peoples for the expansion of each nation's *Lebensraum*. Ultimately the "racially most valuable" people, the Aryans, would rule as the master humans over the inferior peoples. Nazi propaganda defamed particularly the Poles, Russians, and Slavs as "subhuman." Hitler promoted the war in the East as the battle for *Lebensraum*.

The main enemy, in the National Socialist worldview, was **10** "world Jewry," which did not want to recognize these "natural laws." The Jews were said to control international movements of all kinds—of democracy, pacifism, communism, and capitalism—and had destroyed the national "purity" of nations, according to Nazi philosophy.

"Blut und Boden"—The *Lebensraum* myth: Sword over the swastika, 1933

The central aim of the Nazis was therefore the persecution of Jews. Directly after coming to power in Germany, the Nazis began to force citizens of Jewish belief out of all areas by legal, economic, and criminal means, discriminating against them, disenfranchising them, and locking them up.

During World War II, the Nazi regime organized a factory model of mass murder of the European Jews. In the extermination camps, hundreds of thousands of Jews were systematically killed. In total, the number of Jewish victims was around six million. Further victims of Nazi terror included minorities such as the Sinti and

Anti-semitic NS Propaganda, 1942

Roma, homosexuals, and political opponents such as communists and socialists. After the victory of the Allies over Nazi Germany, the ideology of National Socialism was internationally outcast.

1939 | Franco dictatorship in Spain   **1945** | Fall of the Nazi regime   **1989–90** | Democratic revolutions in Eastern Europe

Jan 27, 1945 | Liberation of the concentration camp Auschwitz   **1946** | Communist People's Republic of China   **1991** | Collapse of the Soviet Union

1

THE UNPOPULAR DEMOCRACY:
THE GERMAN REICH 1918–1933

Parliamentary democracy prevailed in Germany in the ❶ revolution of 1918. However, it was never completely accepted by a broad section of the population, and its existence was threatened from the start by radical political forces. The feeling of national humiliation, economic problems, and the internal weaknesses of the democracy made possible the rise of National Socialism under Adolf Hitler, who was named chancellor of the republic in 1933.

Funeral of the victims of the November Revolution, Berlin, Jan 1918

■ The First Years of the German Republic

Hyperinflation and attempted coups from groups from across the political spectrum kept the republic from finding peace and stability in its early years.

The German monarchy collapsed in the wake of social unrest in November 1918. Social Democrat ❷ Friedrich Ebert took over responsibility for the government in the transitional period. The moderate left emerged triumphant in debates at worker and soldier councils over the question of the form of government. A national assembly in Weimar drafted a democratic constitution on January 19, 1919, and established a parliamentary republic with Ebert as president. Fearing Karl Liebknecht would proclaim a socialist republic, another Social Democrat, ❸ Philipp Scheide-

3

Philipp Scheidemann talks to the people, reconstructed picture, 1918

mann, proclaimed the German Republic on November 11.

The radical left felt betrayed by the government due to the lack of social measures. The military suppressed ❹ revolts and volun-

tary military groups, known as *Freikorps* ("Free Corps"), made up of soldiers returning from the war, terrorized the country. Officers of the Freikorps murdered Liebknecht and Rosa Luxemburg, the leaders of the German Communist party.

The right wing considered the government, which had signed the "dishonorable treaty of Versailles" to be agents of the French state—"fulfillment politicians." The signatory of the armistice, Matthias Erzberger, was murdered by right-wing extremists. The ❻ monarchist Kapp Putsch in 1920 and Hitler's 1923

2

Friedrich Ebert, ca. 1918

4

Government troops during the general strike in Berlin, March 3–12, 1919

5

Banknote of the German Reichsbank, November 15, 1923

Beer Hall Putsch, were crushed. The finances of the German Reich were catastrophic; the war had consumed vast sums and the victorious powers demanded reparations. To avoid bankruptcy, more money was printed and ❺ inflation skyrocketed. In October 1923, a US dollar cost 40 billion reichsmarks.

6

Distribution of flyers during the Kapp Putsch, March 1920, in Berlin

The Hitler Beer Hall Putsch 1923

Adolf Hitler, who was previously unknown, attempted to establish a right-wing dictatorship in Germany with a "March on the Feldherrnhalle" (Bavarian War Ministry) in Munich on November 9, 1923. While in prison following the suppression of the putsch attempt, he wrote his ideological work Mein Kampf. Hitler was released early for good behavior in 1924 and promised to seek power by legal means.

After the failed coup of the NSDAP: the accused; in the middle the main initiators Kriebel, Ludendorff, and Hitler, Munich, February 1924

| Nov 9, 1918 | Transitional government under Ebert | Jan 19, 1919 | Weimar constitution passed | 1922 | Inflation begins |
| Jan 15, 1919 | Liebknecht and Luxemburg murdered | Mar 13–17, 1920 | Kapp Putsch | Fall 1923 | "Cabinet of the Great Coalition" |

■ The Fall of the Weimar Republic

After a short interim of stabilization, Hitler's National Socialists received a boost from the world economic depression. With the aid of the German National party, Hitler took over power in Germany in 1933.

The republic seemed to settle down to transient stability after 1924. The economy recovered with a new currency and the regulation of reparations payments under the Dawes Plan. Culturally, Berlin was a world leader. Foreign Minister Stresemann pursued a path of reconciliation with Germany's neighbors, recognizing the western border with France in the ❼ Locarno Treaty of 1925. Germany signed a friendship and neutrality treaty with the Soviet Union and was accepted into the League of Nations.

The election of the committed monarchist Paul von Hindenburg as president in 1925, however, symbolized the republic's disfavor among a wide section of the population. The world economic depression in 1929 strengthened the enemies of the state and initiated the disintegration of democracy. After the collapse of Hermann Müller's Social Democratic government in 1930, President Hindenburg named Heinrich Brüning chancellor by emergency decree, responsible solely to the president and not to the parliament. Brüning's economic policies increased ❽ mass unemployment;

by the beginning of 1933 there were almost six million people out of work.

Growing poverty, fear of losing social status, and the lack of prospects drove many, particularly the middle class and youths, into the hands of Adolf Hitler's rad-

Election poster of the NSDAP, 1932

ical ❾ National Socialist German Workers' party (NSDAP)—the Nazi party—and presented it with an enormous increase in votes in the 1930 Reichstag election. The anti-Semitic and nationalistic smear campaign against the system and the "November criminals" popularized the ⓫ "dagger thrust legend,"

according to which the German politicians of the revolution of 1918 had stabbed the undefeated German army in the back by signing a peace treaty with the Allies. When in 1932 the National Socialists became the strongest party after the elections, the Center Party attempted to profit from the Nazis' mass popularity by joining them in a coalition supporting the "Enabling Act."

On January 30, 1933, President ❿ Hindenburg named Hitler chancellor of the National Socialist–DNVP coalition. "In two months we will have pushed Hitler into a corner so that he squeaks," promised Vice Chancellor Franz von Papen, who was allied with the DNVP—a statement that would quickly prove to be a fatal miscalculation.

From left: Gustav Stresemann, Austen Chamberlain, Aristide Briand, the Locarno Treaty, 1925.

Unemployed workers read job listings, Berlin, 1932

The "Golden Twenties"

Berlin was an open-minded metropolis with a thriving art and cultural scene throughout the Weimar Republic period. Be it the silent films of Fritz Lang, the new Expressionism in painting and poetry, the political theater of Bertolt Brecht, or the glamor of the entertainment industry, personified by Marlene Dietrich, for example—cultural life in the German capital was vibrant and drew intellectuals from all over the world. The victory of National Socialists in Germany abruptly put an end to this creative epoch.

top: Actress Brigitte Helm, 1929
above: Playwright Bertolt Brecht, 1930

Hindenburg and Hitler drive through Berlin, 1933

The "Stab in the Back" propaganda picture, 1924

UNDER THE SWASTIKA: NAZI GERMANY

1933–1939

With Hitler's takeover of power, a twelve-year totalitarian regime began in Germany. In 1939 it brought war and racist terror to the world. The "Führer"-led dictatorship attempted to reform state and society to conform to ❶ National Socialist ideology. Despite the Nazis' brutal suppression of the opposition and single-minded removal of the Jewish population from national life, the world underestimated the nature of the regime and its contempt for human life, and thus World War II erupted.

Imperial eagle and swastika, symbols of National Socialist ideology

■ Setting Up the Dictatorial "Führer State"

Within a very short time, Hitler controlled the state institutions in Germany and the Nazi party and dissolved the democratic structures of the Weimar Republic.

The restructuring of the German state from a democracy to a dictatorship took place between January 30, 1933, and August 2, 1934. When it was over, all power was united in the person of ❷ Adolf Hitler. Without formally repealing the Weimar constitution, the Nazi ideology was able to dominate state and society as apparently legal prerequisites were created to invalidate the democratic constitution.

After the ❹ burning of the Reichstag building in Berlin on February 27, 1933, the Nazi party's private army—the storm troopers or SA—began the first acts of persecution against Social Democrats and Communists.

Moreover, Hitler used the opportunity to suspend basic political rights by emergency decree. This made the persecution of political rivals legal and removed it from state intervention or control.

In the last semi-free election on March 5, 1933, the Nazis failed to gain an absolute majority despite massive intimidation of the public. In the first session of parliament, all the legislators—except the Social Democrats and Communists, who had already been arrested—approved an ❻ "Enabling Act" that transferred full legislative power to Hitler's party government.

The Nazi government did away with German federalism and instituted one-party rule. By 1934, the state parliaments had all been dissolved and replaced by regime-conforming "Reich governors." After the Social Democratic party was banned in July 1933, all of the other opposition political parties disbanded in quick succession or, as was the case with the allied DVNP, were forced to retire. The Nazi party proclaimed itself the state party.

A short while later, Hitler purged his party of internal opposition. Even the SA, which was demanding to take over the country's military power, was seen as a threat. Under the pretense of preventing a putsch, the leadership of the ❸ SA was murdered with the support of the German army on July 30, 1934. This arbitrary action was afterwards legitimized as "national self-defense."

When the president of Germany, Hindenburg, died on August 2, 1934, Hitler claimed the office of head of state and proclaimed himself "Führer and chancellor" of the German Reich. The ❺ German army was compelled to swear a personal oath to Hitler. Germany had irrefutably become a Führer state.

Adolf Hitler, 1937

French caricature commenting on Hitler's liquidation of the SA, 1934

Hitler during his government statement on the "Law to Remedy the Needs of People and Country," known as the "Enabling Act," March 23, 1933

Burning of the Reichstag building, February 27–28, 1933

The German army marches through Berlin, 1934

| Feb 27, 1933 | Burning of the Reichstag building | Mar 10, 1933 | Public book burning | July 1933 | Ban of Social Democratic party |
| Mar 5, 1933 | NSDAP fails to gain absolute majority | Mar 23, 1933 | "Enabling Act" |

■ Control over Society

Propaganda, ideological persuasion, and violence were the methods with which the Nazis controlled and manipulated the German population.

An anarchistic juxtaposition of state and party systems, rather than the hierarchically organized power bloc as suggested by propaganda, characterized the Nazi state. Hitler remained the only point of reference of rivaling power groups. Alongside the terror, successes in foreign affairs and well-directed social measures strengthened the Führer's status among the German people. Thanks to ❿ governmental job creation, unemployment sank by half within two years. By 1939, the massive armament programs intended to make the economy capable of war had even caused a labor shortage.

To pacify the coercively organized economic laborers in the "German Workers' Front," the workers received somewhat extravagant wages, protection

7 Members of the Hitler Youth and the League of German Girls sing, 1937

against job loss, and paid vacations. The ⓫ Nazi party organization *Kraft durch Freude*—Strength through Joy—organized events and inexpensive trips. Thus the regime kept an eye on the "national comrades" even during their time off. The European day of the labor movement, May 1, became a public holiday known as the "Day of National Labor."

Special attention was given to the indoctrination of youth. All youth groups were absorbed by the ❼ Hitler Youth and the ⓬ League of German Girls. Beginning in 1936, all ten- to 18-year-olds had to become members. The Reich Chamber of Culture, under the aegis of ❽ Propaganda Minister Joseph Goebbels, supervised cultural life. Literature that did not conform to the party line was destroyed in public book burnings.

National Socialism's quest for totality was amplified by a network of state surveillance agencies. After the elimination of the SA, Heinrich Himmler's

elite *Schutzstaffel* ("defense squadrons")—known as the ❾ SS—became the most important instrument for fighting political opponents in 1934. All police and secret service departments were placed under its control. The SS took over the administration of the concentration camps. In 1939, about 25,000 "undesirable" persons were serving sentences in five of these camps.

8 Propaganda Minister Joseph Goebbels, 1931

Public Book Burning in 1933

The Nazi student association initiated the public book burnings that took place in the German university cities on March 10, 1933. Following a diatribe from Goebbels against "un-German" literature in Berlin, the works of Walter Benjamin, Erich Kästner, Thomas Mann, Sigmund Freud, and Carl von Ossietzky, among others, were set ablaze. Hundreds of writers emigrated, among them Bertolt Brecht and Stefan Zweig. While in prison, Ossietzky was awarded the Nobel Peace Prize in 1935; after three years in a concentration camp he died in 1938.

Book burnings in Berlin, March 10, 1933

9 Himmler (left) and Hitler inspect a defense squadron, 1935

10 Unemployed people are put to work building the motorway, 1933

11 Poster promoting a *Kraft durch Freude* holiday: "You too can travel now," 1938

12 Poster promoting the building of youth hostels, 1933

| Aug 2, 1934 | Hindenburg dies | | from 1936 | Compulsory membership in Hitler Youth / League of German Girls |
| Jul 30, 1934 | SA leaders murdered | 1935 | Nobel Peace Prize for Carl von Ossietzky | from 1936 | Extensive arms programs |

The Persecution of European Jewry

Through a gradual progression of steps up to 1939, German Jews lost their rights, were dispossessed, and were forced to emigrate.

SA men hang up posters appealing to Germans to boycott Jewish businesses, April 1, 1933

After the takeover by the Nazis, there were uncontrolled outbreaks of violence in many places against the Jewish population by gangs of SA thugs incited by the anti-Semitic newspaper *Der Stürmer*. In response to protests from business and the old elite, the Nazi leadership tried to steer the persecution of the Jews onto a more regulated track through centrally directed actions and sham legislation.

In April 1933 Propaganda Minister Goebbels organized a ❶ nationwide boycott of Jewish businesses. The "Law to Restore Career Civil Service" of April 7, 1933, launched a flood of discriminatory decrees that forced Jewish people out of their professions and by 1939 had completely isolated them socially. Along with government service, the Jews were banned from cultural professions and forbidden to work as ❷ physicians or lawyers.

Eventually every contact with the "Aryan" population was forbidden. The ❹ race laws of 1935

2

Sign of a Jewish physician with a cautionary notice pasted over it: "Warning: a Jew!" 1933

3

Arrested Jewish men in Baden-Baden, November 9, 1938

deprived Jews of all political rights. Every citizen of the Reich had to prove his or her "German-bloodedness." A Jew was defined as anyone who was "descended from, according to race, three full-blooded Jewish grandparents." The whole absurdity of the Nazi race ideology is shown by the criterion for being a "full-blooded Jew" as membership in the Jewish religion.

The Nazi leadership used an attempt to assassinate a German diplomat as a pretext to stage a full-scale ❺ pogrom against the Jews in November 1938. All across Germany on the night of November 9–10, 1938, synagogues were set afire and ❻ Jewish businesses destroyed. Almost 100 persons were murdered and about

30,000 were carried off to ❸ concentration camps. An "atonement payment" of a billion reichmarks ($400 million) was imposed on the German Jews. All Jewish capital assets were confiscated; real estate, stocks, and jewelry were sold under duress. The liquidation of all Jewish businesses and enterprises followed. The economy was thus forcibly Aryanized.

The Nazi leadership next moved on to a program of forced emigration and established a Head Office for Jewish Emigration in 1939. However, financial straits and the restrictive immigration regulations of foreign nations made leaving the country difficult. Emigration was finally banned in 1941 after the new strategy of exterminating the Jews was adopted. The organized mass murder of Jews—along with Sinti and Roma (gypsies), homosexuals, and other minorities—began in Poland.

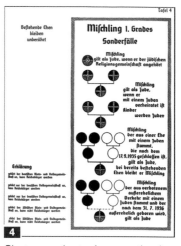

4

Chart purporting to show genetic relationships between the races, 1940

Emigration

A total of almost a million people, the vast majority of them Jewish, were forced or went voluntarily into exile from Germany after 1933. However, the formation of a united, powerful opposition was unsuccessful. The writer Thomas Mann put a face to "the other Germany" with his critical speeches from the United States. Many exiles joined the armies of their host countries during World War II.

Thomas Mann (left) with his family in American exile, 1940

5

Reichskristallnacht 1938: a burning synagogue in Bielefeld

6

The day after: passersby in front of a vandalized Jewish shop

Nazi Foreign Policies through 1939

The Nazi leaders were tactically clever in disguising their plans of conquest as a peaceful policy to revise the Treaty of Versailles.

Hitler had planned a great war since the beginning of his rise to power. In a secret speech to German officers in February 1933 he openly spoke of the goal of "conquering new living space in the East and its ruthless Germanization." In order to restore Germany's position of power necessary to accomplish this, the Nazi leadership successfully ❽ revised the restrictions imposed by the Treaty of Versailles. To pacify their war-weary European neighbors, they veiled their goals in an official policy of rapprochement.

Despite ❼ leaving the League of Nations in 1933, Hitler avowed the German desire for peace and stood by Western cultural heritage. The Reich Concordat with the Vatican, which was meant to secure the rights of the Catholic Church in Germany, nonaggression pacts with other states, and the hosting of the 1936 ❿ Olympic Games seemed to confirm

this. When Saarland clearly voted to join the German Reich in a plebiscite in 1935, the Western allied powers acknowledged the Germans' right to self-determination

Propaganda poster promoting the annexation of Austria: "Bit by bit, Adolf Hitler tore up the Treaty of Versailles!" 1938

and accepted the subsequent violation of the Versailles Treaty. Hitler reintroduced military conscription in 1935, announced

rearmament, and signed a naval fleet agreement with Great Britain. A year later, he occupied the ⓫ demilitarized Rhineland region. Involvement in the Spanish Civil War, the ❾ "Berlin–Rome Axis," and the Anti-Comintern Pact with Japan were coalitions with a clear anti-Soviet orientation that presaged later war alliances.

While the Western Powers had accepted the invasion of Austria in 1938 and its unification with Germany and had even legalized the annexation of the Sudetenland through the Munich Agreement, they gave up their policy of appeasement after the breakup of Czechoslovakia in March 1939 and threatened war if Germany attempted further terri-

The empty seats of the German delegation after it left the League of Nations, 1933

Stamp showing Hitler and Mussolini, entitled "Two nations, one battle," 1938

torial expansion. Poland was invaded by Germany under a pretense on September 1, 1939, and the Second World War had begun.

The reconstituted German Wehrmacht marches into the demilitarized Rhineland on March 7, 1936

The 1936 Olympic Games in Berlin

Germany deceived the world during the Olympic Games of 1936 with a demonstration of cosmopolitan culture. Jazz was allowed to be played in the bars and the persecution of political opponents and Jews was put on hold. The perfectly staged Olympic propaganda film by Leni Riefenstahl also impressed the world and was generally positively received.

above: Under the Third Reich jazz was labeled "degenerate" and prohibited, poster, 1938
right: Still from Leni Riefenstahl's Olympics "Festival of the Nations," 1936

Official English-language poster of the 1936 Olympic Games

| 1936 | "Berlin-Rome Axis" founded | 1938 | Germany invades Austria | Sep 1, 1939 | Germany invades Poland |
| **Nov 9/10, 1938** | Reichskristallnacht | **1939** | Creation of the "Head Office for Jewish Emigration" | **1941** | Ban on Jewish emigration |

1

AUSTRIA: FROM HABSBURG EMPIRE TO GERMAN "OSTMARK" 1918–1945

The multinational state of Austria-Hungary crumbled after the end of World War I, losing three-quarters of its previous territory. The existence of the newly founded Republic of Austria, a small country, was threatened from the beginning by economic problems and political radicalism. The establishment of a partially fascist regime in 1933 could not prevent the Nazi German Reich from absorbing ❶ Austria shortly afterward.

The German Armed Forces cross the Austrian border, 1938

■ The Fall of the Habsburg Monarchy

After the disintegration of the Habsburg Empire in 1918, the German-speaking heartland reconstituted itself as the "Republic of Austria," but the Allies prohibited the merging of this truncated state with the German Reich.

2

Emperor Charles I

World War I, which developed out of Austria's retaliatory strike against ❺ Serbia for the murder of Archduke Franz Ferdinand in 1914, brought the downfall of the Habsburg dual monarchy. ❻ Militarily Austria-Hungary had taken on too much and was dependent on the German troops. When the Austrian fronts collapsed in the spring and summer of 1918, the disintegration of the empire was inevitable. Supply blockages led to civil revolt, mutinies

3

Dr. Karl Renner

took place in the army and navy, and the various nationalities in the empire fought for their independence.

As early as 1917 the Poles, Czechs, and Slavs had formed governments in exile, and in October 1918 Hungary declared itself independent of Austria. The last Habsburg emperor ❷ Charles I refused to participate in the new government. He was deposed in 1918. In 1919, the Austrian national assembly officially re-

pealed the Habsburg right to rule and confiscated their fortune.

On November 12, 1918, the ❹ "German-Austria" Republic was proclaimed; its chancellor was the Social Democrat ❸ Karl Renner. The state also declared itself part of the German republic, but the Allies prohibited this annexation of Austria to Germany in the Treaty of St. Germain in 1919. The treaty also forced Austria to cede further territories: South Tirol was given to Italy and the German Sudeten territories to Czechoslovakia. From the beginning, the much smaller Austrian state had to struggle with severe

economic problems. In 1922, the League of Nations granted the republic a large credit to revitalize the state finances— under the condition that it would irrevocably refrain from a union with the German Reich. The republic slowly began to be consolidated with the introduction of the schilling as currency in 1924.

4

Proclamation of the republic of Austria

5

Anti-Serbian violence in Sarajevo, after the assassination on June 28, 1914

6

Battle against Italy, postcard

1917 | Governments in exile of Poles, Czechs, and Slavs   Nov 1918 | Charles I renounces the throne   1919 | Treaty of St. Germain

Oct 1918 | Hungary's independence from Austria   Nov 12, 1918 | Proclamation of "German-Austria" Republic

Austria's Anschluss with the German Reich

Internal political radicalization led to the establishment of an authoritarian government in Austria in 1933. The Austro-Fascists, however, were only able to delay Austria's eventual assimilation into the Nazi German Reich.

The ideological polarization between the national political parties of the Austrian republic, the Christian Socialists, and the Social Democrats, intensified after 1927. At the same time, clashes between fascist and socialist factions shook the nation. As the government had shown itself incapable of dealing with the continuing economic crisis and social unrest, Chancellor ❼ Engelbert Dollfuss, in a coup-like move, suspended parliament in 1933 and by emergency decree established a dictatorship—"Austro-Fascism"—modeled on that of Fascist Italy. He gave the Home Guard police authority, founded the nonpartisan ❽ Fatherland Front while banning all other political parties, reintroduced the death penalty, and set up detention camps to incarcerate regime opponents. A putsch by the Social Democrats in February 1934 was brutally crushed.

Dollfuss was killed during a coup attempt by Austrian National Socialists in July 1934. His successor, ❾ Kurt von Schuschnigg, dedicated himself particularly to the struggle to maintain Austria's independence now that the

7

Chancellor Engelbert Dollfuss

Anschluss (union) with Germany, desired by some Austrians since the late 1920s, had become a threat with Hitler's accession to power in 1933. It was clear that if this were to occur, Austria would have to subordinate itself to the German Nazi party. Schuschnigg put his hopes in close relations with Italy, which had proclaimed itself a guarantor of Austrian sovereignty and had also dispatched troops to the Brenner Pass on the Austrian border during an attempted Nazi takeover in 1934. Schuschnigg, however, was pressured by Hitler in 1936 to accept the "July Agreement" that obligated Austria to adopt a "more German" foreign policy and to release all Nazis held in custody. Two years later, he was forced to appoint a leading Austrian Nazi, ❿ Arthur Seyss-Inquart, as minister of the interior.

Schuschnigg's last attempt to prevent as-

similation by the German Reich was to call for a ⓬ plebiscite on Austrian independence. The vote was set for March 13, 1938, but on March 12, ⓭ German troops marched into Austria, and two days later Hitler delivered a speech on the Heldenplatz in Vienna in front of cheering masses. The Anschluss was approved by an overwhelming majority in the plebiscite. Even the socialist leader Karl Renner publicly voted for it, and churches were festooned with swastika banners. Austria was then renamed German "Ostmark." In April, the first concentration camp was erected in ⓫ Mauthausen.

8

Federal Chancellor Dollfuss approves a parade by the Fatherland Front

9

Kurt von Schuschnigg (left) pays Mussolini (middle) a visit, 1934

10

Arthur Seyss-Inquart with Adolf Hitler, 1938

11

Detainees liberated from Mauthausen, 1945

12

Poster with Schuschnigg's appeal to vote for the independence of Austria, in March 1938

13

Parade of the German Armed Forces in Vienna on March 15, 1938, after their invasion of Vienna on March 12

1933 | Parliament dismissed   **Jul 1934** | Putsch by National Socialists   **1938** | Seyss-Inquart becomes minister of the interior

1924 | Introduction of the Schilling   **Feb 1934** | February putsch by the Social Democrats   **1936** | July Agreement

SWITZERLAND: ISLAND OF STABILITY 1914–1945

Switzerland, a parliamentary federal republic since 1848, remained ❶ neutral during both world wars despite its position in the center of the European continent. Neither the economic problems of World War I nor its encirclement by the Axis powers in World War II was able to fundamentally endanger the democratic tradition of Switzerland. However, in order to avoid occupation by Hitler's Germany, Switzerland followed a controversial policy of compromise with the Nazis, despite official neutrality, as a result of which it was viewed with skepticism by the Allied powers.

Swiss soldiers protect the border, 1939

■ Strict Neutrality in the First World War

Switzerland's perpetual neutrality, as guaranteed at the Congress of Vienna in 1815, remained intact during World War I. Despite economic and social difficulties, the traditional democracy remained stable.

Even in the 19th century, Switzerland played an exceptional role in Europe. As an independent nation since the late Middle Ages, except for a short time after 1798 when it had been under French control, and without expansionist aspirations, it had long been a venue for international negotiations. The Congress of Vienna had granted the Swiss, in the interest of all of Europe, permanent neutrality, and World War I did not alter this. The small nation did not interfere with the Great Powers' war aims and had no raw materials essential to war. During the war, the Swiss army was provisionally mobilized but never saw action. However, the popula-

Swiss railway line

ce suffered due to a war-related economic crisis, causing the introduction of a war tax. As imports were difficult, attempts were made to strengthen the Swiss economy. The cultivation of grain was promoted, and the ❷ Swiss railway became the first to use electric instead of coal-burning, steam-driven engines.

The growing poverty of the people brought about a leftist-oriented revolt in 1916. However, the great general strike of 1918 was less an attempt at revolution than a call for social change; the strike was ended by military force, but state social reforms worked to relieve the tension. The liberal democratic tradition of the

❸ federal republic, which had existed since 1848, withstood the postwar turmoil unaffected. The Treaty of Versailles unconditionally reaffirmed the neutrality of the Swiss, and ❺ Geneva was chosen as the headquarters for the ❹ League of Nations initiated by U.S. President Woodrow Wilson; Switzerland joined in 1920.

Later, the threat of the Axis powers to Switzerland's strict neutrality in World War II would present a greater challenge than that of World War I.

The Swiss Houses of Parliament in Bern

Liechtenstein

The tiny principality of Liechtenstein, situated between Austria and Switzerland, has been sovereign since 1806. Following the economic crisis in the wake of World War I, Liechtenstein leaned economically and politically on Switzerland. Like its neighbor, it too remained neutral during the Nazi period. To this day, the princes of Liechtenstein have more rights than any of the other European monarchs.

top: Liechtenstein coat of arms
above: Vaduz Castle, Liechtenstein

Meeting of the League of Nations in Geneva, 1934

The League of Nations complex in Geneva

1806	Liechtenstein gains sovereignty		1863	Red Cross founded		Aug 10, 1914	Swiss army mobilized
	1815	Swiss neutrality guaranteed		1882	St. Gotthard Pass railroad built		1918	"General strike"

■ The Nazi Threat

In the 1930s, liberal and neutral Switzerland became the first retreat for German refugees. At the height of World War II, the Swiss were able to maintain their independence only through accommodation of Nazi Germany, although this was limited.

Although economic problems had been increasing in Switzerland since 1927, the influence of emerging front movements that had close ties to the Nazis in the 1930s remained marginal and was unable to shake the parliamentary federal republic. Once the Nazis took power in Germany, many refugees sought refuge in neighboring Switzerland, though often only as an intermediary station. "The boat is full" was a slogan often used to limit immigration; by the end of World War II, more than 20,000 Jews had been turned back at the border.

The latent external threat surrounding the Swiss caused them to move closer together and united them domestically. Switzerland was released in 1938 from its obligations to take part in League of Nations sanctions. The Swiss National Exhibition in 1939, actually an agricultural and industrial show, turned into a demonstra-

10 Advertising poster for the Saint Gotthard Pass railroad, 1924

tion of independence, freedom, and willingness to ❽ defend these ideals. The military mobilization ❼ during World War II was primarily symbolic. Switzerland remained ❾ unoccupied and provided humanitarian services. However, Federal Council member Marcel Pilet-Golaz implemented a highly controversial policy of compromise with the Axis powers—in principle the enemy—that was financially advantageous for the Swiss. The ❿ Saint Gotthard Pass railroad tunnel between Italy and Germany was at the disposal of

6 Gold ingot of the German Reichsbank, 1941

military transports, and restrictions were placed on the freedom of the press in 1939. The economy profited from the increased export and delivery of weapons to the German Reich.

After 1945, lucrative gold and foreign currency transactions also gave a negative edge to Swiss neutrality. ❻, ⓫ Gold that the Germans had plundered—especially Jewish property confiscated by the Nazis—was deposited in Swiss banks. The voluntary economic collaboration resulted in a short-term international isolation of Switzerland after the war.

7 Gas masks are fitted and sold in a pharmacy, 1938

8 Protecting the Swiss border, 1939

9 Swiss soldiers in a peaceful meeting with German soldiers at the Swiss border, 1939

11 Gold ingots in a bank safe, 1941

The International Committee of the Red Cross (ICRC)

The International Committee of the Red Cross (ICRC), a neutral medical and aid organization for the casualties of war, was a Swiss idea, proposed by Swiss businessman Jean-Henri Dunant and founded in 1863. It was the beginning of the growth of a worldwide movement that developed over the course of the 20th century into an aid organization that transcends cultures and nations. The Red Cross was active on all fronts in both world wars and allowed the wounded to recover as patients in neutral Switzerland and provided them with free medical attention. The ICRC was awarded the Nobel Peace Prize in 1917 and in 1944.

Japanese Red Cross first aid attendants in France, 1914

top: US poster, 1914, recruiting for the Red Cross

FRANCE: INSECURITY AND OCCUPATION

1918–1945

1

Despite ❶ victory in World War I, France still felt threatened by its German neighbor. Politically unstable at home and weakened by the war, France initially saw its security as guaranteed only through the pursuit of a "harsh course" against its "traditional enemy." However, in the face of Hitler's aggressive power politics in the 1930s, France seemed almost paralyzed. After the Blitzkrieg in 1940, the German army occupied the north of France and the French Vichy regime collaborated with the Germans.

Victory celebrations in Paris, 1919

■ Turbulence in Domestic Affairs between the Wars

Despite numerous changes of government and economic tension, the antidemocratic movements in the Third Republic were unable to seize power.

In the period between the wars, France had to struggle domestically against the economic, financial, and social consequences of the Great War. The war had cost the lives of about ten percent of the adult male population, in addition to the 4,270,000 wounded. However, in comparison to Great Britain and Russia, France remained relatively stable economically and remained a leading continental power with increased territories. During the 1920s French industrial production grew significantly with state support.

Eventually the effects of the worldwide economic depression reached France, albeit later than in the fully industrialized nations as its ❸ agrarian sector was still very large. The number of unem-

3

French farmer with horse-drawn plow in the 1940s

ployed began to rise in 1931, which shook the stability of the Third Republic. The administrations came and went as if through a revolving door—a total of 41 times by 1940. The few senior ministers who remained in office,

such as Raymond Poincaré and ❷ Édouard Daladier, provided the only elements of continuity in the leadership.

In 1924, the right-wing Bloc National governed with a majority; a leftist socialist reform cartel then took power for two years. Meanwhile, disagreements between the moderate parties strengthened both left- and right-wing radicalism. The Communists consistently won about ten percent of the votes in the ❺ elections, but never really posed a threat to established policies. Right-wing antidemocratic radical groups such as the Action Française and Croix du Feu (Cross of Fire), an organization of World War I veterans, gained influence in the 1930s; the latter attempted a ❹ coup in Feb-

2

Édouard Daladier making a radio address to the French people, 1938

ruary 1934 but it quickly fizzled out.

In 1936, Socialist prime minister ❻ Léon Blum organized and led the leftist Popular Front—a coalition of the Socialists, Radical Socialists, and Communists—in order to avert the rise of a fascist regime like that in Italy. Among other popular reforms, he introduced the 40-hour working week and entitlement to paid holidays.

4

Coup attempt in Paris, February 1934

5

Election posters

6

Leon Blum (left) with the leader of the Communists

1923	French occupy Ruhr area	Oct 16, 1925	Locarno Pact	Jun–Dec 1932	Herriot's radical majority cabinet
1925	French withdrawal from Ruhr area	1932–40	Albert Lebrun presidency	1934	Attempted putsch by radical right

■ Between Retribution and Appeasement: France's Foreign Policy up to 1939

The fear of renewed German aggression fundamentally determined French foreign policy between the wars.

7

Foreign soldiers guard the elections of the referendum in the Saarland concerning a return to the German administration

In the peace negotiations of 1919, France believed its national security could be fulfilled only through the maximum territorial and economic weakening of Germany. In the Versailles Treaty, France was awarded Alsace-Lorraine, German colonies such as Cameroon, the occupation and economic exploitation of the ❼ Saarland, and a large share of reparations. In addition to the agreed reduction of the German army to 100,000 men and the abolition of the General Staff, France demanded the complete demilitarization of the Rhineland to serve as a buffer zone.

Due to the growing differences among the other Allies and the lack of a military security guaran-

8　German poster calling for passive resistance under the slogan: "No! You won't make me do this!" 1923

tee from the United States, which had retreated into extreme isolationism, France pursued an intransigent reparations policy at the beginning of the 1920s—despite the German Reich's inability to meet the immense demands. French president ❾ Poincaré ordered the occupation of the ❿ Ruhr, Germany's industrial center, on January 23, 1923, to enforce the payment of reparations, over the objections of the United States and Great Britain. The new leftist government of 1924 introduced a conciliatory policy of rapprochement toward Germany, however, and because of the population's ❽ passive resistance the Ruhr was evacuated in 1925. Germany guaranteed the inviolability

9

Raymond Poincaré

of her Western borders with France and Belgium in the Locarno Pact of 1925.

France attempted to counter Nazi Germany's aggressive power politics that began in 1933 with a system of international alliances, including the 1935 mutual assistance pact with the Soviet Union and the Anglo-French military alliance. Under the influence of Great Britain, and because of divisions within the Popular Front government, France pursued a policy of appeasement toward Germany in 1938. Prime Minister Daladier and Foreign Minister Bonnet tolerated the annexation of Austria and signed the ⓫ Munich Agreement. The French policy of appeasement, reflecting the desire of both leaders and people to avoid another war, continued until the invasion of Poland.

The Maginot Line

To protect themselves against a new German invasion, the French erected the Maginot Line between 1926 and 1936, a huge barrier of fortifications on the northeastern border with Germany. It was named after the French minister of war and consisted of artillery and infantry emplacements, communications, and bunker complexes that cost about three billion francs and was considered impregnable. When war arrived, Nazi Germany simply avoided the fortifications by invading via neutral Belgium, and France surrendered within six weeks.

top: Draft of the subterranean bunker complex of the Maginot Line
above: French bunker on the Maginot Line destroyed by a German attack, 1940

10

French soldier guarding a confiscated coal wagon, 1923

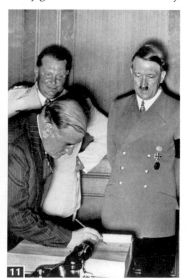

11

Munich Agreement; Daladier signs Hitler's guestbook, 1938

1935	Franco-Soviet mutual assistance pact	Sep 1938	Munich Agreement	Aug 1939	Anglo-French military alliance
1936–37	Popular Front cabinet led by Leon Blum	Nov 1938	General Strike	Sep 2–3, 1939	Germany declares war on France

▪ The Vichy Government, 1940–1944

After Germany's occupation of half of France in May 1940, a German-friendly government based in the town of Vichy was set up to administer the unoccupied regions.

France declared war on Germany after Hitler's invasion of Poland on September 3, 1939, but still refrained from active military engagement, relying on the elaborate fortifications of the Maginot Line. Then in May 1940, German troops suddenly ❷ marched through Belgium into France. The French were stunned by the rapid advance, known as blitzkrieg ("lightning war"), and resistance broke down after only six weeks; ❶ Marshal Henri-Philippe Pétain asked for a cease-fire on June 16, 1940. In order to humiliate France, the resultant ❹ treaty was signed in a railway carriage in the woods of Compiègne—the same place where the French had forced the armistice on the Germans in 1918 to end World War I. The Third Republic had fallen apart.

While German troops occupied the north and west of France, including Paris, an État

Marshal Henri-Philippe Pétain

Français was established in Vichy, in France's unoccupied south. This authoritarian government saw itself as a partner of the German Nazi regime but was recognized by the United States and the Soviet Union, among others. The 84-year-old Pétain became head of state with considerable power at his disposal; his deputy was

❸ Pierre Laval, whom Pétain had arrested at the end of 1940 because he had argued for entry into the war on the side of the Germans. Despite extensive compromises, the Vichy regime continued to come under increasing German pressure. In April 1942, Laval was installed as prime minister and took over the leadership of the state.

In the wake of the Allied landings in North Africa, the German army occupied the remainder of France, turning the Vichy regime into a fascist police state. From the summer of 1942 onward, the French police played a substantial role in the ❺ deportation of French Jews to death camps. The Allied invasions at Normandy on June 6, 1944 and on the Mediterranean coasts led to the collapse of the Vichy regime and the liberation of Paris.

Victory parade of German troops through Paris, 1940

Vichy leaders Henri-Philippe Pétain and Pierre Laval (right), 1942

Armistice of Compiègne: The historic train carriage, where the German surrender in the First World War was signed, is used for the French surrender, 1940

Arrested Jews are loaded onto a truck by the German SS and the French police, ca. 1942

	Jun 5–24, 1940	Battle for France		Jul 10, 1940	Formation of Vichy government led by Pétain
May 1940	Germans invade France		Jun 16, 1940	Armistice signed in Compiègne	Oct 24, 1940	Pétain refuses to enter war

■ The Resistance and the Rise of Charles de Gaulle

The French leader in exile, General Charles de Gaulle, united small resistance groups into a powerful political force in 1943. This formed a provisional French government directly after the Allied liberation in 1944.

After the occupation of Paris by the German army, French fighters—the Résistance—organized in small groups and waged war through ❼ acts of sabotage and strikes against the occupiers and the Vichy collaborators; they also aided the politically or racially persecuted to flee. The Germans dealt harshly with the insurgents: A total of about 30,000 Resistance fighters were executed, and 75,000 died in concentration camps. In 1944, German SS troops wiped out the village of ❻ Oradour-sur-Glane as a retaliatory measure for partisan attacks.

In exile in London, ⓫ General Charles de Gaulle had in 1940 al-

7

French saboteur attaches dynamite to the railway tracks, 1944

8

Meeting of the Free French movement in Algiers, 1943

ready formed the ❽ Free French movement, which saw itself as the legitimate representative of France, and built a government in exile—receiving a death sentence in absentia for high treason from the Vichy government. In May 1943 de Gaulle united the different factions of the resistance, such as Combat and Franc-Tireur, into a National Council of the Resistance. At the same time, the exile government moved to Algiers and recruited North African freedom fighters for the insurgency.

The Resistance supported the advance of the Allied troops after their landing in Normandy in June 1944. They organized a revolt in Paris on August 18, 1944, shortly before the Allies arrived in the capital. A week later, de Gaulle entered Paris. The National Council of the ⓰ Resistance was then recognized by the Allies as the provisional government. De Gaulle was able to unite the somewhat conservative members of the government in exile with the left-wing, and frequently communist, resistance movement.

Pierre Laval was executed in October 1945; Marshal Pétain was sentenced to death but was later pardoned and exiled to the island of Yeu. Acts of mob violence, in-

6

The village Oradour-sur-Glane after an attack by the German SS, 1944

9

A woman suspected of collaboration has her head shaved in public, 1944

cluding lynchings, against citizens suspected of collaboration were frequent, particularly against ❾ women thought to have "fraternized" with Germans.

Charles de Gaulle broadcasting from London, June 18, 1940

"I invite the officers and the French soldiers who are located in British territory or who would come there... to put themselves in contact with me. Whatever happens, the flame of the French resistance must not be extinguished and will not be extinguished. Tomorrow, as today, I will speak on Radio London."

above: Charles de Gaulle inspects French army in exile

10

A rebellion in Paris by French resistance fighters, 1944

11

Charles de Gaulle

| Apr 1942 | Laval becomes president | | Aug 18, 1944 | Resistance organizes revolt in Paris |
| Jun 6, 1944 | Allies land in Normandy | | Aug 25, 1944 | de Gaulle enters Paris |

BRITAIN BETWEEN THE WORLD WARS
1919–1939

The British Empire attained its greatest territorial extent after World War I but lost power due to the internal weakening of the kingdom. The ❶ economic and political problems at no time threatened the democratic traditions of Great Britain but did force it into a defensive peace policy to preserve its interests at any cost. Until 1939, it was indecisive and uncertain in the face of the German Nazi regime's aggressive policies.

London transport workers on strike, 1936

■ Economic Weakness in the Wake of the Great War

After emerging victorious from World War I, structural problems and massive debt plunged Great Britain into an economic crisis that lasted into the middle of the 1930s.

Winston Churchill, 1915

Superficially, the end of World War I brought the United Kingdom only success. The German Reich was bankrupt and its fleet was at Britain's mercy. Furthermore, Great Britain had gained the majority of the German colonial possessions and parts of the Ottoman Empire under a ❹ mandate from the League of Nations. But these territorial gains had been paid for by 900,000 dead and two million wounded Britons, as well as a serious weakening of the economy. The cost of the conflict had increased the national debt tenfold by 1918, and

Great Britain was now indebted to the United States and had lost its position as the world's primary financial power.

Fiscal dependency, outdated technology in essential industrial sectors such as steel and coal, and the weak buying power on the Continent resulted in a long-lasting economic depression. The situation became even more critical when Chancellor of the Exchequer ❸ Winston Churchill restored the pound to the gold standard in 1925, which led to an enormous increase in the price of British exported goods. Unemployment increased

rapidly among the workers. Beginning in 1919 prolonged ❷ strikes demanding social improvement—influenced by the Russian Revolution—repeatedly stopped work in essential industries, greatly damaging the economy. The climax was a miners' revolt in 1926 that was supported by a ❺, ❻ general strike of the labor unions. In the end, the workers' struggle ended in a bitter defeat for the consolidated labor unions. The government then passed the Trade Disputes and Trade Union Act of 1927. This legislation outlawed sympathetic strikes and mass picketing, severely curtailing the ability of organized labor from different sectors to collaborate.

Striking textile workers in front of the union office in Lancashire, 1929

British military police in the British mandate territory of Palestine, 1938

Anti-German Sentiment

Anti-German sentiment in Great Britain during World War I became so strong that in 1917 the royal family decided to change its German surname, Saxe-Coburg-Gotha. The descendents of Queen Victoria's line have used the family name "Windsor," after the royal residence of Windsor Castle, ever since.

above: Windsor Castle

Counter-demonstration by aristocratic British women against the general strike, May 1926

Traffic jam in central London as public transport workers join the general strike, May 1926

| 1919–22 | Wave of strikes by the miners | 1922 | "Transport and General Workers' Union" | Feb 1924 | Recognition of USSR |
| | 1920 | Unemployment insurance introduced | 1924 | Formation of 1st Labour cabinet | Oct 1924 | Conservative election victory |

■ A Bulwark of Democratic Stability

The traditional parties, together with the rising Labour party, attempted to come to grips with the social and economic problems Britain faced. Radical forces in the parliamentary monarchy that were opposed to the system found no support.

The United Kingdom's fundamental parliamentary-democratic constitutional order remained stable between the wars despite the ongoing economic and social crisis. Revolutionary parties of the masses, unlike those on the Continent, stood no chance. The National Fascist party, founded in the 1930s by Sir Oswald Mosley, remained of as little consequence as the Communists.

In 1918, parliamentary law became fully democratized. All males over 21 and all women over 30 were entitled to vote. In 1928, women were given voting rights equal to those of men.

Domestically, the Labour party gained strength during the war. Labour grew at the expense of the Liberals to become the strongest opposition party and broke the traditional Liberal–Conservative two-party system. In 1924 the first Labour politicians came to power with the support of the

8
Stanley Baldwin

Liberals. However, when the Labour prime minister ❼ Ramsay MacDonald recognized the Soviet Union, he was voted out after only eleven months in office, and the Conservative ❽ Stanley Baldwin took over affairs of state. Nevertheless, in 1929 Labour won again and MacDonald formed his second cabinet.

Two years later, when unemployment support was cut back at the height of the economic depression, the Labour government collapsed. Under pressure from ❿ King George V, MacDonald then agreed to head a coalition national government, with a cabinet made up only of Conservatives and Liberals, until 1935. The unity government tried in vain to solve the economic problems with retrenchment and tax increases, but not until government stabilization measures and rearmament began in 1937 was there a noticeable drop in unemployment. In 1940, the Labour party joined an all-party wartime government under ❾ Winston Churchill.

7
Labour Party conference in London, 1929; McDonald (center) became a pariah for the Left

9
Winston Churchill, 1939

Edward VIII

Following the death of his father, George V, Edward VIII reigned for less than a year before Prime Minister Baldwin forced him to abdicate in 1936, because he insisted on marrying the twice-divorced American Wallis Simpson even after the explicit disapproval of the cabinet. Edward was downgraded to "Duke of Windsor" and thereafter led a luxurious playboy lifestyle with his wife, mostly in France.

above: Edward, Duke of Windsor, with his wife, 1937

10
The Royal family, 1929; King George V in the center

1925	Pound stabilized	1927	Trade union law	1934	Beginning of rearmament
1926	Miners and labor unions strike	1929–31	MacDonald's second cabinet	1940	Coalition cabinet led by Churchill

British Foreign Policy between the Wars

The United Kingdom sought to secure the British position of world power by a policy of preserving international peace. Strong nationalist movements in the colonies led to the crumbling of the British Empire.

The conviction that ❷ Great Britain should seek peace at all costs to maintain the empire's worldwide sphere of influence, formed the core of British foreign policy after 1919. The consequent avoidance of conflict, preference for diplomatic negotiation, and striving to protect imperial trade were the key principles of the British "peace and trade" foreign policy up until 1939.

China, France, Italy, Japan, the Netherlands, Portugal, and the United States resolved to reduce the size of Pacific fleets at the ❹ Washington Conference of 1920–1921; in the process, Great Britain agreed to allow the United States equal strength in its battle fleet and so relinquished its traditional naval superiority. In Europe Britain supported the peace efforts of the former belligerents.

1

Locarno Treaty, 1925; from left: Gustav Stresemann, Austin Chamberlain (half-brother of Neville), and Aristide Briand

British Prime Minister Neville Chamberlain

"Ever since I assumed my present office my main purpose has been to work for the pacification of Europe, for the removal of those suspicions and those animosities which have so long poisoned the air... The question of Czechoslovakia is the latest and perhaps the most dangerous."

Arthur Neville Chamberlain, 1938

2

Houses of Parliament, London, ca. 1900

3

Locarno Treaty, signatures

In the League of Nations, Great Britain demanded that the organization take on the regulation of armament production and became the driving force in international disarmament efforts after WWI. Great Britain, Belgium,

In 1925, Great Britain, France, Belgium, Italy, and Germany signed the ❶, ❸ Locarno Treaty, which included a declaration of intent to resolve all conflicts without resort to the force of arms. The British Empire found itself confron-

ted by nationalist movements in many of its colonies. Centuries-old Irish efforts to gain independence culminated in the division of the island in 1921; southern Ireland became independent. Britain, whose complete name since

1801 had been the United Kingdom of Great Britain and Ireland, modified its name in 1927 to the United Kingdom of Great Britain and Northern Ireland. In other parts of the world, the empire also had to relinquish territory. It gave up its protectorate of Egypt in 1923, and in 1932 consented to Iraq's independence. Great Britain and the now autonomous dominions of the British Empire founded the ❺ Commonwealth of Nations in 1926.

To a great extent, Britain remained calm in the face of Japan's imperialistic strivings in East Asia and those of Italy in the Mediterranean. Increasingly, the focus in East Asia was on Hong Kong and Singapore. However, the powerful movements for independence in India were still suppressed by force.

4

Washington Conference, 1920–21

5

Empire Conference establishing the Commonwealth, 1926

| **1920** | Government of Ireland Act | **1921** | Division of Ireland | **1926** | Commonwealth of Nations founded |
| **1921–22** | Washington Conference | **1923** | End of the British protectorate in Egypt | **1932** | Independence of Iraq |

■ Appeasement of Nazi Germany

In an attempt to avoid another war in Europe, Great Britain at first tolerated the aggressive revisionist politics of the Nazi regime. Only after the invasion of Poland in 1939 showed that diplomacy was futile did the British government declare war on the German Reich.

Great Britain had already warned its partners against isolating the German Reich during the peace negotiations in 1919 and later criticized France's huge reparation demands. In the 1920s it put its weight behind the economic and political rehabilitation of Germany, expecting therewith the

6

Chamberlain (left) visiting Hitler (middle) to discuss the Sudeten Crisis, 1938

pacification of Central Europe and an increased market for British goods. Hitler's rise to power did little to change this policy, even if Great Britain did gradually begin to ❾ rearm.

British leaders believed that war should be avoided through negotiation and accepted Germany's more moderate revisionist demands. In the ❼ Anglo-German Naval Agreement of 1935, Hitler was granted a fleet equal to 35 percent of the capacity of the British Navy and parity in the submarine fleet. The deployment of German troops into the demilitarized Rhineland in 1936 and the union with Austria in 1938 were tolerated, although both were clear violations of the Treaty of Versailles. The British prime minister,Neville Chamberlain, even ❻ accepted the annexa-

7

The German envoy Ribbentrop outside the German consulate in London, June 4, 1935

tion of the German-speaking territories of Czechoslovakia under the Munich Agreement in 1938, and appeared to have saved the peace at the last minute.

When Hitler again violated the treaty and marched into Prague in March 1939, Chamberlain recognized the failure of his appeasement policy and began to make the initial ❽ preparations for war. Universal conscription

was introduced, and Poland and Romania were assured of military support in case of a German invasion. Following Hitler's invasion of Poland, Great Britain met its obligations and declared war on Germany. Chamberlain, widely discredited by appeasement's failure, announced his resignation in 1940 and was succeeded by ❿ Winston Churchill.

8

Prime minister Chamberlain (front row, middle) and his war cabinet (Churchill, second row, middle), February 1939

Munich Agreement

In the Munich Agreement, Great Britain and France granted the Nazi regime control over the German-speaking Sudeten territories after Hitler had declared these his "last territorial demands." Although Britain and France had signed defensive alliances with Czechoslovakia, neither felt prepared for war, and the idea of another European conflict

Chamberlain talking to the Italian dictator Mussolini at the Munich Conferences, 1938

aroused dismay among the populations of both countries. Some were also sympathetic to German grievances over the territorial losses imposed after World War I. Czechoslovakia, whose territory was at stake, was excluded from the negotiations, and the agreement that emerged was dubbed the "Munich dictate" by angry Czechs.

9

Production of grenade launchers for the British Navy, 1940

10

Winston Churchill signs autographs, 1940

| Jun 1935 | Anglo-German Naval Agreement | 1937–40 | Government of Neville Chamberlain | Apr 1939 | Reintroduction of universal conscription |
| | 1936 | Death of George V | Sep 1938 | Munich Agreement |

1

Street in an Irish village, ca. 1930

IRELAND: DIVISION AND INDEPENDENCE 1914–1949

In ❶ Ireland in 1921, the nationalist movement won a partial victory in its struggle for independence against Great Britain; in exchange, however, it had to agree to the division of the country. After years of civil war in Ireland over the question of unity, the island was officially divided in the 1940s. While Northern Ireland remained part of the United Kingdom, the majority of Ireland became an officially independent republic in 1949.

■ From the War for Independence to the Anglo-Irish Treaty

Ireland won the status of an autonomous dominion in 1922 after a bloody war of independence, while the northern province of Ireland remained a British possession.

The smoldering conflict between the Irish and the British reignited in 1914 when the British government passed a Home Rule Bill that guaranteed Ireland partial autonomy, including the Protestant parts of the North, which were opposed to the bill. The decision to suspend the bill as war broke out was met with nationalist outrage. The militant Irish Volunteers occupied public buildings in Dublin on April 24, 1916, and proclaimed an Irish Republic in the ❸ Easter Rising. The British military brutally suppressed this revolt; hundreds of people were killed, and the leaders were arrested and executed or condemned to long ❺ prison sentences. Further ❹ radicalization on both sides followed, initiating a new phase of violence.

Under Eamon de Valera, an illegal revolutionary parliament was formed; most of its members were from the Sinn Féin ("We ourselves") political party. A year later the military unit called the Irish Republican Army (IRA) was founded to attack British authority. In 1921 the British government and Sinn Féin agreed to a cease-fire and signed the Anglo-Irish Treaty, which gave Ireland the official status of a "free state." Excluded from this were six counties of the mainly Protestant province of ❷ Ulster, which had voted to remain part of the United Kingdom. In 1922, the Irish Free State gained the status of a dominion. The acceptance of this partial sovereignty was approved by the Irish parliament, the Dail,

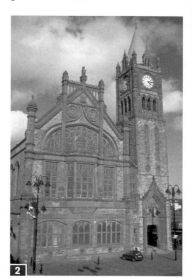

2

Town hall in Londonderry in the province of Ulster, Northern Ireland

by a narrow majority of 64 against 57 votes. On December 6, 1922, the new Irish constitution came into effect.

"Bloody Sunday" of 1920

"Bloody Sunday"—November 21, 1920—was representative of the brutal cycle of violence in Ireland: Following the execution of 14 British officers on the orders of Michael Collins, a leading Irish nationalist, a unit of British soldiers opened fired into an Irish crowd during a Gaelic football match in Dublin, killing many civilian spectators.

Victims of street fighting in Dublin, 1920

3

The city center of Dublin after the suppression of the Easter Rising, 1916

4

Remains of a train derailed by a terrorist attack planned by the IRA, 1916

5

Prison where the Easter Rising leaders were held

From Civil War to Independence

The division of Ireland led to bloody altercations within the Irish independence movement over the question of unity. The southern republic of Ireland gained full sovereignty in 1949 and left the Commonwealth.

The Anglo-Irish Treaty divided not only the country, but also the Sinn Féin independence movement. Supporters and opponents of the treaty now fought among themselves. The radicals under de Valera, the later Fianna Fáil party, accepted the exclusion of ❼ Northern Ireland, but strove for a reunification. The Fine Gael, under Prime Minister Thomas Cosgrave, sought equality with Great Britain. The IRA was divided as well, with one part joining the official Irish army while ❾ radical "irregulars" fought against the govern-

6 US soldiers at base in Northern Ireland during WW II, 1942

ment of the Irish Free State in 1922–1923. Over time, the radicals lost support, and de Valera ordered the end of hostilities. Isolated ❽ acts of terror took place into the 1930s, after which the IRA was

banned. A new constitution introduced universal adult male and female suffrage as well as proportional representation. Ireland became a member of the League of Nations. The constitution established Gaelic (also called Erse) as the official national language. In March 1932 de Valera was elected prime minister and refused the oath of allegiance to the English king. His Fianna Fáil party has stayed in power almost continuously since then, but the desired reunification of the country did not occur and the division became cemented.

Michael Collins and Eamon de Valera

Michael Collins and Eamon de Valera were leaders of Sinn Féin and also symbolically represent its division. Shaped by the Easter Rising of 1916, both were members of the underground government, de Valera as chairman of Sinn Féin and Collins as the founder of the IRA. After the peace agreement with Great Britain, their paths diverged: Collins accepted the secession of Northern Ireland and joined the official Irish army. De Valera fought first violently and then peacefully for unity. While Collins was shot in an ambush in 1922, de Valera stayed at the top of Irish politics until 1973.

8 Extinguishing fires after an IRA bomb attack in London, 1939

7 Parade for the opening of the parliament in Belfast, Northern Ireland, 1925

9 Irish volunteers with cannons and armored cars acquired for their fight against the British army, 1921

After a constitutional change in 1937, southern Ireland called itself Eire. It stayed out of World War II, while ❿ Northern Ireland ❻ participated as part of the United Kingdom. On April 1, 1949, Eire left the Commonwealth, and on April 18, officially proclaimed itself the Republic of Ireland.

10 Monastery of Clonmacnoise, province of Leinster

above: Eamon de Valera, 1932
top: Monument to Michael Collins in Dublin

| Dec 6, 1921 | Anglo-Irish Treaty signed | Dec 6, 1922 | Irish constitution accepted | 1937 | Southern Ireland renamed "Eire" |
| 1922 | Proclamation of the Irish Free State | 1932 | De Valera refuses oath to Crown | Apr 18, 1949 | Eire leaves Commonwealth |

BELGIUM AND THE NETHERLANDS: OBJECTS OF GERMAN POWER POLITICS

1914–1945

While Belgium became the military invasion route for the German armies during both world wars, the Netherlands survived the Great War unscathed. In World War II, however, it could not hold off the ❶ attack of the Germans and became an occupied territory of the Nazi Reich.

German forces invade the Netherlands, 1940

■ Belgium: Victim of Two World Wars

As a strategically important country between Germany and France, Belgium unwillingly became a combat zone in both world wars.

King Albert I of Belgium, ca. 1910

The burned-out library of Louvain, 1914

Battlefield at Passchendaele, 1917

The Locarno Conference, 1925

Before attacking France in 1914, Germany demanded free passage through Belgium in an ultimatum. ❸ King Albert I, who wanted his country to remain neutral, refused, and on August 4, German troops proceeded to occupy the country. The country's neutrality was guaranteed by the Great Powers, which brought Great Britain into the war. The Belgian army mobilized when the country's neutrality was violated, but Liege, Namur, and Brussels soon fell. Almost the entire country was occupied and the strong resistance of the Belgians was answered with brutal retaliations by the German soldiers, notably in ❷ Louvain. The government was forced into exile. Western Belgium, where the French and German troops met, became a battlefield; many cities were ❻ destroyed and parts of Flanders ❹ were utterly devastated.

At the end of WW I, Belgium annexed the German-speaking region of Eupen-et-Malmédy. A military accord was made with France, and a defensive alliance against Germany was signed with Great Britain. In 1925, Belgium joined the ❺ Locarno Treaty, which was meant to secure Belgium's borders. All this was to no avail, however, when Germany again invaded France through Belgium in May 1940. A few weeks later, the Belgian army under King Leopold III, who was taken prisoner, capitulated. The Belgian government escaped to London where it remained in exile for the remainder of the war. Leopold was suspected of collaboration and was forced to resign.

Ypres after German bombardment, 1915

Atrocity Propaganda

Lurid propaganda was used by all sides in World War I. During the Belgian campaign, the British started a rumor that German soldiers hacked off the hands of children so that they would no longer be able to use a weapon. Although not a single example of this was found, the propaganda lived on. The rumors probably arose from the German view that civilians must not resist an occupying power. Thus hostages were taken and franctireurs were shot.

French propaganda postcard, 1914

■ The Netherlands between Independence and National Socialism

Despite economic problems, the Netherlands was able to assert its neutrality until 1940 and remained politically stable. After the country was occupied by German troops, the new rulers implemented Nazi policies in the Netherlands, including the deportation of Dutch Jews to death camps.

The Netherlands survived World War I without internal upheaval, and coped well economically despite sheltering almost a million refugees who flooded out of Belgium in 1914. However, the blockade imposed principally by the Royal Navy had a restrictive effect on Dutch maritime traffic with countries which Britain and France feared could supply Germany. A severe shortage of coal led to the near-paralysis of Dutch industry. With the introduction of universal suffrage in 1917, the constitutional monarchy was democratized further, though a socialist revolution instigated by Pieter Jelles Troelstra was unsuccessful. The outbreak of the world economic crisis in 1929 caused a rapid increase in unemployment in the kingdom, however.

Externally the Netherlands committed itself to strict neutrality, but it was naturally interested

8

Anti-Semitic caricature from the Netherlands, 1939

in maintaining good relations with its German neighbor. For this reason, the government granted asylum to Wilhelm II in 1918.

The Bombardment of Rotterdam

Like Guernica, Coventry, and Dresden, the Dutch city of Rotterdam stands as a symbol of the terror of modern air warfare against civilian populations. During the German Luftwaffe air raid on May 14, 1940, large parts of the city were completely destroyed, around 78,000 people were made homeless, and 900 people were killed.

above: The city center of Rotterdam, flattened except for the church of St. Laurentius, 1940

The 1933 victory of the National Socialists in Germany divided the Netherlands. Dutch supporters of Hitler, who organized themselves under ❼ Anton Adriaan Mussert, remained a minority, but after the first immigration wave of Jewish refugees, fears of ❽ Judaization became widespread, particularly in Protestant circles. The government followed news of German aggression with anxiety and ordered a general mobilization in 1939.

The army of the Netherlands was no match for the German attack in May 1940. After the bombardment of Rotterdam, the government capitulated and fled to London along with the royal family. The Nazi Reich's commissioner, Arthur Seyss-Inquart, began to align the Dutch state with the economic and social policies of the Nazi regime. Dutch citizens had to do forced labor, the concentration camps Westerbork and Vught were set up, and the ❿ systematic extermination of Jews began. While some volunteer ❾ Dutch SS divisions formed and others collaborated, a

7

Meeting of the Dutch National Socialist movement led by Anton Adriaan Mussert (middle), 1941

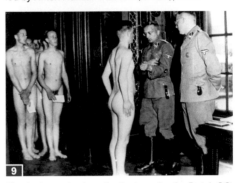

9

Physical examination of volunteers for the Dutch SS divisions, 1940

resistance movement that fought the regime with raids and acts of sabotage also established itself.

In September 1944, the Allies reached the Netherlands, and ⓫ liberated it on May 5, 1945. The Dutch East Indian colony, occupied by the Japanese in 1942, was returned after the war.

11

US forces liberate the Netherlands, 1945

10

Official sign during the German occupation of Holland reads: "No admittance for Jews!," 1941

1939	Mobilization	**May 14, 1940**	Bombardment of Rotterdam	**Jun 1940**	Belgian government in exile in London
May 10, 1940	German invasion of the Netherlands	**May 14, 1940**	Capitulation of the Netherlands	**May 5, 1945**	Liberation of the Netherlands

ITALY UNDER FASCISM 1919–1945

The economic crisis and the dashed expectations of acquiring a colonial empire after World War I radicalized Italy's political right and led in 1922 to the establishment of Europe's ❶ first fascist dictatorship under the leadership of Benito Mussolini. He cleverly exploited Italian aspirations to "Great Power" status. After moving closer both ideologically and politically to the German Nazi regime, "Il Duce" led Italy into World War II against the Allies on Germany's side.

Meeting of the Fascist chamber in 1939

■ The Rise of Mussolini

Mussolini's Fascist movement emerged victorious in 1922 out of the domestic turmoil that followed World War I. The ambitious Mussolini turned the state into a personal dictatorship, while retaining a nominal monarchy.

Benito Mussolini, 1940

By extending the possibility of territorial gains and financial advantages, Great Britain, France, and Russia convinced the formerly neutral Italy into World War I in 1915. Emerging on the victorious side at the end of the war despite a marginal military contribution, Italy nevertheless resented how it had been sidelined during the peace negotiations. With half a million dead and an economic depression, internal divisions brought the country to the brink of civil war.

The nationalist right, under the slogan of "Mutilated Victory" and

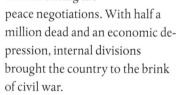

❸ King Victor Emmanuel III

led by ❷ Benito Mussolini, turned into a violent and thuggish mass movement. In Rome and elsewhere, the ❺ Fascisti fought fierce street battles against socialist and communist groups, while the moderate parties were incapable of controlling the situation. When Mussolini marched on Rome in October 1922 and demanded the power of state, ❸ King Victor Emmanuel III acquiesced and appointed him prime minister, invested with extensive powers.

With the king's approval, Mussolini used the internal crisis that resulted from the murder of Socialist leader Giacomo Matteotti in 1925 to resolutely build up a "leader dictatorship." All opposition parties were outlawed, the parliament was dissolved, individual civil rights were repealed, and Mussolini's personal power was institutionalized. The Church and

the king retained their rights within the framework of the regime. In 1929, Mussolini and Pope Pius XII concluded the ❹ Lateran Treaty, which granted the Vatican autonomous status.

Mussolini initially maintained his distance from Hitler and the German Nazi regime, even promising to protect Austria from a forced union with Germany. In 1935, he formed the Stresa Front with France and Great Britain to prevent further violations of the Versailles Treaty by Germany. However, dreams of empire soon saw him change his policies and alignments.

Signing of the Lateran Treaty in 1929; Mussolini (right) and Cardinal Gasparri, (seated)

The 1922 "March on Rome"

The Fascist demonstrations of October 27–31, 1922, became known as the "March on Rome" and served as a model for Hitler's followers. Fascist groups advanced to within a few miles of Rome following Mussolini's declaration in Naples that he would use force if necessary in

The March on Rome, 1922

order to take over the government. The large protest marches, attended by around 30,000, that converged in Rome on October 30 in fact took place without Mussolini—he had already been made prime minister the day before.

March of the Fascist youth organization "Balilla" in Italy, 1939

| Apr 26, 1915 | Secret London treaty | 1919 | Fascisti gather around Mussolini | Nov 1922 | Mussolini gains unlimited authority |
| Aug 26, 1915 | Italy declares war on Germany | Oct 1922 | "March on Rome" | 1929 | Lateran Treaty |

■ Alliance with the Nazi Regime

During the 1930s, Italy and the German Reich increasingly leaned toward each other. Mussolini hoped to realize Italy's imperialist dreams of a new Mediterranean empire by fighting alongside Hitler in World War II. However, abject military failures soon left him dependent on Hitler.

Mussolini's campaign against ❻ Ethiopia (Abyssinia prior to WWI) in 1936 was the beginning of his cooperation with Hitler's Nazi regime and of the so-called ❼ Berlin–Rome "Axis." Germany was the only nation that supported the unprovoked Italian attack on a nation that had long been independent. Following a full-scale invasion that involved the use of tanks, bombers, and chemical weapons against the non-mechanized Ethiopian army, Victor Emmanuel III was proclaimed "emperor of Ethiopia."

The Italian-German relationship strengthened in the ensuing years. Italy resigned from the League of Nations in 1937 and did not protest when Hitler annexed Austria into the German Reich in 1938. Together, Italy and Germany supported the coup led by General Francisco Franco in the Spanish Civil War. Italian Fascism also moved closer to National Socialism ideologically. Whereas the racial supremacy doctrine had not initially been part of the Italian fascist agenda, in 1938 most of the Jews in Italy lost their civil rights and were excluded from public offices. In May 1939, the two ❽ dictators concluded the "Pact of Steel," a friendship and alliance agreement that defined the conditions for a common European war.

While Italy still reacted hesitantly to Germany's invasion of Poland in 1939, the rapid German victory against France erased all doubts and Italy declared war on the Allied powers on June 10,

6 Italians enter Gondar in Ethiopia, 1935

8 Hitler on a state visit to Italy in 1938

1940. Mussolini's goal was to conquer the ❾ Mediterranean region, including Greece and North Africa, and found a new "Roman" Empire. The Tripartite Pact of September 27, 1940, committed Italy, Germany, and Japan to wage war against any nation siding with the Allies. Military failures soon ensured ❿ Italy's complete dependence upon Germany's po-

litical and military leadership and fanned the flames of internal crisis that ultimately culminated in Mussolini's downfall. Following airstrikes and the Allies' invasion of Sicily, the king forced Mussolini to resign on July 25, 1943, and had him arrested. When General Eisenhower announced a cease-fire with Italy a little while later, German troops occupied Rome. Mussolini was freed by German paratroopers and under the protection of German troops founded the fascist "Italian Social Republic" in Salò, northern Italy. On July 9, 1944, Rome was taken by the Allies, and following the surrender of German armed forces in Italy, Mussolini's puppet government was dissolved. Communist partisans ⓫ executed the former dictator on April 28, 1945, as he was fleeing to Swizerland.

7 Italian Fascist symbols being erected in preparation for Mussolini's visit to Berlin in 1937

9 Italian torpedo boat in the Mediterranean Sea, 1942

10 German Stukas flying across the Mediterranean region to help the Italians, 1941

11 The bodies of Mussolini and his girlfriend Clara Pettaci, who were publicly hanged by partisans in 1945

| 1936 | Ethiopia conquered | Jun 10, 1940 | Italy declares war on the Allies | Jul 25, 1943 | Mussolini taken prisoner | Apr 28, 1945 | Mussolini murdered |
| | May 1939 | "Pact of Steel" | Sep 27, 1940 | Tripartite Pact | Jul 9, 1944 | Allies take Rome |

Spain and Portugal 1914–1945

In Portugal and Spain, strong right-wing authoritarian movements gained influence in the 1930s. While a dictatorial system was quickly established in Portugal, a bloody and devastating ❶ civil war with international involvement raged in Spain between leftist and rightist forces from 1936 to 1939. The victorious General Franco erected a brutal and long-lasting military dictatorship in Spain.

Spanish civil war, the front at Malaga, 1936

■ Portugal: The Salazar Regime

In the 1930s, Premier Salazar used the political turmoil of the postwar period to build up a dictatorial system, which remained largely uninvolved in world politics.

❸ Portugal supported the Entente in World War I, even sending a poorly prepared division that was destroyed on the Western Front, but domestically chaotic conditions had reigned since the founding of the republic in 1910. The government changed hands 44 times before the republic finally collapsed in ❷ May 1926 following a military coup. The new head of government, General António de Fragoso Carmona, named ❹ António de Oliveira Salazar as his finance minister in 1928. Salazar succeeded in the rapid economic consolidation of the state.

Salazar founded the fascist União Nacional in 1930, which under his leadership shaped politics in Portugal well beyond World War II. In 1932 he became prime minister and in 1933 institutionalized the "New State" (Es-

Traditional fishing on the Atlantic coast of Portugal, photography 1930s

tado Novo) through a new constitution and a dictatorial government on a corporative basis, which economically bound employers and employees in a ❻, ❼ state-controlled, hierarchical political system and society.

In international affairs, Salazar supported the insurgents under General Francisco Franco during

the Spanish Civil War of 1936–1939, and after Franco's victory, the two countries signed a nonaggression pact. Salazar at first pursued a neutral course in World War II but in 1943 joined the Allies and allowed the stationing of air force and naval units on the Portuguese ❺ Azores Islands.

Military parade in 1928 on the anniversary of the May 28, 1926, coup

António de Oliveira Salazar, ca. 1950

Portuguese backup troops embark and are sent to the Azores, 1941

Mounted members of the state-controlled paramilitary organization "Légion Portuguesa," 1936

Parade of the state-controlled youth organization "Mocidade," 1936

1923 Military coup led by de Rivera	**1928** Carmona becomes head of government	**1931** 2nd Republic in Spain founded
1926 Republic of Portugal dissolved	**1930** "União Nacional" founded	**1932** Salazar becomes premier

Spain: Civil War and the Franco Dictatorship

Domestic tensions in Spain erupted in the Spanish Civil War in 1936. This led to a fascist dictatorship under Francisco Franco in 1939.

Spain was shaken by political unrest for more than 20 years following World War I. Corruption, separatist aspirations—for example, in Catalonia—and the long struggle to pacify the protectorate in the northern part of Morocco against Abdel Krim, leader of the independence movement, weakened the parliamentary monarchy and led to a military coup by General Miguel Primo de Rivera in 1923. He installed a personal dictatorship that was tolerated by King Alfonso XIII. Despite the successful conclusion of the Moroccan war, however, he had to step down in 1930 due to unresolved social problems and the overstretching of the economy in the boom years of the twenties. In the San Sebástian pact of 1930, republican political parties, as well as ❶ intellectuals such as José Ortega y Gasset, resolved to overthrow the monarchy. In 1931, they were successful and the king was forced to leave the country. The Second Republic was founded, but quickly came under fire from radical political forces on both the left and right. Violent ❿ uprisings and revolts for social reform by the unionized workers occurred in 1933, as did a strengthening of the fascist

International Brigade

Many left-wing idealists, including artists from throughout the world, fought in the International Brigade against Franco's troops. André Gide, George Orwell, Egon Erwin Kisch, and Ernest Hemingway, among others, came from France, Great Britain, Germany, and the United States as fighters or reporters for the republic.

above: Volunteers of the International Brigade, 1936

Insurgents burn churches and monasteries, 1931

movement. In 1933, the antidemocratic ❾ Falange party was formed; it later became a decisive instrument of Franco's dictatorial government. General strikes and political murders further widened the gulf between the conservative-nationalist forces and the republicans and radical socialists. General Franco's right-wing revolt against the leftist Peoples' Front government in 1936 ignited a three-year ⓬ civil war that aroused international attention and was waged with foreign military support on both sides. The republic broke up in January 1939 following the capture of Barcelona by ❽ Franco's troops.

Franco built a dictatorial regime in devastated Spain, outlawed the formation of political parties, and suppressed all opposition. More than 350,000 opponents were executed and hundreds of thousands incarcerated.

Franco's regime remained largely neutral in World War II, despite joining the Anti-Comintern Pact. Combat units dispatched to fight Bolshevism on the Eastern Front were sent back in 1944. As the defeat of the Axis powers loomed, Franco approached the Allies and curbed the persecution of Communists.

Francisco Franco, 1935

Young Spaniards learn to march in the manner of the Falangists, 1935

Guernica

The total destruction of the small Basque city of Guernica by the German Luftwaffe on April 26, 1937, during the Spanish civil war, offered a foretaste of the bombing raids of World War II. The attacks were directed exclusively at the civilian population in order to break the morale of the Republican troops. Picasso's famous oil painting "Guernica" was meant to condemn this terrible act of destruction to the world.

Destroyed Guernica, 1936

Students call for the Republic, 1931

Spanish refugees on the border to France, 1939

1933	Constitution of the "New State"	**July 1936**	Military revolt led by Franco	**1939**	Spanish-Portuguese Alliance
1933	"Falange Espanol" founded	**Sep 1939**	Franco becomes head of government	**Jan 1939**	Republic dissolved

SCANDINAVIA AND THE BALTIC 1917–1944

Following World War I, all of the Scandinavian countries moved toward the development of democratic welfare states. In international affairs, only Sweden was able to maintain the Scandinavian tradition of neutrality throughout World War II, while Denmark and Norway were occupied by German troops, and Finland fought hard to preserve its recently won independence. The newly created independent ❶ Baltic states found themselves squeezed between the aggression of Germany and Russia.

1

Freedom memorial in Riga, Latvia, built in 1935

■ The Baltic Republics' Brief Independence

With German aid, the Baltic states became independent following World War I. From 1939 on, they were invaded and occupied first by Hitler and then Stalin. After World War II they were annexed and became republics of the Soviet Union.

In the Treaty of Brest-Litovsk of 1918 between Germany and Russia, the Bolsheviks had been forced to guarantee the independence of their Baltic provinces in northeastern Europe. Through long struggles, Estonia, ❷ Latvia, and Lithuania established themselves as liberal constitutional states by 1920. Germany sought to play the role of guarantor of their sovereignty against attacks from Poland and the Soviet Union. In 1920, the former German port of Memel was taken over by Lithuania; in 1924, it gained autonomy until it was once more assimilated into Hitler's fascist Reich in

3

Ministers of State sign the nonaggression pact: (seated from left to right) Munsters of Latvia, Ribbentrop of Germany, Selter of Estonia, 1939

5

Arrival of the Red Army in Vilnius, Lithuania, July 1944

1939. Under the ❸ Nazi-Soviet Pact of 1939, the Baltic states were at the mercy of Hitler and Stalin. In the accord's secret protocol, the Nazi regime recognized the whole Baltic region and Finland

as a ❻ Russian sphere of influence. Hitler had shortly beforehand signed a nonaggression pact with Latvia. In 1940, the Red Army marched into the Baltic States. Stalin forced Lithuania, Latvia, and Estonia to accept Soviet naval bases and garrisons; Russia had long sought access to warm-water ports and control of the Baltic Sea. The German army retook the territory during its invasion of Russia and carried out a systematic elimination of the Jewish population. Germans were ❹ resettled further west. In the hope that Germany would support the independence of the small republics after the war, many ❼ anti-communists and anti-Semites from the Baltic area, especially Lithuania, volunteered for the Waffen SS. As the Soviets began to push westward, Estonia, Latvia, and Lithuania again fell to the ❺ Red Army in 1944. After the war, they were incorporated into the Soviet Union and did not regain their independence until the fall of the USSR.

2

Parliament of the republic of Latvia in the capital Riga, ca. 1930

4

Arrival of Baltic Germans in Stettin as part of the resettlement, Oct 1939

Volunteer Corps

Long after the official end of World War I, German volunteer corps continued to fight against the Red Army in the Baltic states. They were officially supported by the Western governments that sought to crush the nascent Bolshevik Revolution in Russia. After many bitterly fought battles, the volunteer corps were defeated and returned to Germany in mid-December 1919.

Volunteer corps soldiers return from the Baltics to Berlin, 1919

6

Soviet Socialist propaganda after the annexation of Latvia

7

Volunteers from the Baltic SS divisions being inspected by a Nazi official, 1944

■ Scandinavia and Finland through World War II

While the Scandinavian countries were all able to remain neutral during the First World War, only Sweden avoided being pulled into the hostilities by German aggression during the Second World War.

Sweden, Denmark, and Norway did not join the conflict during World War I, although the Entente occasionally boycotted Sweden because of its lively trade with the German Reich, and Norway sent out its merchant fleet against the Central Powers. Still, the nonaligned status of the Scandinavian countries was never challenged by either side and, after the war, there were no social upheavals. The Scandinavian monarchies became parliamentary democracies in the interwar period and steadily developed as welfare states. The Social Democrat majority reduced the effects of the economic depression on the population through increased state services.

Finland was a special case in the Scandinavian world due to its proximity to ➓ Russia. As a former dominion of the czar's empire, Finland took advantage of the turmoil of the Russian Revolution to declare its independence on December 6, 1917. Despite a nonaggression treaty signed in 1932, the relationship with the Soviet Union remained tense, and in accordance with the Nazi-Soviet Pact that assured German acquiescence, the Red Army invaded Finland on November 30, 1939, in order to prevent future German threats to the Soviet

9
Norwegian fascist leader Vidkun Quisling (right) and Heinrich Himmler, 1942

Union moving through Scandinavia. However, only after Soviet bombing of Finnish cities and fighting which inflicted grave losses on the Russians was the ➓ "Winter War" decided in the Soviet Union's favor, and it was able to retain only about 10 percent of ➑ Finland as the Western powers threatened to intervene. Following Hitler's invasion of the Soviet Union in 1941, Finland allied with Nazi Germany against the Soviet Union.

Sweden emerged from World War II unscathed. Through making concessions to Nazi Germany, such as permission to allow German troops through Swedish territory, it was left in peace and granted refugees asylum in the country until the end of the war. At the end of 1943, though, Sweden began to lean more decidedly toward the Allies.

➓ Denmark and ➌ Norway were occupied by German troops on April 9, 1940. Resistance developed in Norway from the beginning. About 40,000 Norwegians were deported into concentration camps, and a Norwegian fascist leader ➒ Vidkun Quisling was appointed prime minister by the occupying forces in 1942.

When the Germans began deporting Jews from Denmark in 1943, the situation became critical. Martial law was imposed following strikes and acts of sabotage. Danish fishermen carried 7,900 Jews to safety over the straits to Sweden. Denmark was liberated by British troops, who did not have to fire a shot, in May 1945. The German occupying forces in Norway also surrendered without offering any resistance.

8
Swedish volunteers fighting for the Finnish against Russia, 1940

10
Finnish soldiers fleeing from the Red Army are brought home under the protection of German soldiers, 1918

11
German armored convoy in Denmark, 1940

13
German soldiers in Norway, 1940

12
Finnish soldiers on skis, 1939

1939–40 | Soviet-Finnish Winter War   **1940** | Norwegian exile government in London   **1944** | Red Army annexes the Baltic Republics

Apr 9, 1940 | German occupation of Denmark and Norway   **1942** | V. Quisling made prime minister

POLAND 1914–1939

After 123 years of foreign rule, Poland was restored as a ❶ sovereign state after World War I, but the existence of the nation was constantly threatened from without because of border disputes. Internal political strife and unresolved problems with minorities also affected the country. Germany and the Soviet Union carved up Poland between them in 1939.

■ The Polish State until 1921

Poland proclaimed itself an independent state in 1918. The wrangling over the final positions of the borders, however, dragged on until 1921.

Celebration of Polish independence, painting, 1918

Conquest of Kiev by the Red Army, 1920

Polish delegation at the Riga Conference, 1921

Polish workers take up arms during the dispute over Upper Silesia, 1921

Polish soldiers, 1915

Since 1795, the Polish territories had been divided between Prussia, Austria, and Russia. The outbreak of World War I revitalized the Poles' hopes for the restoration of their sovereignty. Polish ❸ legionnaires supported the Central Powers, which proclaimed the restitution of the Polish hereditary monarchy in 1916. The looming defeat of the Central Powers and the assurances of the Entente Powers regarding Poland's sovereignty initiated a change of mood in favor of the victorious powers.

After the overthrow of the czar, the provi-sional Russian government recognized the Polish right to self-determination in March 1917, and in 1918 in the Brest- Litovsk Treaty relinquished its Polish territories. Following the capitulation of the Central Powers, Jozef Pilsudski proclaimed Poland independent on November 11, 1918, and named himself the provisional head of state of the republic. He built the state of an independent Poland.

The Treaty of Versailles in 1919 granted the new nation the province of Poznan as well as broad sections of West Prussia to create the "Polish Corridor," a narrow strip of territory along the Vistula River with access to the Baltic Sea. Pilsudski, however, sought the restoration of the borders of 1772, which would include the Russian-dominated Byelorus-sia, Ukraine, and Lithuania. The Lithuanian Vilnius territory was

brought under Polish sovereignty through military action. A Polish advance on ❷ Kiev in March 1920 then triggered the Polish-Soviet War. The Soviet counteroffensive failed with the Polish victory in the Battle of Warsaw (the "Miracle on the Vistula"). The subsequent Treaty of ❹ Riga on March 18, 1921, moved the Polish–Russian border about 150 miles (241 km) to the east.

The League of Nations divided the ❺ disputed Polish-German Upper Silesian territories in 1921. Poland received the coal-rich ❻ eastern Upper Silesia; the oth-er territories went to Germany. The city of Danzig was declared a free city, a further sore point in the Polish–German relationship.

"God, let my native soil stay German!" Propaganda poster during the Upper Silesia dispute, 1921

| 1916 | Kingdom of Poland proclaimed | April–Oct 1920 | Polish-Soviet War | Mar 1921 | Treaty of Riga |
| Nov 11, 1918 | Poland regains independence | 1921 | Military alliance with France | 1926 | Coup led by Pilsudski |

■ Brief Sovereignty

Even the domestic transition from a democracy to an authoritarian state could not prevent Poland's powerful neighbors Germany and the Soviet Union invading Poland and dividing the country between them in 1939.

After the boundaries were agreed upon, Poland re-formed as a democratic constitutional state in 1921. The internal consolidation of the newly formed nation was made difficult from the outset by its underdeveloped economy and the nationalist protectionism that was prevalent in inter-war Central Eastern Europe. The fierce rivalry among the political parties meant the rapidly changing governments failed to coordinate the diverse administrative and economic systems created during the partition and to integrate the minorities. Less than 70 percent of the population living within Poland's new borders was Polish,

7

Funeral of Jozef Pilsudski, 1935

and the minorities were granted only a restricted franchise and influence in parliament. There were numerous Ukrainian uprisings in East Galicia.

The founder of modern Poland, ❽ Pilsudski, proclaimed himself to be the savior of the nation and carried out a military coup in 1926. While formally retaining the democratic constitution, he set up a dictatorial regime that suppressed the opposition. The regime was based on his personal prestige and deteriorated after his ❼ death in 1935. A succession of military leaders determined the course of the state thereafter.

Due to border disputes, Poland was continually threatened by its powerful neighbors, Germany and the USSR. It signed an al-

liance with France in 1921, but this had little effect. Nonaggression treaties negotiated with the Soviet Union in 1932 and with Germany in 1934 quickly proved to be nothing more than a ❾ temporary cease-fire. In a secret protocol of the Nazi–Soviet nonaggression pact of August 23, 1939, also known as the Ribbentrop-Molotov Pact after the foreign ministers of the two countries who negotiated the secret clause, the two powers agreed to partition Poland. The German "Blitzkrieg" poured across the Polish ❿ western border on September 1, 1939; Soviet troops invaded the eastern part two weeks later. The

8

Polish leader Jozef Pilsudski at a military parade, 1926

simultaneous attack ensured that the ill-equipped Polish army's brave resistance was short-lived, and on September 27, the Germans occupied Warsaw.

9

Hitler revokes his nonaggression pact with Poland, 1939

"Free City" of Danzig/Gdansk

Hitler used the status of Danzig (Gdansk in Polish) as a free city under international law as a pretext to unexpectedly start a war against Poland in 1939. The internationally mandated city had, since its establishment in the Treaty of Versailles, been a source of contention to German nationalists. Danzig had a German majority and it was an economically important port city.

Nazi victory parade through the streets of Danzig/Gdansk, Poland, 1939

10

German soldiers tear down a barrier on the frontier with Poland, 1939

1932	Nonaggression pact with USSR signed	1935	Pilsudski dies	Sep 1, 1939	Germany invades Poland
Jan 26, 1934	Nonaggression pact with Germany signed	Aug 23, 1939	Anglo-Polish alliance	Sep 27, 1939	Occupation of Warsaw

HUNGARY AND CZECHOSLOVAKIA 1914–1945

Out of the remnants of the dual monarchy of Austria-Hungary, the new states of ❶ Hungary and Czechoslovakia emerged in 1918. However, both became caught in the web of the expanding German Reich in the 1930s as a result of their geographical proximity to Germany. Under German pressure, Czechoslovakia was divided up in 1938 and dissolved as a nation before a part of it was annexed by the German Reich. Hungary's radical right-wing regime was sympathetic toward the Nazis and fought on the side of the Axis powers in World War II, following which the government crumbled with the end of World War II.

Elizabeth-Bridge in Budapest, Hungary, built 1897–1903

Hungary: From Republic to Right Wing Regime

Following the first postwar revolutionary years, an authoritarian regime established itself in the drastically reduced state of Hungary. It was sympathetic toward Germany during World War II.

Following the collapse of the Habsburg dual monarchy in 1918, Count Mihály Károlyi used the middle class–democratic "Aster Revolution" in Hungary to take

Participants in the peace conference of Trianon

Hitler and Horthy, 1941

over the government, proclaiming a republic on November 16. From the beginning, it was burdened by party conflicts and territorial losses. Hungary was compel-

led to vacate areas in the south and east of the country as a result of the Treaty of Versailles in 1919. The Czechs occupied Slovakia, the Romanians Transylvania, and the Serbs southern Hungary. The treaty also forced the reduction of the Hungarian army and obliged the nation to pay reparations. Károlyi resigned in protest, and the Communists, led by ❷ Béla Kun, proclaimed a Soviet republic in March 1919.

Opposing pressure from the right and waging a war against Czechoslovakia and Romania over lost territory brought down

the leftist regime. At the end of the war, the ❸ Treaty of Trianon in 1920—by which Hungary lost two-thirds of its territory—ushered in the peace. Revisionist demands from then on determined Hungary's politics and encouraged nationalist movements.

In 1920 Hungary once again became a monarchy. The parliament chose ❹ Miklós Horthy as regent of the empire and established a right-wing regime. The central domestic problem was a financial crisis that was only temporarily relieved by a loan from the League of Nations in 1923. The economic depression of the 1930s brought a further shift to the right. The national socialist ❺ "Arrow Cross" gained popularity, and internally and in foreign affairs the government sought to move closer to Hitler's Germany. Anti-Semitic laws restricted the rights of the Jews in public life.

Germany's and Italy's "Vienna Arbitrations" (1938 and 1940) satisfied some of Hungary's territorial demands: Part of Slovakia and the areas occupied by Romania were returned to

Communist leader Béla Kun holds a speech before the public, 1919

Tragedy following the pogroms of the national socialistic "Arrow Cross," 1944

Hungary. In alliance with Germany, Hungary marched into Yugoslavia in 1941 and participated in Hitler's Russian military campaign. When in 1944 Hungary sought a cease-fire, German troops occupied the country, but quickly lost it again to the advancing ❻ Red Army. By April 4, 1945, the Soviets had conquered Hungary completely.

Monarchy

With the proclamation of March 23, 1920, Hungary became a monarchy without a monarch. The Hungarian people rejected the claims to the throne of the former Austrian emperor and Hungarian king, Charles IV. When Charles attempted to seize the crown on his own authority, he was arrested in October 1921 and sent into exile on Madeira.

The former emperor Charles in exile with his family, 1921

Russian soldier on the lookout, 1945

■ The Republic of Czechoslovakia 1918–1938

The Czechoslovakian republic, founded in 1918, was broken up in 1938 and added to the German Reich as the "Protectorate of Bohemia and Moravia."

During World War I, Czech and Slovak emigrants sympathetic to the Allies and escaping military service in the Austrian forces formed governments in exile in the United States; in the Pittsburgh Treaty of 1918, they resolved to unite the two nations in one state after the war. In 1920, the National Assembly chose the Czech ❽ Tomás Masaryk, who had formed Czech regiments in the Allied service, as president of the new parliamentary democratic republic. He remained in power, together with the long-standing foreign minis-

7
Konrad Henlein, nationalist gymnastics teacher

ter Edvard Benes, until 1935 but failed to form a common national identity among the assorted ethnicities of the different states. The population of the new multinational state was only about 60 percent Czechs and Slovaks; alongside Hungarians, Ukrainians, and Poles, the Sudeten Germans were the largest minority with almost 25 percent. Encouraged by the Nazis' takeover of power in Germany, the Sudeten Germans increasingly aspired to autonomy.

Together with ❼ Konrad Henlein's Sudeten German Homeland Front (from 1935, the Sudeten German party), Hitler precipitated the Sudeten Crisis in 1938. Neither the 1920–1921 alliance with France and Poland nor the ❾ "Little Entente" with Yugoslavia and Romania were able to withstand the territorial claims of the Nazi

regime. In the Munich Agreement between the Great Powers, Czechoslovakia had to relinquish the ❿, ⓫ Sudetenland to Germany. The breakup of the state could no longer be prevented. Poland and Hungary were granted territories in the border regions. The day after Slovakia proclaimed its independence under German protection on March 14, 1939, German troops marched into the remains of Czechoslovakia and placed it under the rule of the German Reich as the Protectorate of Bohemia and Moravia. Czechoslovakia was dissolved. There was hardly any rebellion against the German occupation. The first ⓬ revolt did not take place until May 1945 in Prague.

Benes, now president, worked on rebuilding a Czechoslovakian state from his exile in London. The government in exile concluded an agreement in 1943 on the occupation of the territory by the Red Army. On September 10, 1945, Czechoslovakia reconstituted itself under the protection of the Soviets.

8
State President Tomás Masaryk, 1926

9
Meeting of the "Little Entente," founded in 1920, Kamil Krofta (right), foreign minister of Czechoslovakia

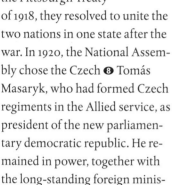
10
Wehrmacht soldiers take down the border sign to the Sudetenland, 1938

Slovakia

Following Slovakia's declaration of independence, a fascist satellite state of the German Reich was created there. It participated in the German invasion of Poland in 1939, joined the Tripartite Pact in 1940, and from 1941 was involved in the extermination policies against the Jews. Following its occupation by the Red Army in April 1945, Slovakian president Jozef Tiso and three ministers were hanged.

11
Sudetenland 1938: Evacuation of Czech citizens

12
Corpses following the Prague revolt, 1945

Father Jozef Tiso is congratulated following his election

1938 "Sudeten Crisis"	**Nov 2, 1938** First arbitration decision of Vienna	**Sep 10, 1945** Czechoslovakia reconstituted
Sep 29, 1938 Munich Agreement	**Mar 15, 1939** Protectorate of Bohemia and Moravia	**Apr 4, 1945** Red Army conquers Hungary

THE SOVIET UNION 1917–1939

The Russian czar was deposed in 1917, even before the end of World War I. The radical left-wing Bolsheviks emerged victorious out of the dispute between the democratic transitional government and the revolutionary Soviet Council of Soldiers' and Workers' Deputies. They came to power in the October Revolution in 1917 under the leadership of ❶ Lenin, ended the war, suppressed counterrevolutionary uprisings in a civil war, and constituted the first Communist-ruled state in the world: the Union of Soviet Socialist Republics (USSR). After Lenin's death in 1924, the Soviet Union became an increasingly centralized personal dictatorship under Stalin in the 1930s. Stalin oversaw a massive industrialization program and forcibly collectivized agriculture, while millions fell victim to the regime's repression.

Lenin at the unveiling of the Marx-Engels memorial on the Place of the Revolution in Moscow, 1918

■ The End of the Czar's Empire

The deposing of Nicholas II in 1917 resulted in a tension-filled coalition between the liberal government and the Soviet Council of Soldiers' and Workers' Deputies.

The large numbers of war dead, supply shortages, and corruption during the course of ❷ World War I led to growing dissatisfaction with the czarist autocracy among the Russian people. The ❹ calls for an end to the war became louder not only in the civilian population but also in the military. Avowals of friendship and brotherhood with the enemy even took place among the soldiers.

The situation escalated in March 1917 when military units in St. Petersburg refused ❺ Czar

Demonstration, 1917

Nicholas II's order to deal severely with striking workers. The military allied itself with the strikers and forced the czar to abdicate on March 15, 1917, in the February Revolution. Nicholas and his family were ❼ executed on July 17, 1918, by the Council of Ekaterinburg, where they were confined due to alarm at the rapid approach of White Russian forces which wanted to release the czar.

A provisional government under Prince Lvov was set up. It proclaimed the right of political freedom and was supported by moderate Social Democrats, the Mensheviks. Parallel to this, in many cities workers and soldiers organized into ❸ Soviet councils

that demanded more social changes and saw themselves as a counter to the power of the provisional government.

In April 1917 the Communist revolutionary leader of the Bolsheviks, Vladimir Ilich Ulyanov, known as ❻ Lenin, returned to St. Petersburg from his exile in Switzerland. In his "April Theses," he demanded an immediate peace settlement and the redistribution of land to the peasants. He also demanded an end to the coalition of the provisional government and exclusive power to the Soviets. The Bolsheviks' attempted coup in July 1917 failed, however.

Russian prisoners of war in East Prussia, 1915

Meeting of the Petrograd Soviet council, March 1917

Czar Nicholas II

Palace in Ekaterinburg, where the czar and his family were executed on July 17, 1918

The Russian Calendar

Until 1918, the Russian calendar was based on the old Julian calendar, from which the name "February Revolution" derives. According to the Gregorian calendar customary in the Western world, it was March 15. Similarly, the "October Revolution" took place on November 7 according to Western dating.

Lenin leading the people in the Russian Revolution, painting by Alexandre Gerassimov, 1930

| Mar 15, 1917 | February Revolution | July 1917 | Bolsheviks attempt coup | Mar 1918 | Government moved to Kremlin in Moscow |
| April 1917 | Lenin returns from exile | Nov 7, 1917 | October Revolution | Jul 17, 1918 | Czar Nicholas II murdered |

■ The Bolshevik Victory

A civil war broke out after the October Revolution as western governments armed the counterrevolutionary "White Army." By 1922 the Red Army had emerged victorious.

As the liberal provisional government under the new prime minister, ❽ Aleksandr Kerensky, continued the war and did not give in to the demands for social improvement, the conflict between the Soviets and the government became increasingly critical in the second half of 1917. Lenin and the Bolsheviks once again planned an armed uprising against the government after September 1917.

The ❾ October Revolution finally erupted on November 7, 1917. ⓫ Leon Trotsky led the Bolshevik Red Guard in occupying the most important points in St. Petersburg and ⓬ stormed the Winter Palace, the seat of the provisional government. Kerensky's government was arrested, and Lenin formed the Council of People's Commissars, the first Soviet government.

The Bolsheviks ended the war against the Central Powers with the Treaty of Brest-Litovsk on March 3, 1918. The harsh terms

9
Cartoon: *The Proletarian's Hammer Strikes Back*, 1917

11
Leon Trotsky, 1917

dictated by Germany were accepted by Lenin, as Russia was in turmoil. Large property owners and industry owners were expropriated without compensation, banks were nationalized, opposition parties were banned, and the democratic parliament was abolished. The newly founded security agency, the Cheka, was meant to secure the exclusive authority of the Bolsheviks. The first phase of the revolutionary reformation of Russia ended with

the move of the Soviet government to the ⓭ Kremlin in Moscow in March 1918.

But the government was still by no means secure. A counterrevolutionary alliance of monarchists, Mensheviks, and nonsocialist powers had formed a ❿ "White Army" in 1918 that fought the Bolsheviks' ⓮ "Red Army" in a bloody, almost three-year-long civil war. Despite support of the Whites from Russia's World War I allies, the tightly led Red Army finally prevailed at the beginning of 1922. With Georgia, Ukraine, Armenia, and Azerbaijan, the Reds conquered even states that had declared their independence after the Treaty of Brest-Litovsk. The Polish-Russian war of 1920–1921 and the terrible famine in Russia in the winter of 1921–1922 no longer posed serious threats to Bolshevik power. By 1922, the new socialist state

8
Aleksandr Kerensky (on car) at a parade, 1917

10
General Yudenich of the White Army forces with his staff, 1919

had almost reached the same extent as the former Russian empire.

In the same year, the Russian Soviet Federated Socialist Republic united with the Soviet republics of Ukraine and Belarus to form the Union of Soviet Socialist Republics (USSR). The Soviet Union was the world's first Communist country and was hailed by socialists around the world.

12
Storming of the Winter Palace, 1917

13
Lenin's mausoleum (right), Red Square, Moscow

14
Red Army cavalry, 1919

| **1918** | Founding of the White Army. | **1920–21** | Polish-Russian War | **1922** | Founding of the USSR |
| **Mar 3, 1918** | Treaty of Brest-Litovsk | **1921-22** | Red Army prevails | | |

Stalin's Rise from 1924 to 1929

After Lenin's death, Stalin took over the leadership of the party and by 1929 was undisputed leader of the country. In foreign affairs, the Soviet Union was primarily concerned with consolidation.

After Lenin fell ill in 1922, internal power struggles over succession within the party determined the domestic development of the country. Stalin used his power as general secretary of the Communist party to place his followers, particularly Kamenev and Zinoviev, in important government and party posts and give his office a key position in the party structure. Although Lenin in his "political will" had recommended the replacement of Stalin—whose ambitious nature he suspected—as general secretary, Stalin was able to overcome his rivals after Lenin's ❷ death on January 21, 1924. However, civil war and international intervention to crush the revolution created permanent fears.

By 1929 Stalin had been able to eliminate his competitors in the party and government leadership through shifting coalitions. In 1927, he forced his most powerful rival, Leon Trotsky, out of the party and in 1929 had him expelled from the country; Trotsky

2
Lenin lying in state, 1924

was murdered by the Soviet secret service in his ❸ Mexican exile in 1940. Whereas Trotsky had maintained that the Soviet Union could be secured if ❶ Communist revolution were continued in the highly industrialized nations of Europe, Stalin primarily concentrated on the ruthless establishment of a socialist social order in his own country from 1928 on. With the increased industrialization and ❹ forced collectivization of the economy, Stalin's dictatorship became a bloody system of suppression in the 1930s.

The Communist state had been recognized by most of the European nations by 1924. The priority of the Soviet Union's foreign relations under Stalin was to secure its

own system of rule. The USSR joined the League of Nations in 1934 and signed diverse nonaggression pacts and treaties of mutual assistance. After Nazi Germany's rearmament in the 1930s, the Western powers' concessions in the Munich Agreement reinforced Stalin's reservations with respect to the capitalist nations, especially after their betrayal of democracy in the Spanish Civil War. Stalin therefore decided for the ideologically paradoxical ❺, ❼ alliance with Germany. This allowed the Soviet Union to participate in the ❻ division of Poland and was intended to avert major military conflict. Hitler broke the treaty on June 22, 1941, when German forces began to invade.

1
"Workers of the World Unite!," Soviet poster, 1932

3
Trotsky's arrival in Mexico, 1937

Joseph Stalin, the "Man of Steel"

Stalin's real name was Iosif Vissarionovich Dzhugashvili. He was the son of a shoemaker and was set to become a priest, but because he had organized demonstrations and strikes, he was excluded from the Orthodox seminary in 1899. Only after Lenin's arrival in St. Petersburg did Stalin, a member of the Russian Social Democratic party, join the radical Bolsheviks. Lenin regarded his organizational talent highly, and only later recognized his immense hunger for power.

above: Soviet propaganda poster, Lenin and Stalin, 1944

4
Collective farm, 1931

5
Foreign Minister Molotov and Hitler in Berlin, 1940

6
German-Soviet meeting at the demarcation line in occupied Poland, 1939

7
French cartoon satirizing the Nazi-Soviet Pact, 1939

Jan 21, 1924	Lenin's death	1928	Stalin forces farm collectivization	1934	USSR joins the League of Nations
1927	Leon Trotsky expelled from the Party	1932	"Social Realism" movement		

Stalin's Reign of Terror in the 1930s

Stalin's personal dictatorship of state and party reached its bloody pinnacle with his large-scale political purges in the 1930s.

After the 1920s, Stalin's dictatorship was linked to a growing personality ⓬ cult and the development of the state as a tight, centrally controlled administrative machine. Stalin's policies were declared socialist dogma, and in 1936 the hegemony of the Communist party at all levels of society and state was officially established. The state secret police kept the population under surveillance and eliminated any opposition with ⓫ shootings, forced labor, and deportations to Siberia.

Without regard for human life, forced farm collectivization was introduced in 1928; the farms were to be combined into great production cooperatives. The farmers who owned medium and large tracts were defamed as "enemies of the people" and "exploiters"; their land was expropriated, and they

9
Dead children, winter of 1921-1922

were sent off to ❽ work camps in Siberia. A temporary, massive collapse of agriculture was the result; in the Ukraine four million people ❾ starved to death.

Between 1935 and 1939, Stalin eliminated all potential or imagined opponents in the "Great Purges." The ⓭ persecution took place at all levels of party, state, economic, and cultural groups. Millions of people were sent to penal or work camps, accused of being "vermin," spies, or saboteurs. Opposition to official views was labeled "deviationist" and

the holders were often accused of acting on behalf of foreign powers. Between 1937 and 1938, Stalin had the majority of the military leadership elite eliminated; 35,000 officers were arrested, and about 30,000 were executed. Non-Russian peoples also were victims of Stalin's persecution. The ❿ Volga German Republic was dissolved in 1941 and its inhabitants put into camps.

Prominent party members were accused of being "counterrevolutionaries" in three great public show trials and sentenced to death. Of the members of the party's Central Committee elected in 1934, two-thirds did not survive the years 1937 and 1938.

By the end of the wave of terror in 1939, practically the entire revolutionary elite of 1917 had been extinguished and replaced in all areas of the party structure by "apparatchiks" whose loyalty to Stalin was assured.

8
Forced laborers in a quarry, 1930

10
Meeting of a community of Volga German farmers to organize collectivization, 1931

11
Mass graves from the Stalin era near Kursk, only discovered in 1987

Social Realism

In 1932 "social realism" was enforced in all cultural fields. Literature and the visual arts were supposed to educate the Soviet citizens in the spirit of socialism. The central motif was the "working hero," representing socialist progress. Sculptures and murals of working men and women adorned buildings across the Soviet Union.

above: Poster, 1942

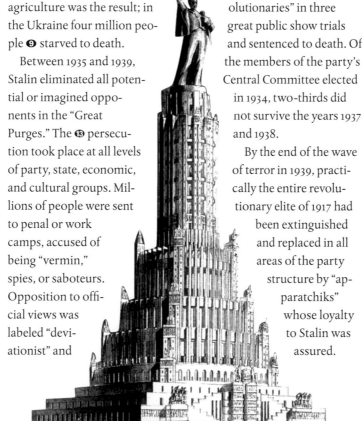
12
Model of the Soviet Palace of Culture including a memorial to Lenin, almost 1600 feet (500m) tall, designed by Boris M. Iofan 1933

13
1937 order for a mass arrest of senior party figures signed by Stalin

1936 Stalin consolidates his leadership position	**1940** Trotsky assassinated in Mexico	**Jun 22, 1941** German invasion of the Soviet Union
1935–39 Stalin's "Great Purges"	**1939** Nazi-Soviet Pact	**1941** Republic of Volga Germans dissolved

SOUTHEAST EUROPE BETWEEN THE WARS

1914–1945

In the wake of the Ottoman Empire's decline, independent kingdoms were founded in almost all of the states of southeastern Europe at the start of the 20th century. In the powder keg of the Balkans, Croatia, Serbia, and Slovenia united after 1918 to form the new state of Yugoslavia. German troops occupied Yugoslavia in World War II. The ❶ advance of the Red Army after 1944 then brought all of the Balkan states under the influence of communism. Greece alone was able to maintain its independence from communism after the war.

Red Army occupies Bulgaria; Communists build a new government, Sept. 1944

■ Greece

Greece was shaken by domestic crises following World War I and a lost war against Turkey. When the Germans occupied the country in 1941, the Greeks successfully resisted.

At the outbreak of World War I, Greece's ❷ King Constantine I was determined to protect the neutrality of his country, while Prime Minister ❸ Eleutherios Venizelos favored entering the war on the side of the Entente. Against the will of the king and the Greek people, he asked the British and French to set up a base in Thessaloniki. Constantine abdicated in 1917 in favor of his son Alexander, whom the ❺ Entente forced to declare war on the Central Powers through a coastal blockade. As a reward for this, Greece was granted a sizable amount of territory after the end of the war in 1918. The conflict with Turkey over

❸ Eleutherios Venizelos

Izmir led to a two-year war that ended in defeat for the Greeks. More than a million Greek inhabitants were driven out of Turkey, and Turks in Greece emigrated back.

The republic was proclaimed in 1924. However, after several dictatorships, domestic stability was restored when Prime Minister Venizelos took office in 1928. The world economic crisis hit Greece hard, and in 1932 Venizelos was not reelected. Radical right- and left-wing groups were able to build up their strength during the depression. In 1935, the Royalists repealed the constitution and declared a monarchy under ❻ King George II. The king was unable to

bring about domestic peace, though, and so ❼ Gen. Ioannes Metaxas seized power in a coup in 1936 and established a military dictatorship based on fascist ideology. Through an attempted invasion by the Italians in 1940, which the Greeks were able to repulse, Greece was dragged into World War II. German troops oc-

Constantine I, King of the Hellenes

cupied the country in 1941. The Communists organized a partisan resistance movement against the occupiers and brought a large part of the country under their control. The ❹ German troops withdrew in October 1944. When the conservative republican government in exile was installed in Athens under the protection of the British, the Communists incited a revolt that, after clashes with British troops, was ended in a cease-fire. Despite an agreement, the government, with British assistance, was in control only in the cities.

German tank in Athens, 1944

French and British troops in Thessaloniki, 1915

King George II oversees a maneuver, 1940

General Ioannes Metaxas (second from the right)

| 1916 | Rival government in Thessaloniki | 1918 | Proclamation of the "Kingdom of the Serbs, Croats, and Slovenes" | 1935 | Monarchy under George II proclaimed |
| 1917 | Constantine I abdicates | 1924 | Proclamation of the Republic of Greece | 1928 | Venizelos takes power |

■ The Balkan States

With the founding of Yugoslavia at the end of World War I, a new state came into being in the Balkans. Along with Bulgaria and Albania, it was caught in the sphere of influence of the Axis powers in World War II.

Following the disintegration of the great empires in the First World War, Montenegro, Bosnia-Herzegovina, and Croatia united with the Kingdom of Serbia. On December 1, 1918, King Peter I proclaimed the "Kingdom of the Serbs, Croats, and Slovenes," which was renamed Yugoslavia in 1929. The state was unstable, however, due to social and economic problems, particularly the opposition of the Croats to the almost exclusive Serbian leadership. During the 1930s, it increasingly came under ❾ German influence, and in 1940 Yugoslavia was partitioned by Hitler's troops and divided among the Axis powers. The Communists under Tito took the leadership of the partisan fighters against the occupiers and in 1944 agreed with the royal government in exile concerning a provisional government.

Bulgaria suffered great losses following World War I. Having already suffered territorial losses in the Second Balkan War, Bulgaria, as an ❽ ally of the Central Po-

wers, was put under a heavy burden of reparations by the Treaty of Neuilly. It lost Western Thrace to Greece, thus depriving it of access to the Aegean. To protect itself from the territorial claims of

10 Czar Boris III of Bulgaria together with his family, 1940

its neighboring countries, Bulgaria under ❿ Czar Boris III moved closer to the Axis powers in 1939, and in 1941 it became a signatory of the ⓫ Tripartite Pact. Following the invasion by the Red Army in 1944, the Communists took over government in Sofia. Bulgaria

then signed a treaty with the Soviet Union and declared war on Germany.

In 1912–1913, Albania gained its sovereignty after the Balkan wars, but during World War I, the country was contested by the hostile Great Powers. Albania was the only Balkan state whose territory remained unchanged after the war; the claims of Greece, Yugoslavia, and Italy were disallowed at the Paris Peace Conference. Italy, which had occupied the north of the country during World War I, recognized Albania's independence in 1921. ⓬ Ahmed Bey Zogu, who governed the Albanian republic as president from 1925 and then from 1928 as King Zog I, unsuccessfully sought to rid the country of Italian influence. In April 1939, Mussolini occupied the country, and ⓭ King Victor Em-

9 The Yugoslavian prince regent Paul with his wife on a state visit to Berlin, 1941

8 Caricature of Bulgaria's entry into the war, which was "pushed" by the Central Powers, 1915

manuel III of Italy was installed as king of the Albanians. Italy used the country as a base in World War II. Resistance formed against the occupying power, although the Albanian Communists and nationalists also fought against one another after 1943. The Communists prevailed in 1944, and Enver Hoxha took over the leadership of the country.

11 Yugoslavia becomes a signatory of the Tripartite Pact, 1941

12 Ahmed Zogu, president of Albania from 1925 and king from 1928, photo, 1930

13 Reception of the Albanian delegation in the Roman Quirinal palace on the occssion of the proclamation of King Victor Emmanuel III as king of Albania, 1939

| 1936 | Ioannes Metaxas attempts military putsch | 1941 | Bulgaria joins the Tripartite Pact | 1944 | Tito government in Yugoslavia |
| Apr 1939 | Italian troops occupy Albania | 1940 | Italian invasion of Greece | 1941 | Greece occupied by German troops |

1

Mustafa Kemal Atatürk, "Father of the Turks"

THE DECLINE AND FALL OF THE OTTOMAN EMPIRE 1914–1945

Between 1878 and 1918, the Ottoman Empire lost over three-quarters of its territory. The remaining parts were occupied by the Allies after World War I. The downfall of the Empire gave ❶ Mustafa Kemal (later "Atatürk") and his followers the opportunity to carry out reforms. After a four-year struggle for independence, the Turkish Republic was declared and an era of political and social upheaval ensued.

■ The End of the Ottoman Empire

The Ottoman Empire disintegrated during World War I. The occupation by victorious foreign troops was followed by a succession of wars for independence.

When World War I erupted, the already weakened Ottoman Empire at first sought to remain neutral. However, upon the instigation of the Young Turk minister of war, ❷ Enver Pasha, Turkey ❹ entered the war in November 1914 on the side of the Central Powers. Three of Turkey's five armies were placed under the command of the German general Liman von Sanders. The Turkish navy attacked British and French shipping in the Black Sea. The consequences of the war were fatal to the empire. With British support, Arabia was able to free itself from Ottoman control; part of Palestine was promised to the Jews in the Balfour Declaration as a national homeland; and after the defeat of the Central Powers, the Entente occupied most of what was left of the empire. In the Treaty of Sèvres in 1920, the Turkish state lost its sovereignty.

Resistance to the occupying regime was organized under the leadership of Mustafa Kemal. The struggle for independence began in 1919 when Kemal and the ex-naval officer Rauf Bey convoked a nationalist congress at Erzerum on July 23. The Congress created the Nationalist Party, which established its headquarters at Ankara, overthrowing the feeble regime in Istanbul on October 5, 1919, and achieving overwhelming victory at the subsequent elections. Its first success came with the recognition of the eastern borders by the young Soviet Union. France was also forced to renounce its territorial claims in 1921. The ❺ war against Greece, which sought to annex Constantinople and large parts of Anatolia, ended with the expulsion of not only the Greek army but also a large portion of the long-established ethnic Greek civilian population.

3

The town square in Izmir

2   Enver Pasha

The fight for independence ended with the destruction of ❸ Izmir. The occupying powers concluded the Peace of Mudanya with the government on October 11, 1922. International recognition of the Turkish state followed a year later with the Treaty of Lausanne.

The massacre of the Armenians, color print from the French newspaper *Le Petit Journal*, 1916

The Genocide of the Armenians

After the turn of the 20th century, attacks against the Christian Armenian minority occurred frequently in Turkey. In 1915, under the pretext of treason—the Armenians supposedly having collaborated with Russia—Turks began a campaign that cost the lives of an estimated 1.5 million Armenians. Most died on "death marches" into the desert. To this day, Turkey denies that a genocide took place, but the United Nations and the European Union recognize a genocide.

4

Turkish soldiers who fought with the Central Powers

5

Mustafa Kemal with his unit during the Greek-Turkish war, 1921

| **from 1915** | Forced relocation and massacre of Armenians | **1920** | Treaty of Sèvres | **1923** | The republic is proclaimed |

| **from 1919** | Struggle for independence under Mustafa Kemal | **1922** | Sultanate abolished |

■ The Founding of the Turkish Republic

Following the successful conclusion of the struggle for independence, Mustafa Kemal proclaimed the Republic of Turkey in 1923. A phase of intensive modernization began.

❽ Mehmed VI, the last Turkish sultan, had hardly any influence over political events, as the reform movement under Kemal had already won the upper hand in internal political affairs. In the course of the struggle for independence, Kemal formed an opposition government to the sultan's court. He abolished the sultanate in 1922, before he was even elected as the first president, and later also eliminated the caliphate and other religious courts. Kemal proclaimed the republic on October 29, 1923, and moved the capital to Ankara.

The following 15 years of Kemal's governance saw radical political and social change for Turkey. The "clothing reform" of 1925 banned the ❿, ⓫ veil for women and the fez for men. In the same year, the Gregorian calendar and the metric system were adopted, followed later by the ❻ Latin alphabet. Legal systems were absorbed piecemeal from

various European nations: Swiss civil law, German commercial law, and Italian criminal law were taken over and implemented. The enforcement of monogamous marriages and social equality between men and women were introduced, though they succeeded

"Kemalism"

The political and social ideology named after Kemal Atatürk is based upon the "Six Pillars," which was formulated in 1931 by his party. The six pillars are: nationalism, laicism, republicanism, statism, modernism, and populism. Its goal is the building of a modern, Western-oriented nation in which economic and social development is state-directed. Although the state religion was abolished and the clerics strictly excluded from state affairs, Islam still plays a major role in the national concept of a Turkish identity. In 1925 religious opposition parties were banned.

top: Memorial of the 1928 Republic of Istanbul; Kemal Atatürk with his comrade-in-arms

only partially; in 1930, women were given voting rights and, four years later, the right to stand for office.

Kemal, who was honored with the epithet "Atatürk" (Father of the Turks), died in 1938. His successor as president was his comrade-in-arms ❾ Ismet Inönü, who sought to continue Turkey's modernization.

Internationally Turkey strove to maintain its sovereignty. During World War II, Turkey remained neutral. In 1934 it signed the ❼ Balkan Entente with Greece, Romania, and Yugoslavia. Turkey also became a charter member of the United Nations. When the Soviet Union once again attempted to exercise control over the region of the Bosporus and Dardanelles straits, Turkey sought closer ties with the United States.

Atatürk champions the Latin alphabet on a visit to the provinces, 1929

Turkish envoy, second from left, signs the Balkan Entente, September 4, 1934

This was fundamental to US containment policy, which focused on checking the spread of Communism in Europe. In 1952, Turkey was admitted to NATO after it fought alongside the US in the Korean War.

The last sultan, Mehmed VI, at his enthronement 1918

From left: Ismet Inönü, Kemal Atatürk, and a young female pilot, 1937

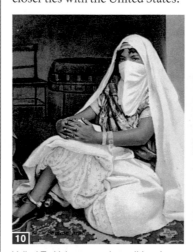

Veiled Turkish woman, in traditional Turkish dress, 1917

Young Turk after the "clothing reform," ca. 1935

1923	Caliphate abolished	1930	Introduction of women's right to vote	1938	Atatürk dies
1923	Treaty of Sèvres revised	1925	Soviet-Turkish nonaggression pact	1930	Pact of friendship with Greece

THE REORGANIZATION OF ARABIA 1918–1945

With the end of ❶ World War I and the disintegration of the Ottoman Empire, the Arab world faced a new beginning and a period of political restructuring. The desires for national independence and self-rule of the countries that had previously been Ottoman provinces, collided with British and French "Great Power" colonial interests in the oil-rich region and led to constant tension. In Palestine, Arab and Israeli territorial claims, which could not be resolved by the British Mandate, overlapped. The foundation for the present-day conflict in the Middle East was laid.

Capture of Jerusalem by the British under General Allenby, December 1917

■ Postwar Political Reorganization in Syria, Lebanon, and Palestine

Great Britain and France divided the territories of the defeated Ottoman Empire between them following World War I. In Palestine, Great Britain failed to successfully mediate between Arab and Jewish interests and solve the territorial conflict.

Rebellion against British rule in Palestine: "Holy War" against the British supremacy is declared, 1915

Castle in the desert, near Qasr al-Azraq, Jordan, in which Lawrence of Arabia had his battle headquarters

Arabs celebrate the fall of the Ottoman Empire and the liberation of Mecca, June 1916

fought on the side of the Entente. The British officer and archaeologist Captain T. E. Lawrence, later known as "Lawrence of Arabia," successfully organized an ❸ uprising of the Arabs against the Turks, which significantly contributed to the downfall of the Ottoman Empire. At the 1920 Conference of San Remo, however, the Entente powers disregarded their promise of Arabian independence and focused instead on consolidating their influence. France was given a League of Nations mandate to rule over Syria and Lebanon, while Great Britain took control, also as the mandatory power, over ❷ Palestine and Iraq. When Syria declared itself an independent "United Kingdom" in the same year, the French military intervened and banished King Faisal. In other colonial areas as well, resistance to the Europeans took on

In order to weaken its World War I opponent, the Ottoman Empire, the British government supported the nationalist dreams of the Ottoman provinces of Syria, Lebanon, and Iraq, promising them ❹ independence if they

strength. In Iraq the British had to defend against numerous insurrections, and in Palestine the British occupation was unable to satisfy the demands of the League of Nations for a balancing of Arab and Jewish interests.

Lawrence of Arabia

Thomas Edward Lawrence, known as "Lawrence of Arabia"

The archaeologist Thomas Edward Lawrence from North Wales became legendary as Lawrence of Arabia through his leadership in the battle for Arabian independence. From 1916 to 1918, he worked toward inciting an Arab rebellion against the Ottomans. After the war, he saw the imperialist reorganization of the region as a betrayal of his Arabian friends; he refused all awards and lived reclusively until his death in 1935.

Oil Production in the Near East

The major powers' demand for oil had increased steadily since the beginning of industrialization. In 1920, the oil-rich provinces of Baghdad, Mosul, and Basra were combined under British mandate to form present-day Iraq. The British shared the rights to the oil deposits with France, the US, and the Netherlands. The payment the Iraqi government received in exchange for oil was a small fraction of the profits.

Oil production in Iraq, 1937

■ Palestine: A Religio-Political Conflict Is Born

After 1917, Arabic and Jewish national movements collided over the issue of the religio-historically sensitive region of the territory of Palestine.

5 Street scene in Jericho, ca. 1900

6 Transjordanian emirs

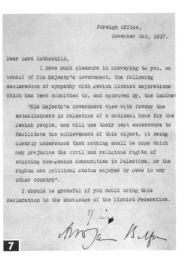

7 Balfour Declaration for the settlement of Jewish immigrants in Palestine, 1917

Even by the end of the 19th century, the Arab nationalist movement had provided for a revitalization of Islam and had increasingly begun to defend itself against the secularization promoted by Ottoman rule. At the same time, Jewish nationalism—Zionism—also increased, seeking to unite Jewish people throughout the world in the "Land of the Fathers," in Ottoman-controlled **5** Palestine. As the Zionist cause was thus anti-Turkish, and as many of the young men of the exiguous Jewish population of Palestine enrolled in British forces and provided military intelligence, Great Britain promised the Jews a "national homeland in Palestine" in the **7** Balfour Declaration of 1917. Conflicting expec-

tations were thereby created in the Arab and Jewish nationalist movements, both of which expected their own to be fulfilled when the Ottoman Empire collapsed and Great Britain conquered Palestine.

Negotiations between the Zionists and Arab nationalists led to the Weizmann-Faisal Agreement in 1919, in which the Arabs accepted the **8** immigration of the Jews as long as Arab independence in Palestine was secure. These initial declarations on both sides were forgotten, however, when territorial conflicts began.

Arab **9** resistance against the Zionist settlement of Palestine became increasingly strident. In response, the British government restricted Palestine to the area west of the Jordan River and created the semi-independent **6** Emirate of Transjordan in the east. During World War II, Transjordan fought with the British including the 1941 invasion of pro-German Iraq.

The conflict between Jews and Arabs increa-

sed when Nazi persecution increased Jewish immigration to the region during the 1930s. The Arab Palestine Uprising in 1936–1939 demanded an independent state and an end to Jewish immigration. In response, Jews demanded the right to unlimited immigration and demanded the creation of a Jewish state in Palestine at a 1942 New York conference.

8 View of the camp of Jewish immigrants in Palestine, 1920

Jewish Immigration to Palestine

The first wave of Jewish immigration to Palestine occurred in 1881 after the pogroms against the Jews in Russia. The increasing anti-Semitism throughout Europe around the turn of the century strengthened the Zionist movements, which demanded the creation of a Jewish "homeland secured by public law" in Palestine. In 1896 Theodor Herzl published the programmatic book The Jewish State, *in which he laid out the conditions of national Jewish self-rule, and a year later he called the first Zionist congress. Despite Arab protests, the Jewish proportion of the Palestine population increased from less than 10 percent at the turn of the century to 30 percent at the end of World War II.*

Arrival in the port of Tel Aviv, 1936   Theodor Herzl

9 Anti-Zionist demonstration by Arabs in the region controlled by the British mandate, March 1920

1920–21 Creation of the Emirate of Transjordan	**1936–39** Arab Palestine uprising	
1920 Founding of Iraq under British mandate	**1932** Independence of Iraq	**1946** Independence of Jordan

1 Mountainous region in Loristan, Iran

IRAN AND AFGHANISTAN: BATTLE FOR INDEPENDENCE CA. 1900–1945

Afghanistan and ❶ Persia (Iran after 1935) had to defend themselves against the imperialist interests of the Great Powers in the first half of the 20th century, and both were more or less successful in their struggles for independence from Great Britain. Domestically, those in power strove for modernization based on the Turkish model; this was more fully realized in Persia than in Afghanistan. During the World Wars, the Entente powers and then the Allies used Iran against its will as a military base for their troops.

■ Persia/Iran: Modernization in the Shadow of the Great Powers

In 1905 Persia was divided between British and Russian spheres of influence, with a neutral zone in between. Then, during World War I, it was occupied by Russia, Great Britain, and Turkey.

After the Bolsheviks came to power in 1917, Russia withdrew from Persia and recognized its sovereignty. In response, Britain occupied the country in 1919, but it was unable to force a protectorate treaty upon Persia and ultimately also withdrew. For fear of Soviet expansion, the British demanded that a stable Persian government be set up.

❷ Colonel Reza Khan, the minister of war, took power through a coup in 1921 and consolidated Persian central authority. In 1925, he had the parliament depose the last of the Qajars and elect him shah. As Reza Shah Pahlavi, he began in an authoritarian manner to westernize the country cultur-

6 Mohammad Reza Pahlavi, 1937

ally, intellectually, and industrially, following the example of Atatürk. For example, he had the Trans-Iranian Railway built and introduced European legal systems through the passage of civil and criminal codes. From 1929, men were required to wear Western-style clothing, women gave up the ❸ veil, hospitals and new roads were built, and in 1935 the first modern university opened in Tehran. Nevertheless there was little progress in the country because the system existed to serve the shah. Through land reform, the shah forced the ❺ nomads to settle in specially

3 Women wearing the chador, 1930

5 Nomadic boy with lamb, 1937

constructed villages. Revolts against his policies were brutally ❹ crushed and opposing tribal leaders were killed.

Internationally, Persia strove to maintain its autonomy. In 1933, it forced a new agreement upon the Anglo-Persian Oil Company under conditions more favorable to Persia and in 1935 changed the official name of the state to Iran. Nevertheless, the attempt to remain neutral during World War II again failed, as British and Soviet troops in 1941, and later also Americans, occupied the country to keep the great oil reserves out of German hands. The presence of a large number of German agents in Persia was a cause of anxiety for Britain. The shah, who sympathized with the Axis powers, was compelled to abdicate and was sent into exile. His son ❻ Mohammad Reza Pahlavi became his successor to the throne and cooperated with the Allies. Roosevelt, Stalin, and Churchill reassured Iran of its

2 Reza Shah Pahlavi, 1925

4 Persian prisoners, ca. 1928

postwar independence at the ❼ Tehran Conference in 1943 and held out the prospect of economic aid. Accordingly, the United States and Great Britain left the country in 1945, the Soviets one year later.

7 Stalin, Roosevelt, and Churchill at the Tehran Conference

| Dec 30, 1906 | Persia's constitution on Belgian model | Aug 8, 1919 | Treaty of Rawalpindi | 1926 | Reza Shah Pahlavi enthroned |
| 1919 | 3rd Anglo-Afghan War | Aug 8, 1919 | Independence of Afghanistan | 1926 | Soviet-Afghan nonaggression pact |

■ Afghanistan: Liberation from British Influence

Afghanistan was finally able to achieve its independence from Great Britain in 1919. Only limited state reforms after the Turkish model could be achieved over the opposition of conservative forces.

❽ Afghanistan was able to maintain its neutrality in World War I under Amir Habibullah. At first it did not defend itself when British India occupied parts of southeastern Afghanistan beyond the Durand line. In 1919, however, ⓫ Amanullah—the son and successor of Habibullah, who had been murdered the same year—started the Third Anglo-Afghan War by crossing the frontier into India in May 1919 and was able to make initial gains against the British. In the Treaty of Rawalpindi on August 8, 1919, Great Britain finally released ❾ Afghanistan into

9
Street scene in Afghanistan

11
Amanullah watches a German Army exercise in Berlin, ca. 1925

independence, recognizing the Durand line as the border.

Amanullah Shah identified with secularly oriented young Afghans and introduced a sweeping modernization program following the model of laicized Turkey. He sent young men abroad to study and planned a wide, if unrealistic, program of public works. However, his plans to give women equal rights, secularize the legal system, and institutionalize the protection of religious minorities crumbled against the resistance of the conservative forces in the country that held tight to their ❿ tribal traditions and religious supremacy. In 1929, internal revolts led to

Amanullah's abdication.

Following nine months of bloody rule by Habibullah II, Mohammad Nadir Khan seized Kabul in October and, as Nadir Shah, took power. Taking into account conservative political sentiment, he proceeded cautiously to continue his predecessor's reform policies. He fell back on the Sharia—Islamic law—as a legal foundation and made ⓭ Sunni Islam the state religion.

Under his successor Zahir Shah, Afghanistan was also able to maintain its neutrality throughout World War II. A nonaggression pact had already been signed with the Soviet

8
Rock face with Buddhist cave monasteries and "Little Buddha," Afghanistan

10
Afghan dignitaries, ca. 1910

Union in 1926. The Allies accepted Afghanistan's neutral position, although they insisted that ⓬ Zahir Shah expel the diplomatic representatives of the Axis powers from the country.

Young Afghan Movement

The Young Afghan movement developed against the backdrop of British domination at the beginning of the 20th century. Influenced by pan-Islamic enlighteners of the 19th century and the ideas of the Turkish politician Atatürk, they wanted to renew the nation.

12
Mohammad Zahir Shah, 1937

13
The Blue Mosque in Kabul, Afghanistan

| 1933 | Agreement with "Anglo-Persian Oil Company" | 1935 | Name changed to "Iran" | Nov 28–Dec 1, 1943 | Tehran Conference |
| 1935 | First modern university in Tehran | | 1941 | Occupation of Iran by British and Russian troops |

INDIA'S PATH TO INDEPENDENCE   UNTIL 1947

❶ Mohandas Gandhi (also known as Mahatma) was the most significant figure of India's struggle for independence from Great Britain. His program of passive resistance and noncooperation was supported by the public and became a powerful protest movement that forced the British to make more concessions, until India was at last granted independence from the British Empire in 1947. The Muslim minority in India also was given Pakistan as a separate state in the same year.

Mohandas Kamarchand Gandhi, known as Mahatma Gandhi

■ Gandhi's Nonviolent Struggle

The British massacre in Amritsar in 1919 gave new impetus to the Indian independence movement. Gandhi's campaign of civil disobedience then developed into a powerful political force.

Jawaharlal Nehru

Despite military loyalty to the British in ❸ World War I, the Indian independence movement's hopes for political equality were not fulfilled at the end of the war. Although high-level political reports proposed more representative government, particularly at a local level, together with the admission of natives to all levels of the public service, additional emergency laws further restricted the Indians' right to partake in decisions, which only strengthened the nationalist Indian National Congress party led by Gandhi and ❷ Jawaharlal Nehru.

After the British bloodily suppressed a protest meeting in 1919 in Amritsar, Gandhi carried out his first campaign of "civil disobedience" and "noncooperation." It rapidly grew into a powerful mass movement and made Gandhi the undisputed leader of the dominant Congress party. He called for a boycott of the British organs of state and championed the revitalization of the basic Indian ❹ crafts industry.

The success of the campaign was reinforced when the Muslim League, led by ❺ Muhammad Ali Jinnah, also joined it. The British participation in the destruction of the Ottoman Empire had increased their aversion for the occupiers. Gandhi broke off the campaign in 1922 when excited ❻ demonstrators violated the ban on violence. Gandhi was sentenced to six years in prison but was released in 1924. It was not until 1930 that he became politically active again.

Indian troops in World War I

Gandhi at the spinning wheel

Gandhi with Muslim leader Muhammad Ali Jinnah

Political unrest in Calcutta

Noncooperation and Passive Resistance

Noncooperation and passive resistance were methods that Gandhi had used in his successful battle for the rights of the Indian minority in South Africa. He also followed this path in India, because he believed that British rule was made possible only through the cooperation of the Indian people and that this method could thus force political change. He believed that the Indians should defend themselves by "holding fast to the truth" ("satyagraha"), an ancient Indian idea. If one refers to a truth, one has to prove it and alone carry the burden of proof. One should do no harm to anyone, except, at most, oneself. For that reason, Gandhi equated "holding fast to the truth" with nonviolence.

| 1919 | British massacre in Amritsar | 1920–22 | First "Satyagraha" campaign | 1928 | Nehru's report | 1930–32 | "Round Table"-conferences |
| 1920 | Constitutional reform | | | 1924 | Gandhi released | 1930 | Second "Satyagraha" campaign |

Independence and Division

The British reluctantly gave in to the pressure of the Congress party and granted independence to India and the separate Muslim state of Pakistan following World War II.

The refusal of the British to grant India its demands for sovereignty in 1930 triggered a second mass movement. To protest against the British monopoly of the salt industry, Gandhi led several thousand people in a demonstration march to the salt fields on the coast. Numerous nonviolent protests followed throughout the country. A constitutional conference in London in 1931 brought only partial success: The salt monopoly was lifted by the

7

Gandhi on the way to sign the Gandhi-Irwin Pact, 1931

❼ Gandhi-Irwin Pact, but the demand for national self-determination was again rejected.

The Government of India Act passed by the British Parliament in 1935 allowed the Indians to build autonomous governments at the provincial level but left the central government under the British unchanged. The act had to satisfy a huge range of opinion and at the same time see to the protection of Indian minorities. In 1936, the Congress party emerged as the winner of the elections in the provinces; however, in protest against the British governor's emergency laws, they only partly took over their ministerial offices. When the viceroy, Lord Linlithgow, proclaimed India's entrance into World War II in 1939 without guaranteeing later independence, the ❽ Congress party refused its support and called for renewed ❾ civil disobedience. ❿ Gandhi answered a halfhearted British concession in 1942 with the demand to "quit India." Thereupon the complete leadership of the Congress party was arrested. The

8

Indian National Congress party

10

Prison cell crowded with arrested supporters of the independence movements

11

Mass exodus of Hindus and Sikhs from Pakistan, 1947

course of the war and the mounting inner tension in India, however, increased the pressure on Great Britain to find a cooperative solution.

The Muslim League had distanced itself from the Hindu-based Congress party at the end of the 1930s. Muhammad Ali Jinnah, who held the view that Hindus and Muslims were two distinct nations, increasingly demanded the creation of a separate state in the north of the subcontinent after 1940. In order to avoid a bloody civil war between Hindus and Muslims, the British decided after World War II to partition the country in two. In 1947, ⓫ Pakistan (the Muslim areas) and India (the Hindu areas) were granted independence as dominions. Gandhi, who unwaveringly spoke for peace between Muslims and Hindus, was assassinated in 1948 by a fanatical Hindu.

9

Women demonstrate for Indian independence from Great Britain

The "Salt March"

The "Salt March" to the ocean caused a great international sensation. Mahatma Gandhi and his followers took only a few lumps of salt from the ocean, but thus symbolically violated the British salt monopoly. Sixty thousand participants were arrested, Gandhi among them. This number of prisoners far exceeded the capacity of British jails.

Demonstrations against the British monopoly on the salt trade in India

1935	Government of India Act		1940	"Pakistan Resolution" of the Muslim League		1947	Indian Independence Act
Sep 12, 1931	Gandhi-Irwin Pact	1939	Congress government resigns	1942	"Quit India" resolution	Jan 30, 1948	Gandhi murdered

CHINA BETWEEN EMPIRE AND COMMUNISM 1911–1949

For more than a century, between 1811 and 1949, China was characterized by the ❶ fight against Japanese expansionist aspirations, the struggle for national unity, and bloody domestic ideological disputes. The internal power struggle between the Republicans and the Communists was briefly set aside in the face of Japanese imperialism. Following World War II, with Soviet aid, Communism prevailed and restructured the country politically and economically.

Guards with machine guns along the Great Wall of China

■ Civil War and Japanese Aggression

The end of the Empire saw political chaos and territorial breakup in the Republic of China. Japan exploited the turmoil, launching a military invasion as it sought to build an empire in Asia.

At the end of 1911, Republican revolutionaries led by Sun Yat-sen and Gen. ❷ Yuan Shikai forced the last emperor of the Qing dynasty, P'u-i, to abdicate. A republic was proclaimed in 1912. Yuan's attempt to found a new dynasty failed in 1915 due to resistance in the provinces. The government disintegrated with his death in 1916, and until 1928 China experienced continuous civil war. Warlords ruled, particularly in the north of the country. Japan sought to capitalize on the chaos for its own purposes. Its "21 demands" of 1915 sought the colonization of the whole country.

China entered World War I in 1917 hoping to gain allies in its defense against Japanese imperialism. When by 1919 these expectations proved illusory, Chinese nationalism increased. Sun Yat-sen began militarizing the Republican National Party (Kuomintang) in 1923 with the aim of unifying the country. After Sun's death in 1925, Chiang Kai-shek took over the leadership of the party. With the capture of Beijing in 1928, he succeeded in subduing the warlords in the north and became president of the republic. By 1937 Chiang had essentially restored China's unity, but his government ground itself down in domestic conflicts with the Communists.

Japan had already occupied ❸ Manchuria on the Chinese mainland in 1931 and proclaimed the state of Manchoukuo. When Beijing was attacked in 1937, Chiang had no choice but to form a ❹ united front with the Communists in order to defend the country. The Japanese army, however, continued to advance further into the country. Following the violent ❺ subjugation of Nanjing, known in China as "the rape of Nanjing," the government was forced to withdraw to the west.

When the United States declared war on Japan in 1942, China received American material and military support. Following the Japanese surrender to the Allies, the Japanese left Nanjing, and the puppet state of Manchoukuo disintegrated.

Yuan Shikai gives the order to cut off the emperor's traditional plait, 1912

Chinese soldiers in the battle against the occupying Japanese forces in Manchuria, 1932

Communist meeting to discuss the "united front," 1937

Japanese troops invade and lay waste to Nanjing, 1937

P'u-i, the Last Emperor

P'u-i, the last Chinese emperor, had just turned five when he was forced to abdicate in 1912. In 1924, he placed himself under the protection of the Japanese, who proclaimed him emperor of their puppet state, Manchoukuo, in 1934. At the end of World War II, P'u-i fell into Soviet captivity and was detained in custody for "reeducation" until 1959.

The Chinese imperial couple P'u-i and Wan Jung, ca. 1934

| 1912 | National People's Party (KMT) founded | Feb 15, 1912 | General Yuan Shikai's presidency | 1917 | China enters WW I | 1921 | CCP founded |
| Feb 12,1912 | Last emperor abdicates | 1915 | Japan's "21 Demands" | 1916–28 | Civil War | 1919 | Start of "Fourth of May Movement" |

■ The Rise of Communism under Mao Zedong

The influence of the Communist Party under Mao Zedong grew steadily through the 1920s and 1930s. Despite being brutally persecuted by the government, the Communists were able to prevail over the Republicans after World War II.

With China's entry into World War I and the Bolshevik victory in Russia, Western revolutionary thought penetrated China and found expression in the "Fourth of May Movement." The Chinese Communist Party (CCP) emerged in 1921 from the movement's Marxist study groups. With Soviet help, the groups became an important power in the country.

In the wake of national unification efforts, the Communists at first united with the Republican party in 1922. The influence of the Communists steadily increased, however, culminating in a rift between the parties in 1927. ❻ Chiang Kai-shek's forces then persecuted the Communists. During the worst attack, in

7 Execution of a Chinese communist student, 1927

The Fourth of May Movement

Named after the date of a Beijing student demonstration against the pro-Japanese government, the Fourth of May Movement became a nationwide political emancipation movement of intellectuals, students, and workers in 1919. Its demands, along with national independence, included the rejection of traditional Confucianism, more civil rights, and social reform within the state.

Student demonstration, 1919

Shanghai on April 12, 1927, thousands of Communists and union members were ❼ massacred. The CCP then withdrew its ❽ People's Liberation Army into the countryside and built up a local government. After carrying out an agrarian revolution, it set up a Soviet-style republic in Yiangxi province in southeastern China.

To evade the pressure from the "extermination campaigns" of the Republican government, the CCP was forced to move with its troops to the north of the country. Under their new undisputed

leader, ⓫ Mao Zedong, the Communists managed to escape in 1934–1935 on the "Long March" through western China to Yan'an, which they built up to be their central base.

The CCP steadily expanded its control during the ❾, ❿ war with Japan. When the Soviet Union occupied Manchuria in 1945, the CCP seized power there. By 1949 Communists controlled the whole of the Chinese mainland with Soviet support. Mao proclaimed the People's Republic of China on October 1, 1949.

6 Chiang Kai-Shek, Koumintang politician, with his wife, 1927

The "Long March"

The Communists' Long March to the north of China took place in 1934–1935 over a distance of some 6000 miles. Many soldiers gave up along the way; others died of illness, of exhaustion, or in battle. In the end, only about 8000 of the original 90,000 reached Yan'an. The CCP later used the Long March as a symbol of the socialist struggle in China.

Mao Zedong

11 Mao Zedong speaking at a Communist conference, 1933

8 Communist fighters on the "Long March," 1935

9 Shanghai shortly after a Japanese air-raid bombing, 1937

10 Japanese infantrymen with Chinese prisoners during WW II

Apr 12, 1927 Communists executed and persecuted		**1931** Japan occupies Manchuria	**1937–45** Sino-Japanese War
1923 Militariziation of the Republican National Party	**1928** Beijing taken and China united	**1934-35** "Long March"	**Oct 1, 1949** Proclamation of the PRC

IMPERIAL JAPAN AND SOUTHEAST ASIA

1914–1945

Aggressive expansionist policies and increasingly fascistic nationalism characterized the politics of the Japanese empire from 1914 to 1945. Beginning in 1931, Japan waged a brutal war of conquest against China that lasted almost 15 years. Japan overextended itself with its surprise attack on the ❶ United States in 1941, and despite its military strength, supremacy over the whole of east Asia was clearly unsustainable. The country's inevitable defeat was hastened when the US destroyed two Japanese cities with atomic bombs. Most of the southeast Asian nations won their independence after the war, though some had to fight prolonged conflicts with the Western colonial powers.

US bomber attacks Japanese destroyer, ca. 1943

■ Development of Japanese Imperialism up to 1931

Japan expanded its sphere of influence when it gained control of the former German colonies in the Pacific after World War I. Nationalist ideas and the imperial cult increasingly gained influence in the economically flourishing country as it sought to expand into Asia.

Japan further developed its position of supremacy in East Asia after the death of Emperor ❹ Meiji in 1912 and the ascension to the throne of his son Yoshihito. At the outbreak of war in 1914, the Japanese foreign minister stated that while Japan had no desire to become embroiled in war, she would stay loyal to her alliance with Great Britain and protect its interests. When Germany refused to relinquish its lease hold and naval base at ❸ Tsingtao in the Chinese province of Shantung,

Government building in Tsingtao, capital of Kiaochow, 1913

Japan joined World War I on the side of the Entente. Japanese forces occupied all German colonies in the Pacific: the Marshall, Marianas, Palau, and Caroline Islands. After the war, the League of Nations transferred these islands and Tsingtao to Japan to administer as mandated territories. Although Tsingtao was given back to China in 1922 under the Shantung Treaty, the islands' territorial status quo was confirmed in other international treaties. In

the ❷ "Four Power Treaty," France, Great Britain, Japan, and the United States agreed to respect one another's Pacific possessions and to help in case of an attack by an outside power. In the "Nine Power Treaty" of 1922, Japan guaranteed China national sovereignty.

Economically, after a short postwar weakness, a period of strong growth began in Japan. Even the ❻, ❼ devastating earthquakes around Tokyo and Yokohama in 1923 only slightly affected this trend. The global economic depression after 1929, however, brought this to an end, particularly affecting ❺ silk farmers.

The country became formally democratized after the war. The electorate was broadened tenfold to 14 million,

"Four Power Treaty," November 1921

and universal suffrage was introduced in 1925. Politically more important, though, was an ultra-nationalistic group of military officers that over the course of the 1920s gained increasing influence with the government and emperor through extraparliamentary committees such as the "Secret State Council" and the "Military Senate." They pushed for conquests to secure new resources.

Damage wrought by earthquakes, 1923

Victims of the earthquake, 1923

Emperor Meiji in military uniform, portrait, late 19th century

Japanese silk painting, ca. 1850

■ Japan's War of Conquest in China 1931–1945

The decade-long Japanese conquest of China began with the occupation of Manchuria in 1931. Domestically, the right-wing military hierarchy tightened its grip on power in the empire, silencing more moderate civilian voices.

❾ Emperor Hirohito took the throne in 1928, but from 1932 on, the army emerged as the sole power factor in the country. Japan rejected the Washington accords of 1922, which had sought to avoid a naval arms race. Chauvinistic and antidemocratic military groups determined Japanese politics behind the scenes in the 1930s, leading to the official collapse of the entire parliamentary system. In 1940, the old political parties were compelled to dissolve, and a sort of conglomerate party emerged in their place: the Imperial Rule Assistance Association (*Taisei Yokusankai*). A new government under Prime Minister Prince Fumimaro Konoe nationalized the economy and put restrictions on important civil rights.

8 Marco Polo Bridge near Beijing

At the instigation of the military, Japanese troops invaded **❿** Manchuria in 1931 and managed to occupy the entire region in a few months. They created the puppet state of Manchoukuo headed by the former Chinese emperor P'u-i, who was named **⓫** emperor of Manchoukuo in 1934. Japan continued its expansion and colonization of China, also seizing Yehol province. China, militarily inferior and divided could do little to resist the occupiers. In 1935, Shanghai was captured in a brutal campaign.

Japan gradually pulled away from international agreements. When the League of Nations refused to recognize Manchoukuo in 1933, Japan announced its resignation from the organization. In 1936, it terminated the naval fleet agreement, and soon after, Japan declared its withdrawal from the London disarmament conference and signed the **⓬** "Anti-Comintern Pact" with Nazi Germany.

The **⓭** Sino-Japanese War began in July 1937 with a clash between Chinese and Japanese soldiers on the **8** Marco Polo Bridge near Beijing and lasted until September 1945. Within a short time, Japan had annexed the north of China and almost the entire coast. Further advances into the interior were halted in 1938 only by the rugged mountains of central China. The devastating war claimed enormous losses among the Chinese population; estimates range as high as 20 million dead—the majority of them civilians. With its defeat at the end of World War II, Japan was forced to withdraw from China completely.

Poem by Ushiyama Kinichi

In honor of the German–Japanese alliance:

"The alliance has been created, blood brothers equal,
The countries of both united strive to ascending power,
Brilliant the culture, the justice commanding awe,
German soul, how you equal the Japanese."

Japanese and Nazi banners on the occasion of the visit of the Japanese foreign minister to Berlin, 1941

9 Emperor Hirohito, 1930

10 Japanese soldiers in occupied Manchuria, 1945

11 Emperor P'u-i on a state visit to Japan with Emperor Hirohito, Tokyo, 1935

12 Signing of the Anti-Comintern Pact, November 25, 1936

13 Japanese infantry in winter uniform, in front of armored train, ca. 1937

The Struggle for East Asia in World War II

Japan fought the Allies for hegemony over the entire East Asian region in the War in the Pacific of 1941–1945. The dropping of the atomic bombs on Hiroshima and Nagasaki forced Japan into unconditional surrender.

Japanese surprise attack on Pearl Harbor, December 7, 1941

US war plane takes off from an aircraft carrier, 1944

Japanese destroyer opens fire on British cruiser, 1943

The outbreak of war in Europe in 1939 did not alter Japan's imperialist aims: the project of "reordering east Asia." Its goal was to unite the entire region—from India to Manchuria to Australia—as the "Greater East Asia Co-Prosperity Sphere" under the political and economic hegemony of Japan, using the "divine emperor" Hirohito to legitimize this claim to dominance ideologically.

As a safeguard against interference, Japan signed the Tripartite Pact with Germany and Italy on September 27, 1940, although it did not commit itself to aid in case of war. Japan also signed a neutrality pact with the Soviet Union on April 14, 1941. An attempt at rapprochement with the United States, which had canceled its trade agreement with Japan in 1939, failed. When Japan-

ese troops marched into Saigon in July 1941, US president Roosevelt imposed an oil embargo on Japan. As a result, Prime Minister Konoe resigned, and his extremely nationalist successor, General Hideki Tojo, decided to attack the Americans.

On December 7, 1941, the Japanese bombed the US Pacific Fleet base at ❶ Pearl Harbor, Hawaii. The resulting entry of the United States into the hostilities turned the European war into a world war.

In the ❷, ❸ War in the Pacific, Japan was able to conquer all of east Asia by 1942. In rapid succession, Japan occupied the Philippines, Hong Kong, Singapore, and Burma. It advanced to India's borders and was on the brink of conquering Australia. The situation finally began to change with the British invasion of Burma in 1943. Then, after American landings in the Mariana Islands and the crushing defeat in the aircraft carrier battle at ❹ Saipan, the war cabinet under Tojo stepped down.

When the Americans captured the islands of Iwo Jima and Okinawa and cut off fuel supplies, Japan's defeat became inevitable, as the desperate deployment of ❺ kamikaze pilots showed. Despite this Japan refused to surrender on the terms that the Allies demanded. On August 6 and 9, 1945, the US dropped atomic bombs on the Japanese cities of Hiroshima and Nagasaki, a demonstration that forced Hirohito to announce Japan's ❻ unconditional surrender.

US troops march across the island of Saipan, 1944

Japanese kamikaze pilots praying before their final flight, 1945

Japanese soldiers taken prisoner in Guam, 1945

Atomic Attacks on Hiroshima and Nagasaki

The United States ended World War II with the dropping of atomic bombs on Hiroshima and Nagasaki and ushered in the nuclear age. The devastating destructive force of the new weapon shocked the world. Between them the two bombs are thought to have caused more than 200,000 civilian deaths, perhaps half instantly and half in the fallout.

Atomic explosion over Nagasaki, April 9, 1945

The morality of the attacks are still disputed. Strategically, it saved the lives of US soldiers and served as a demonstration of American power, improving the US position in negotiations over the postwar world order.

| Sep 27, 1940 | Tripartite Pact | Apr 14, 1941 | Soviet-Japanese neutrality pact | Dec 8, 1941 | US and Great Britain declare war on Japan |
| 1939 | US terminates trade agreement | 1941 | Ho Chi Minh founds Viet Minh | Dec 7, 1941 | Attack on Pearl Harbor |

■ East Asia's Path to Independence

The states of east Asia emerged from Japanese rule and decades of colonial domination following the end of World War II.

At the beginning of the 20th century, nearly all of east Asia was ruled by the western colonial powers: Indochina belonged to France; the Philippines to the United States; India, ❼ Malaya, and the northern part of Borneo to Great Britain; and today's Indonesia to the Netherlands. On the mainland, only ❽ Siam (present-day Thailand) was officially independent, but even it was subject to French and Japanese influence. Korea had been a Japanese protectorate since 1905.

Internally, resistance groups such as the communists, which appeared for the first time in Indonesia in 1914 and in other East Asian countries toward the end of the 1920s, posed little threat to the colonial rulers. Only in Burma in 1937 did domestic dissent achieve a significant goal, when an uprising of nationalist students triggered the country's breaking away from the British Indian empire, and Burma was granted partial autonomy.

Japan's plans for a Greater East Asia Co-Prosperity Sphere im-

7
Japanese inspect a captured British plane, Malaya, 1941

plied driving the Europeans out of the region, which all east Asian resistance groups welcomed in principle. But it also promoted a split in the anticolonial resistance. Left-wing groups did not want to be ruled by a Japanese divine emperor and formed anti-Japanese communist people's armies, for example, in the Philippines and Malaya. In contrast, nationalists hoped that a pro-Japanese position would help them gain national sovereignty more quickly. A ❾ volunteer army in

Burma supported the Japanese, and there was a similar body in India. The reaction in present-day Vietnam was different. When Japan occupied the eastern part of the country in 1941, the nationalists and communists joined together against the Japanese under the leadership of Ho Chi Minh in the League for the Independence of Vietnam, the ❿ Viet Minh.

Following Japan's surrender in 1945, the colonial powers gradually withdrew from the region. Vietnam, Korea, the Philippines, Indonesia, Cambodia, Laos, and Burma proclaimed themselves sovereign states by the end of the 1940s. Malaya gained independence only in 1957. The humiliating loss of British Singapore and Hong Kong greatly reduced the power and prestige of the colonialist powers in southeast Asia.

Ho Chi Minh

Ho Chi Minh ("He who enlightens") was the charismatic leader of the Vietnamese liberation movement and in 1945 became the first president of the Democratic Republic of Vietnam. In the 1960s he was the figurehead of the Vietnamese struggle against the military intervention of the United States. Ho was born in 1890 in Annam, went to France in 1917, and was a founding member of the Communist Party there. After his deportation to Moscow in 1923, he became the Comintern functionary in Southeast Asia. An advisor to the Chinese Kuomintang troops in the Soviet Union in 1938, he returned to his homeland only after the Japanese invasion in 1941.

Ho Chi Minh, ca. 1960

8
Bangkok, capital of Siam, ca. 1930

9
Japanese soldiers in Burma, 1944

10
Ho Chi Minh (foreground) with Viet Minh forces, 1950

Jun 3–7, 1942	Battle of Midway	**Aug 6 and 9, 1945**	US air force drops atom bombs on Hiroshima and Nagasaki
Jan 2, 1942	Manila occupied	**Jun 1944**	Naval battle at Saipan
		Sep 2, 1945	Democratic Republic of Vietnam constituted

1

THE BRITISH COMMONWEALTH: EMANCIPATION OF THE BRITISH COLONIES 1914–1945

Step by step, in the wake of strengthened and ever more vocal national movements, the colonies of the British global empire were granted independence. At first they became self-governing dominions of the British Empire, following which the colonies became completely autonomous in 1931 under the Statute of Westminster. A community of equal and sovereign states under the protection of the British crown, the ❶ British Commonwealth took the place of the British Empire.

Crown of George V, Emperor of India, 1910

■ Dominion: The Preliminary Stage to Independence

Great Britain granted numerous colonies domestic self-rule as "dominions" at the beginning of the 20th century, yet it was not until 1931 that they officially gained complete independence.

2

London Conference, 1926

4

Arthur James Balfour, British foreign secretary

(King George V photo caption:) **3** King George V

In 1867, Canada became the first British crown colony to be granted independence. It was followed in the early 20th century by Australia, New Zealand, Newfoundland, the South African Union—composed of Cape Province, Natal, Transvaal, and the Orange Free State—and, in 1922, Ireland. As dominions, they became sovereign nations with self–rule according to international law. But the bond with Great Britain, particularly in issues of world and security policies, stayed intact, and

the ❸ British monarch remained the formal head of state. When Britain declared war on Germany in 1914, the ❺ dominions were automatically also at war. After the war, however, they defended themselves against having British will imposed. In 1919, they individually signed the Treaty of Versailles and joined the League of Nations.

At the ❷ London Conference of 1926, the "Balfour Formula" promised the dominion's independence, which came into effect in 1931 with the Statute of Westminster. As "autonomous communities within the British Empire, equal in status," they were free of British influence in legislation, domestic and foreign policies but "united by a common allegiance to the Crown, and freely associated as members of

the British Commonwealth of Nations" (❹ Balfour). All of the sovereign colonies voluntarily joined the Commonwealth, from which they could withdraw. Australia joined in 1942 and New Zealand in 1947. Newfoundland was a special case. It was once again directly governed by Great Britain from the 1930s and became a part of Canada in 1949.

5

Canadian soldiers on the western front, 1916

The Dominion of South Africa

The Dominion of South Africa began setting the foundations for the future apartheid state in 1910. The British and the white "Afrikaners," descendents of Dutch colonists, were united in the suppression of the black Africans. For non-whites, ownership of land was allowed only within reservations, forms of employment were greatly restricted, and migration to urban areas and sexual relations with whites were prohibited. In 1912, black Africans founded the African National Congress as a common protest organization against injustice.

right: Durban, in the South African province of Natal, ca. 1910
left: Mausoleum of John Langalibalele Dube, ANC founder, Inanda, Natal

■ The Disintegration of the British Empire

At the end of World War I, the British Empire was larger than ever before. But financial burden and powerful independence movements in the colonies brought the empire to a gradual collapse after World War II.

The British Empire expanded one last time after the First World War. Great Britain took over the League of Nations mandates of Palestine, Iraq, and the former German colony of ❻ Tanganyika. It also gained influence over New Guinea and Namibia because the former was governed by the British dominions of Australia, the latter by South Africa.

In terms of actual control, however, British power was becoming ever weaker in the re-

7
Australian soldiers in the service of the British crown, Burma, 1944

6
Young Bantu women, 1936

gions it controlled. The motherland was suffering under a difficult economic crisis and thus reduced funds and the size of its administration and military in the colonies. In addition, after ❽ World War I the African and Asian peoples demanded, if not complete ❿ independence, at

least more self-determination and an end to denigration at the hands of white Britons. In contrast to the dominions that had been granted independence and could decide whether or not they wanted to become members of the newly founded British Commonwealth, the remaining colonies

were compelled to do so. Britain's situation worsened further after ❼ World War II. Financial problems and increasingly powerful movements aiming for ❾ independence in the colonies accelerated the breakup of the empire. In 1947, India, the most important of the British colonies, shook off British rule. Burma and ⓫ Ceylon followed in 1948. The phase of decolonization could not be halted.

8
Indian soldiers, 1914

Crown colonies

The British world empire possessed Crown colonies on every continent except Antarctica after 1918. In Asia, these included India, Burma, Malaya, North Borneo, British New Guinea, and Sarawak. In Africa—apart from the special status of Egypt—there were the Gold Coast (Ghana), Sudan, St. Helena, Nigeria, British Somaliland (Somalia), Sierra Leone, Aden, British East Africa (Tanzania, Uganda, and Kenya), and Gambia. In the Americas, British Guyana, British Honduras, and the islands of Barbados, Jamaica, Bermuda, and the Bahamas were all British possessions.

9
Independence negotiations between the British viceroy Lord Mountbatten and the leader of the Indian Muslim League, Mohammed Ali Jinnah (right), 1947

10
Gandhi when he was an activist in South Africa, 1913

Luxury hotel in Aden, ca. 1890

11
Tea harvesting in Ceylon

AFRICA UNDER COLONIAL RULE THROUGH 1939

With the exceptions of Ethiopia and Liberia, Africa was completely divided up among the European colonial powers by the end of the 19th century. In World War I, German colonial masters were replaced by British, ❶ French, or Belgian rulers. The same thing happened to the Italian colonies in World War II. The South African Union had been granted the status of a dominion since 1910, and Egypt gained limited sovereignty in 1922. Only after World War II did liberation movements start to organize in the rest of Africa.

1 Frenchman with natives from Cameroon, ca.1917

■ Africa in the First World War

Germany lost its African colonies with its defeat in World War I. They were placed under mandates by the League of Nations in 1920 although still administered as colonies.

The African war zones during World War I were Egypt and particularly the German colonies. The British, French, and Belgians and their colonial troops were able rapidly to conquer Togo, Cameroon, and ❺ Southwest Africa. Only in German East Africa (present-day Tanzania) was the ❷ Askari colonial force under General von Lettow-Vorbeck able to

defend the colony through the end of the war; the army there ceased hostilities only after receiving explicit instructions to do so from Berlin in November 1918.

The colonial powers in World War I relied on troops from the native peoples. Segregated from the white soldiers and paid much less, almost half a million Africans fought on the side of the ❸ French, for example; Senegalese and Moroccan tirailleurs were also deployed in ❹ Europe. The desire for independence increased after the end of the war. In the eyes of the returning soldiers, the colonists had morally discredited themselves in the "war of the white tribes." The reinforcement of

2 Askari colonial forces fighting on the side of Germany in World War I

the peoples' right to self-determination through the Treaty of Versailles initiated the trend toward decolonization.

New forms of colonial rule represented a first step toward formal emancipation of the colonies. In 1920 the former German colonies were placed under the mandate of the League of Nations. This theoretically imposed limits on the powers of the colonial administrators, as they now had to answer to a larger and officially organized international public. In practice, however, little changed for the African people; they remained at the mercy of European power interests.

3 Colonial troops in the service of France

4 African soldiers of the French Army fighting at the western front near Verdun during World War II

5 Farmers in southwest Africa

Liberia

How notions of colonists' superiority—which stemmed from the racism of European and American colonists—became embedded in African politics can be seen in the case of Liberia. It was founded as an American colony for the settlement of free slaves and had been a republic since 1847. According to the constitution, only American immigrants had civil rights— the native population was treated as slaves. The settlers' feeling of superiority was similar to that of the white settlers in other colonies. It was not until the 1940s, under President William V. S. Tubman, that native Africans were granted the vote.

President William Tubman

African Economic Development

The world economic depression of 1929 abruptly ended Africa's economic upswing. World War II later placed more instruments of power in the hands of the colonies.

World War I had proven to the warring colonial powers the extent of Africa's economic potential and its importance in supplying both raw materials and manpower for the war effort. The same powers then began the systematic economic development and exploitation of the continent by developing its ❼ infrastructure following the war. A ❻ railroad network spanning all of Africa, corresponding almost to that of the present day, had been built by the end of the 1920s.

6 Oldest steam engine of the Zambesi Sawmill Railway, built 1925

8 Worker in a copper factory in the Belgian Congo

The global economic depression of the 1930s interrupted the modernization push that had meant relative prosperity for the inhabitants. European import goods were suddenly unaffordable, and about half of the African wage earners lost their jobs. The Africans stood helpless in the face of these developments, while the white colonial authorities attempted to stabilize profits through tax increases, among other things. Many Africans tried to earn their living in urban

❽ industrial areas, thus beginning the expansion of the cities; in the countryside, there was a return to older forms of exchange such as bartering.

The outbreak of World War II in 1939 improved material conditions and brought a noticeable economic improvement. As the white population for the most part had to return to their homelands for military service and the need for raw materials increased, many new jobs were created. This strengthened the influence of the indigenous population. Europe's dependency on a functioning colonial economy presented the Africans with the opportunity to obtain pay increases and better working conditions. In 1940 Great Britain passed the Colonial Welfare Act, with the goal of preventing further strikes in the areas they controlled. In 1951, it became the first colonial power after the war to grant an African state—❾ Libya—sovereignty, thereby launching a wave of more or less violent decolonization.

7 Distribution of radio stations over the African continent, 1936

The Pan-African Movement

The importance of the pan-African movement grew after World War II. Active participation in the war and the experience of being economically indispensable reinforced the self-confidence of the Africans in re-

Traditional and modern methods for crossing the desert, 1911

lation to the colonial powers, as they realized the reliance of their colonial masters on their countries and resources. Serious efforts toward autonomy were still absent, however; past Western influences were still too strong for a return to the traditional order, yet too weak for the formation of national states along the European model.

Independence movement in Senegal, 1947

9 Modern housing estate for Italian colonists in Tripoli, Libya, 1935

ETHIOPIA AND EGYPT: BETWEEN SUBJUGATION AND INDEPENDENCE

UNTIL 1945

Ethiopia and ❶ Egypt hold a special position in Africa's colonial history. Egypt had been occupied by the British since 1882 and was formally tied to the Ottoman Empire until 1916. However, it was never fully subjugated and was able to bring about the withdrawal of the British army in 1936. Ethiopia (known as Abyssinia before the First World War) was conquered in a brutal campaign by Mussolini's army but was restored to independence in 1941.

1

US transport plane delivering supplies to the Allied troops in Egypt, 1943

■ Egypt: Between Sovereignty and British Custodianship

Egypt was an important field of operations for the British military in both world wars. Even as a sovereign state, it was bound to Britain in World War II through alliance commitments, though some nationalists looked to the Axis powers for help in ending British influence.

In 1882, British troops occupied Egypt and took control of the country, albeit without terminating its official status as part of the Ottoman Empire. Widespread reforms were carried out under the leadership of Sir Evelyn Baring. At the outbreak of World War I, however, Great Britain officially declared Egypt a protectorate, imposing martial law and cutting the last ties to the Ottomans.

3   Memorial to Saghlul Pasha, founder of the Wafd party, Alexandria

British troops halted an Ottoman-German offensive against the Suez Canal in 1914 and then used Egypt as a base for attacks on Syria and Palestine.

In 1919, Great Britain prohibited the participation of the Egyptian nationalist ❸ Wafd party in the Versailles conferences, resulting in fierce strikes and unrest that were answered with arrests and hangings. In response, the British granted the country independence in

1922, while still maintaining its military presence and remaining in charge of foreign affairs in order to protect their own interests. When ❷ King Fuad I died in 1936, Great Britain reaffirmed Egypt's sovereignty in an alliance treaty and withdrew its troops, except from the Suez Canal zone. It insisted, however, on the right of intervention in case of war, and so Egypt was once again occupied during World War II and used as a military base in fighting the Italo-German alliance. The ❻ British army defeated German forces in 1942 at El Alamein and forced a withdrawal to Libya. Egypt's ❹ King Farouk I was forced to replace his pro-Axis government with a pro-British one. It was not until 1945 that Egypt officially declared war on Germany. With the exception of their forces securing

2   King Fuad I

the ❺ Suez canal, the British once again withdrew from the country in 1946 but still retained explicit control of Sudan.

4

King Farouk I at his wedding, 1938

6

Tank division of the Anglo-Egyptian Army, mobilized to counter the Italian threat in Ethiopia, 1940

5

The Suez Canal, a key waterway for international trade, 1940

| 1882 | British occupation of Egypt | Oct 1896 | Treaty of Addis Ababa | 1930 | Haile Selassie I enthroned | Oct 1935 | Italy invades Ethiopia |
| 1894 | Italian invasion of Abyssinia | | 1922 | Egypt gains independence | 1930 | Ethiopia joins League of Nations |

■ Ethiopia under Haile Selassie I

Due to its modern state structure, Ethiopia was long able to maintain its independence. Italy occupied the country only between 1936 and 1941.

7 Italian infantry during the invasion of Ethiopia, 1935

8 Haile Selassie wearing the imperial robes, 1930

The Treaty of Addis Ababa in October 1896, following the uprising under Emperor Menelik of Shoa, ensured the independence of Ethiopia—then still known as Abyssinia—for 40 years, while Eritrea remained under Italian control. Ethiopia held fast to its course of modernization even after the death of Menelik II in 1913. His grandson Lij Yasu was deposed by public proclamation and succeeded by Menelik's daughter. Ras Tafari Makonnen became king in 1928 and two years later was enthroned as emperor under the name ❽ Haile Selassie I. He enshrined suffrage and civil rights in a new constitution and brought his country into the League of Nations in 1930. No international intervention took place, however, when Italy seized control of ❼, ❿ Ethiopia under the Fascist leadership of Benito Mussolini. In October 1934, Italy manufactured a frontier incident and used it as a justification for war after Ethiopia refused impossible conditions. From October 1935 until May 1936, Italy fought a campaign with modern aircraft, tanks and chemical weapons against Ethiopian cavalry, which provoked an international scandal.

On May 5, 1936, Italian troops captured the capital Addis Ababa. The emperor was forced into exile in London, and Ethiopia was combined with Eritrea and Italian Somaliland to form the colony of Italian East Africa. The people bitterly resisted the invaders in a ❾ guerrilla war and in 1940 supported the British offensive against the Italians in Africa. Haile Selassie returned from exile and retook the throne, ruling up until 1974.

9 Ethiopians fight guerrilla war, 1941

10 Ethiopian tribal chief, captured by Italian soldiers, 1936

The Rastafarians

The Rastafarians are members of a religion created after the crowning of Haile Selassie (Ras Tafari). They believe him to be the one true god. Particularly popular in the Caribbean region, the Rastafarian movement considers its members to be the descendents of the Ethiopian kings from the line of Solomon and the Queen of Sheba. It combines social demands with the aspiration to return to Africa. Its members are supposed to pursue natural lifetyles, and they wear their hair in dreadlocks. The Rastafarians are best known for reggae music, which developed in the 1940s and gained global popularity.

King Solomon receives the Queen of Sheba

May 5, 1936 Italians occupy Addis Ababa	**1941** Ethiopia liberated	**Feb 1945** Egypt declares war on Germany
1936 British army withdraws from Egypt	**Dec 1940** British reoccupy Egypt	**Oct 1942** Battle of El-Alamein

1

EUPHORIA AND DEPRESSION: THE US BETWEEN THE WARS 1917–1945

Following the end of World War I, the United States returned to its traditional isolationism. This period saw the beginning of an economic ❶ boom, but blind faith in progress led to euphoric overconfidence in the financial markets. When the speculation bubble burst in the stock market crash of 1929, the entire world economy collapsed. The interventionist New Deal policies of Franklin Delano Roosevelt's government alleviated many of the effects of the Great Depression. In 1939, the officially neutral United States began de facto support of England in the war against the Axis powers, and in 1941, it officially entered the war.

Building the Empire State Building, built 1930–1932

■ Isolationism and Prosperity

The United States withdrew from Europe after the First World War. Technical progress and spectacular growth rates in the "Roaring Twenties" made the increase in general prosperity seem as if it would never end.

After a long period of hesitation, the United States under President Woodrow Wilson entered World War I in 1917 with the goal of bringing longterm peace to Europe. After the victory over the Central Powers, Wilson succeeded in having the formation of a League of Nations, intended to help secure future world peace, included in the Treaty of Versailles. The US Senate, however, was concerned about potential restrictions on American foreign policy. Wilson, who suffered a stroke while campaigning for the treaty in 1919, was unable to avoid the Senate's refusal in 1920 to ratify the Versailles Treaty and, by extension, the United States' entry

2

The luxury lifestyle: a couple standing in front of their limousine, ca. 1935

into the League of Nations. His successor, ❺ Warren G. Harding, concluded separate peace agreements with the former war enemies in 1921. Until well into the 1930s, the principle of nonintervention in European conflicts remained the determinant of US foreign policy.

Domestically, rapid industrial modernization produced a prospering economy and increasing affluence within the population. Construction and the automobile industry particularly boomed. Efficient production me-

3

Arrest of women wearing too-revealing bathing suits, New Jersey, 1920

thods, reductions in prices, and rising incomes for the first time allowed the development of a consumer society, with new forms of mass entertainment such as radio, movies, and sports. Glittering parties, ❷ limousines, and the newly rich "self-made men" shaped the glamorous image of the ❻ Roaring Twenties.

In contrast, social ❸ conservatism and xenophobia molded the intellectual climate, particularly in rural America. The most visible expression was Prohibition. The racist ❹ Ku Klux Klan gained in popularity, particularly in the South.

4

Members of the Ku Klux Klan at a meeting, 1940

Prohibition

In 1920, Prohibition—a ban on the consumption and sale of alcohol—became a federal law. Thereupon, however, smuggling and the trade in privately distilled ("bootleg") liquor immediately began to flourish, and alcohol continued to be dispensed in illegal bars known as "speakeasies." In 1933, the law was repealed.

Hiding alcohol during prohibition: a candlestick is used to conceal an alcohol bottle, ca. 1926

5

Warren Gamaliel Harding, 1923

6 Two ladies wearing 1920s Charleston dresses

The World Economic Crisis and Entrance into the War

The American stock market crash in 1929 sparked a worldwide economic crisis that surpassed all previous recessions. The United States entered World War II under the leadership of President Roosevelt.

The flourishing economy of the 1920s led to excessive investment and stock buying. When in October 1929 the overextension became clear, ❽ prices on the New York Stock Exchange plummeted. The crash in prices led to the bankruptcy of a third of all American banks. Mortgages were foreclosed and farmers ruined. Lack of capital and companies going out of business resulted in the collapse of industrial production and the domestic market. The gross national product, private incomes, and foreign trade shrank to half their previous size by 1933. The result was record ❼ unemployment. By 1933, almost 15 million Americans had lost their jobs.

7

An unemployed man with a banner demanding work rather than charity, Detroit 1932

8

Investors observe the share prices at the stock market, 1929

9

After the aerial attack by the Japanese: wrecked ships in the port of Pearl Harbor, December 7, 1941

The crisis rapidly spread to the European nations due to the global nature of the economic network. Europe, which had become the United States' largest debtor after World War I, had financed its postwar upswing with American credit. This was no longer available after 1929, causing bankruptcies throughout Europe as well, and high unemployment followed, particularly in industrialized countries such as

Germany. Interrelated drops in prices and production eventually led to a worldwide recession that reached its low point in 1932.

While the crisis strengthened antidemocratic forces, particularly in Germany, US President ❿ Franklin Roosevelt began to build up a welfare state after his election in 1932. His "New Deal" policies fought unemployment through government employment programs and antipoverty efforts and set up the first stages of a social safety-net system with the ⓫ Social Security Act. But the crisis was reversed primarily by the national armaments program of 1938.

Although the United States had established its neutrality in 1935, in

the face of German power politics Roosevelt began to speak in 1937 of a future fight for survival between democracy and dictatorship. The defense budget was increased in 1938 and a military draft was introduced in 1940. Once war broke out in Europe in 1939, the United States officially reaffirmed its neutrality but, from 1940 on, supported especially Great Britain with arms deliveries for the war being waged against

the Axis powers.

After the Japanese attack on the US fleet at ❾ Pearl Harbor in December 1941, the United States entered the war, taking over the leadership of the alliance against the Axis. Its immense resources of manpower and materials proved decisive for the Allied victory in 1945. Roosevelt, who against political tradition was elected president for third and fourth terms, died on April 12, 1945, before the end of the war.

10

President Roosevelt in the Oval Office at the White House, Washington, 1936

11

Postmen in New York submit requests for social security, 1935

LATIN AMERICA 1914–1945

Due to a booming export economy after World War I, ❶ Latin America experienced a period of relative domestic stability. However, social tension resulting from the world economic depression in the 1930s brought authoritarian regimes backed by the military to power almost everywhere. These regimes gained popularity due to their social reforms. In international affairs, almost all the Latin American states proclaimed solidarity with the United States and declared war on Germany and Japan during World War II.

"Christ the Redeemer" statue in Rio de Janeiro, built in 1931

■ Pan-Americanism and Economic Strength

In the 1920s, the economic strength and domestic stability of the Latin American countries led to greater equality with the booming United States.

After the civil wars and coup attempts of the initial phase of independence, the Latin American countries achieved internal consolidation after the 1880s. Politically, from the start of World War I, European influence in Latin America began to weaken, while US supremacy gradually increased. The Pan-American Union, an organization of all American states, was founded in 1889 for the promotion of mutual solidarity, but it soon developed into an instrument through which the United States could influence the economies and politics of the nations to the south. Domestic tension—

such as the general strike in Buenos Aires in 1919, uprisings in Brazil in 1924, and the brief intermezzo of a military dictatorship in Chile in 1924–1925—remained the exception during the general peace of the interwar period.

The opening of the hemisphere to the world market played an essential role in this stabilization. The thriving ❷ export of raw materials created high growth rates through the end of the 1920s, and

US President Franklin D. Roosevelt, 1936

the ❹, ❺ building industry flourished as well. As everywhere else, though, the world economic crisis would abruptly end the economic growth and cause political turmoil.

The economic successes of the 1920s enabled the Latin American states to gain more equality in the Pan-American Union. At a conference in Santiago, Chile, the Latin American countries were able to achieve the election of the chairman of the Pan-American Union's administrative council; until then, the US secretary of state had held this office. ❸ President Roosevelt adopted the "Good Neighbor" policy in 1930, which aimed to combine US claims to hemispheric leadership with mutual respect and solidarity on both sides. In 1933, the United States signed a resolution that banned intervention in the domestic affairs of other American nations. American troops were withdrawn from the Dominican Republic, Haiti, and Nicaragua. Faced with the outbreak of war in Europe in 1939, a common

Selecting coffee beans, Brazil

defense against foreign threats took priority at the Pan-American Union conference in 1940 in Havana. When the United States declared war on Japan and Germany on December 11, 1941, the Central and South American nations entered the war one after another.

Salvador de Bahia, Brazil: elevator connecting upper and lower city, built in 1930, photo, 2004

Copacabana in Rio de Janeiro, 1935

| 1889–1890 | Founding of the Pan-American Union | 1924 | Rebellion in Brazil | Oct 24, 1930 | Putsch by General Vargas in Brazil |
| 1919 | General strike in Buenos Aires | 1924–25 | Military dictatorship in Chile | | |

Latin America's Crisis during the Depression

In Latin America, social unrest resulting from the world economic depression brought military-supported dictatorships to power during the 1930s. In Brazil, Getúlio Vargas established a personal dictatorship that combined subjugation with social charity.

The global economic crisis hit the ❽ export-dependent economies of Latin America especially hard and led to an economic breakdown. As a result, political uprisings took place everywhere. Dictatorships, mostly of military origin, came to power promising to create jobs and fight ❻, ❾ poverty.

Many Latin American states attempted to reduce their dependency on foreign trade and investments through government-controlled economic policies. Consumer goods were to be produced domestically and the corresponding industries set up. Brazil exemplified this model. ❼ Getúlio Vargas, a failed candidate at the 1929 elections, led a revolt in 1930 in the wake of the world economic depression. He

7

General Getúlio Donelles Vargas

instituted wide administrative reforms. After defeating the 1932 insurrection in Sao Paulo, his status was legitimized by an election in 1934, and he then governed from

6

Slum area in Buenos Aires, Argentina

8

A boy harvesting coconuts, 1935

1937 with dictatorial authority, alternately supported by the communists and the fascists. Attempts to overthrow him from both sides were suppressed. Following Portugal's example, Vargas established an authoritarian state he called the "New State" (*Estado Novo*), in which the individual person or minority factions were subordinate to the national whole. Social conflicts were to be regulated not by a "class struggle" but by cooperation between institutions and organizations. Despite the authoritarianism, the reforms made Vargas popular, particularly among the poor. Trade unions were allowed, and pension and health insurance schemes were set up. The state also guaranteed a minimum wage.

Although at the outset of the Second World War Vargas declared himself favorably disposed towards the Axis, after the United States declared war, in 1942, Brazil entered the war on the side of the anti-Hitler coalition, and in 1944 it sent troops to Europe—the only Latin American country to do so. An expeditionary corps of more than 25,000 men fought on the Italian front until the end of the war. Nevertheless, after the defeat of Hitler by the democracies, Vargas's position as dictator became unsustainable. Vargas was ousted by the military in

1945, yet, as a result of his enduring popularity, he was elected president once again in a free election in 1950. However, political scandal led him to commit suicide in 1954.

Argentina

Several generals and conservative politicians including Uriburu and Justo, backed by the armed forces, came to power in Argentina in the 1930s, but they were unable to solve the economic problems or control the growing domestic radicalism. The country doggedly avoided entering the war in favor of the Allies and even occasionally indirectly supported the Axis powers. The Army, however, was very much in favor of Germany, and it rebelled in 1943: Colonel Juan Domingo Perón, vice president and war minister since 1943 and later president (1946-1955, 1973-1974) granted German secret agents asylum in Argentina.

President Perón with his wife Evita in Buenos Aires, 1952

Entry papers of Josef Mengele, a doctor in the concentration camp of Auschwitz, who settled in Argentina in 1945 under a false name

9

A boy offering a captured sloth for sale, 1935

1

THE SECOND WORLD WAR 1939–1945

With its attack on Poland in September 1939, the German Nazi regime under Hitler initiated the most devastating military conflict in world history to date. Before the unconditional surrender of Germany and Japan in 1945, World War II claimed the lives of some 62 million people. The heavily ❶ ideological aspect of the war led to incomprehensible crimes against humanity. World War II fundamentally altered the international political situation. The victorious United States and the Soviet Union became the leading world powers.

Allied forces propaganda poster, 1943

■ Blitzkrieg: German Victories up to 1940

A heavily armed Germany controlled almost the entire European mainland in 1940. It failed to conquer only Great Britain.

Germany's invasion of Poland on September 1, 1939, ignited the Second World War. France and Great Britain declared war on Germany, although they did not actively intervene in the Eastern European conflict. Poland's army, which in part still operated with cavalry units, was ❹ no match for the Wehrmacht and Luftwaffe. Poland capitulated after the bombing of Warsaw on October 6. In accordance with the secret agreement with Germany, ❺ Soviet troops invaded Poland from the east on September 17 and immediately integrated the eastern parts of the country into the Soviet Union. Germany annexed areas in northern and southern Poland and from the remainder formed the ❷ "General Government of Poland," which would become an area in which Nazi racial fanaticism would play out.

In order to cut Germany off from raw material sources in Scandinavia at the beginning of the war, the British ❻ Royal Navy blockaded the German merchant marine traffic in the Baltic Sea. A German–British "race to Scandinavia" began in April 1940. Germany occupied Denmark without resistance. Norway was conquered by June, despite heavy British and Norwegian resistance and serious losses on the part of the German navy. Sweden was forced into cooperation with Germany.

Starting on May 10, 1940, German troops rapidly invaded the Netherlands, Belgium, and Luxembourg. Even France could not put up sufficient resistance to the German blitzkrieg tactics; it surrendered on June 22. Three-fifths of France was occupied by Germany; in the southern part of the country, the ❸ pro-German Vichy government was created.

In order to free up resources for his *Lebensraum* ("living space") policies against the Soviet Union, Hitler hoped for a peace settlement with Great Britain. When Britain refused to surrender, German ❼ air attacks began in August 1940 to prepare the island for invasion. After heavy losses against the Royal Air Force, they were terminated in October.

4

Polish war prisoners, September 1940

5

German and Russian soldiers allied in Poland, 1939

6

British submarine returning from Norwegian waters, 1940

Stamp of the General Government, 1941
2

3

Vichy, le 29 août 1940.
Je sais que c'est avec vous que la France redeviendra ce qu'elle aurait toujours dû rester.

Ph. Pétain

Youth organization established under Pétain, similar to the Hitler Youth, 1941

"Blitzkrieg"

The swift, initial successes of the German army are known as the blitzkrieg ("lightning war"). Sudden, unexpected, coordinated assaults by the combined German armed forces did not give the enemy time to organize a stable defense and thus won them many victories.

7

German fighters approaching England, 1940

Sep 1, 1939	German invasion of Poland	starting Sep 27, 1939	Bombardment of Warsaw	Apr 9, 1940	Occupation of Denmark
Sep 17, 1939	Soviet attack on Poland	Oct 6, 1939	Capitulation of Poland	Apr 9–Jun 10, 1940	Occupation of Norway

■ The Balkan Campaign and the War in North Africa (1941–43)

The failed attempts at conquest by its alliance partner Italy forced Germany into costly campaigns in the Balkans and Africa.

8 Hungarian artillery, 1941

9 Training German *Luftwaffe* troops in Romania, 1940

10 Romanian refinery goes up in flames following British bombardment, 1943

11 Landing of German paratroopers on the Greek island Crete, 1940

Germany, Italy, and Japan joined together in the Tripartite Pact on September 27, 1940, to form the Axis. However, Japan and Italy pursued their war aims in "parallel wars." **9** Romania and **8** Hungary joined the Axis powers in 1940 and Bulgaria in 1941.

Italy under Mussolini aspired to domination of the complete Mediterranean region, which Mussolini resolved Italy should control rather than Great Britain, as well as conquests in Africa, but it failed in its offensives. This repeatedly obliged its alliance partner Germany to supply military support. Deployment on these additional fronts weakened the **10** German army and with it the entire military position of the Axis powers.

In October 1940, Italy attacked Greece, which was supported by Great Britain, from its province Albania, but British troops forced the Italians back into Albania. In order to restore the reputation of the Axis powers, secure access to Romanian oil wells, and shield the planned German attack on the Soviet Union from a threat from the flank, Hitler decided in April 1941 on a **11** Balkan campaign, resulting in the rapid surrender of the armed forces of Yugoslavia and Greece. Yugoslavia was crushed, and British troops withdrew from Greek territories.

Another failed Italian offensive against British-dominated Egypt in 1940, which resulted in the annihilation of the Italian units in Libya, forced Germany to intervene militarily in North Africa. The highly efficient German Africa Corps under General Erwin Rommel forced the British out of Libya and back to the Egyptian border between February and April 1941. In January 1942, German tanks began to move into the **12** Egyptian desert in an advance which, had it been successful, would have brought the Germans to the oil fields of Iraq, but they were halted at the Battle of El Alamein. By February 1943, a **13** British counter-offensive had pushed the Germans back all the way to Tunisia. The fighting in Africa ended on May 13, 1943, with the capitulation of the German-Italian armies.

Erwin Rommel

Erwin Rommel, 1942

Erwin Rommel, the "Desert Fox," was respected even by his foes for his strategic military skills. After he had ordered the retreat out of El Alamein against Hitler's orders, he was transferred to the French front. Although he was not actively involved in the putsch attempt against Hitler, he sympathized with the military resistance movement and, as a long-time confidant of Hitler, urged him to initiate peace negotiations in 1944. Following the failed assassination attempt of July 20, 1944, he was branded a traitor and forced to commit suicide.

12 Motorcycle soldiers during the war in the North African desert, 1942

13 General Bernard Law Montgomery, commander-in-chief of the British troops in North Africa, 1942

| **May 10, 1940** | Beginning of the Western Campaign | **from Aug 1940** | Air "Battle of Britian" | **May 13, 1943** | Capitulation of the Axis powers in Africa |
| **Jun 22, 1940** | Capitulation of France | **Sep 2, 1940** | Tripartite Pact | **April 1941** | Beginning of the Balkan Campaign |

■ Operation Barbarossa: The German invasion of the Soviet Union

The German attack on the Soviet Union was initially devastating and forced the Russians to withdraw all the way to Moscow in the winter of 1941. Despite appalling casualties suffered in the Battle of Stalingrad in 1942–1943, the Red Army managed to break out and surround the German besieging forces. This victory marked a crucial turning point in the war against Nazi Germany.

Hitler had planned his ❷ ideological "main war" against the Soviet Union since the summer of 1940. In violation of the German-Soviet nonaggression pact, Operation Barbarossa began on June 22, 1941. A vast army of more than three million soldiers, 3,500 tanks, and 2,000 aircraft invaded the Soviet Union.

As Stalin had not been expecting a German attack at that point in time and the ❶ arming and reorganization of his army was not yet complete, it seemed that the German intention of crushing the Soviet military within a few weeks was realistic. By encircling the Soviet armed forces, the Germans were able to obliterate a significant proportion of them, and by October they had reached as far as Moscow.

Workers in the Soviet armaments industry, 1941

With all his energy, Stalin in the meantime had organized his defenses. A considerable part of the armament industry was moved east, and areas abandoned to the invaders were first stripped of all resources. ❹ Appeals to patriotism—the war became known as "the Great Fatherland War"—and revulsion at the savagery of the occupation forces toward civilians rallied the Russian people. The sheer size and boundless resources of the country inevitably worked in their favor. Thanks to the neutrality pact signed with Japan in 1941, Stalin was able to redeploy troops from the Far East to the Moscow front. Meanwhile, Ger-

man operations were slowed by extreme weather conditions and the vast distances; the advance on Moscow became bogged down in mud. The Germans were not prepared for the onset of the Russian ❺ winter with −40°F (−40°C) temperatures. Despite a collection drive for winter clothes among the German population, many soldiers froze to death. The German army retreated for the first time. The defeat outside Moscow shattered German plans for a quick victory. Supply difficulties and the long-term materiel superiority of the Soviets undermined German hopes for outright victory.

The real turning point was the Battle of Stalingrad in the winter of 1942–1943. After besieging the strategically important city in the summer of 1942, the 250,000 German soldiers were surrounded by Soviet troops. The entire army ultimately surrendered, following fighting that inflicted ❻ great losses on both sides and on the city's civilian population.

Nazi propaganda in Russian against "Jewish Bolshevism," 1942

Treatment of German ❼ prisoners matched that suffered by Soviets during the invasion. After the last German offensive at ❸ Kursk, the Red Army gradually regained lost territory and in January 1945 finally crossed over the eastern border into Germany.

Partisans place dynamite at a railway near Kursk, 1943

Soviet propaganda poster: "For our home! For Stalin!," 1944

German soldiers supplied by air at Stalingrad, 1942

Fallen German soldiers near Stalingrad, 1943

German prisoners of war near Stalingrad, 1943

■ Wars of Ideology and Extermination

During the campaign of conquest against the Soviet Union, the Nazi leadership put its genocidal program into action.

8 Ukranians murdered by the Soviet secret service, accused of collaborating with the Germans, 1942

In accordance with their ideology, the Nazi leaders planned the war against the Soviet Union not simply as a military operation but rather as a "war of two ideologies"—a "battle of extermination" against what they called the "Jewish-Bolshevik" system. The Polish campaign had already been presented as a struggle of the German "master race" against Slavic **9** "subhumans" and as a struggle for *Lebensraum* ("living space") in the East. Tragically, the invaders were initially greeted as liberators in many of the Soviet republics, such as **8** Ukraine, which were suffering under Stalin's regime. In a number of countries, notably Lithuania, anti-Semitism was very strong, and the local population eagerly joined in the massacres of Jews. Nevertheless,

from 1941 the German occupiers brought their own terror and destruction to the Soviet Union.

According to Hitler's personal instructions—the "Commissar's order" of June 6, 1941—all captured political leaders of the Red Army were to be shot immediately. This was primarily carried out by Heinrich Himmler's SS troops who followed in the wake of the army, but the army was also involved in Nazi extermination policies. "Ruthless measures" were also to be taken against Soviet prisoners of war. More than 3.3 million of them died from starva-

10 Soviet propaganda poster urges Russians to take revenge on Nazi Germany, 1943

tion, torture, execution, or slave labor.

In June 1941, four SS task forces followed the German army east and immediately began mass executions to eradicate "racial inferiors" systematically, particularly **11** Jews, who were rounded up, shot in fields and forests, and buried in mass graves which they themselves had to dig. The organized mass murder of the European Jews had already started in Poland.

The "General Plan East" of 1942 resulted in the decimation of the Slavic peoples through the deportation and forced labor of about 30 million and the step-by step "Germanization" of Eastern Europe. The conquered regions of Byelorussia and Ukraine were placed under the Reich's Ministry for Occupied Eastern Territories. As a result of the triumphs of the Red Army, the realization of this plan became impossible.

The violence and inhumanity of the German occupiers radicalized the resistance on the Soviet side. Propaganda chief Ilya Ehrenburg called for violent **10** revenge. Many German prisoners of war died under wretched conditions. Soviet resistance groups also waged a **12** partisan war against the German occupiers. This in turn was crushed with violence as villages were razed and children were shot.

When the Red Army reached German soil in 1945, the Soviet soldiers treated the German

9 "The Subhuman," cover page of a Nazi propaganda magazine,1942

Ilya Ehrenburg

The Russian writer and journalist, born in Kiev, wrote in the journal Soviet News on March 8, 1945: "The only historic mission, as far as I can see it, is modestly and honorably to diminish the German population."

above: Ilya Grigoryevich Ehrenburg, 1935

population with the same brutality. The Soviet Union lost a total of 28 million people in World War II, of whom more than half were civilians, far more than any other country.

11 Execution of Jews by German troops, near Sniatyn, Poland 1941

12 Byelorussian partisan with his daughters, 1944

Sep 16–Nov 18, 1942	Conquest of a large part of Stalingrad by German troops	Nov 22, 1942	Encircling of German troops in Stalingrad
after Nov 19, 1942	Russian counteroffensive	Jan 31–Feb 2, 1943	Capitulation of Germany in Stalingrad

■ The Murder of the European Jewry

After unleashing the war, the Nazi leadership radicalized the persecution of Jews and introduced systematic mass murder in the occupied East.

The racist policies of the Nazis were spread all over Europe with the German military victories throughout the war until 1941. The isolated position of the Jews was intensified. By 1941, Jews in all of the German-controlled territories were forced to wear the ❶ yellow Star of David. The organized concentration and deportation of European Jews in Polish ghettos began in the summer of 1940. Many Jews were used as ❷ slave labor follo-

❶ Yellow Star of David from the Nazi period, 1941

wing the principle of "extermination through labor." Under the direction of SS leader ❹ Himmler, the number of concentration camps in the occupied territories increased to 22 by 1944, with 165 labor camps annexed to them.

In the summer of 1941, Hitler decided to have all Jews within the areas over which he had control murdered. Under the chairmanship of ❸ Reinhard Heydrich, high-ranking bureaucrats at the Wannsee Conference in Berlin in January 1942 defined the groups of persons to be killed and planned the cooperation of the departments most effective in the implementation of the murder operations.

The mass executions by the SS following the invasion of the Soviet Union marked the be-

ginning of the organized genocide to which almost the entire Jewish population of the Baltic states, Byelorussia, and Ukraine fell victim. Extermination camps, in which Jews were murdered primarily with poison gas, were erected in Poland from autumn 1941: Treblinka, Belzéc, Majdanek, Sobibor, and Chelmno. Millions of Jews were transported in cattle cars from all parts of Europe to these camps. The largest "death factory" was ❻, ❼ Auschwitz-Birkenau. At least a million persons died in its ❺ gas chambers alone. From arrival at Birkenau to completed cremation generally took no more than 90 minutes. When the Red Army was closing in at the end of 1944, the gassing was stopped and the camps disban-

Jewish slave labor in the Warsaw ghetto, ca. 1942

ded, yet innumerable people still died on the death marches to the West in the spring of 1945.

A total of about six million European Jews fell victim to Nazi racist fanaticism. At least 500,000 other "undesirables," primarily Sinti and Roma ("Gypsies"), were also ❽ murdered.

❸ Reinhard Heydrich, 1940

❹ SS leader Heinrich Himmler

❺ Gas chamber in Auschwitz

❻ Selection process at the ramp in Birkenau, 1944

The Concentration Camp Theresienstadt

Theresienstadt, 35 miles outside Prague, served as a stopover on the way to the extermination camps. In Nazi propaganda films, the world was shown peaceful life in a camp designed with the needs of the people in mind. Even the foreign representatives of the Red Cross who visited Theresienstadt were fooled.

Theresienstadt, today the Terezín Memorial

❼ Identification photos of a Hungarian boy in the concentration camp Auschwitz, 1942

❽ Corpses of prisoners in the concentration camp

| 1940 | Founding of the "Viking Division" | **Jul 31, 1941** | Hitler initiates the "Final Solution of the Jewish Question" |

| **Summer 1941** | Building of the concentration camp Auschwitz | **Sep 1941** | Jews forced to wear the Star of David |

■ Pillage and Persecution: The German Occupation Policy

Alongside the reordering in the East modeled on the Nazi ideology, economic exploitation characterized the German occupation policy in all the captured lands. More than a few locals cooperated with the Nazi occupiers.

In Poland, Denmark, Belgium, France, Yugoslavia, Greece, parts of the Soviet Union, and later Italy, Hungary, and Slovakia—in the whole area under German control or influence—the Nazi occupation policy was designed for, in addition to the extermination of the Jews, the exploitation of the countries for German war aims. Local ❾ industries and agriculture were made subordinate to the requirements of the German war economy. In order to meet the need for armament materials in the course of the war, Nazi leaders also increased the use of foreign workers in the homeland. At first,

10

Foreign worker from Eastern Europe, wearing the sign *Ost* ("East"), 1943

only prisoners of war were forcibly transported to Germany and coerced to work, but later it was ❸

civilians, too. German industry employed a total of around 12 million forced laborers during the war.

Whereas in the Eastern countries the subjugation of the Slavic peoples took priority, German administrators actively tried to enlist the ⓫ support of the local populations in the occupied countries of Western and Northern Europe. In these areas, the people mostly maintained a passive wait-and-see attitude; only a few put up any resistance, and there were some who were even willing to cooperate with the Germans.

9

German soldiers at the fish market in Copenhagen, 1940

The mass deportation of Jews from all over Europe to the extermination camps would not have been possible without collaborators. In addition, a total of 21 ⓬ foreign volunteer units provided support to the German army in its campaigns of conquest. The first were the Norwegians, Danes, Finns, Dutch, and Belgians who formed the "Viking Division" in 1940. The Germans received a particularly great influx of support at the beginning of the attack on the Soviet Union. A captured Russian lieutenant general, ⓮ Andrei Wlassow, built up an anti-Communist army of prisoners of war and Russian volunteers in 1942. When Germany's defeat became foreseeable, military support sank. Nevertheless, at the beginning of 1945, the volunteer units still comprised around a million non-Germans.

11

Poster promoting the international unit of the Waffen SS in France, 1941

12

Mohammedan volunteers as mountain soldiers of the Waffen SS, 1944

13

Poster for the recruitment of Dutch people for work in the agricultural sector in the East, 1942

14

General Andrei Wlassow inspecting his troops, 1944

■ The War Conferences of the Allies

Following the German attack on the Soviet Union, the United States, Great Britain, and the Soviet Union formed a common alliance against Germany. At several conferences, the "Big Three" decided upon the essential outline of a postwar European order.

The German attack on the Soviet Union in the summer of 1941 pushed the contrasting ideological and political power interests of the three great powers— the United States, Great Britain, and the Soviet Union—into the background in favor of an anti-Hitler coalition. In October they signed a mutual armament agreement. The United States had already obligated itself in March 1941 to support all enemies of Germany through the Lend-Lease Act. In January 1942, the United States and Britain created a ❶ joint military staff for strategic coordination of the war. Throughout the war convoys endured harsh weather conditions and extreme danger to transport valuable cargoes and supplies to Russian Murmansk. Despite the Japanese attack on

Atlantic Charter, 1941: Churchill talking to Roosevelt (left)

Pearl Harbor, US President Franklin Roosevelt and British Prime Minister Winston Churchill agreed that victory over Germany should be the first priority. In the ❷ Atlantic Charter of August 14, 1941, they announced "the end of Nazi tyranny" to the suppressed countries of Europe, proclaimed the right of free selfdetermination of nations, and declared the rejection of political and economic imperialism as the principles of the future postwar order. Tensions developed within the anti-Hitler coalition in 1942 because Stalin was worried that the territories in Poland and the Baltic region he had gained under the Nazi-Soviet pact would not be recognized and was aggravated by the continual postponement of a "second front" in the West that would relieve pressure on the Red Army. Stalin even explored the possibilities of peace talks with Hitler. However, he aligned himself with the demand by the United States and Britain for Germany's unconditional surrender

at the conference at ❹ Casablanca on January 24, 1943. In ❺ Tehran, at the first conference of the "Big Three" in late 1943, Roosevelt and Churchill took the successes of the Red Army into account and agreed to the "shifting west" in favor of the Soviet Union.

Shortly before Germany's final military defeat, the ❻ partition of Germany into four occupation zones with a common control council and with the participation of France was decided at ❸ Yalta in February 1945. Roosevelt and Churchill agreed to give Stalin a free hand in politically reor-

Churchill (left) and Dwight D. Eisenhower, commander in chief of the Allied Forces from 1944, March 1945

ganizing Eastern and Southern Europe in exchange for his aid in the war against Japan after Germany's capitulation. This paved the way for the foundation of the Communist "satellite states" of the Soviet empire after 1945.

Conference at Casablanca, 1943: Roosevelt and the French general Henri Giraud (right)

Conference at Tehran, 1943: Stalin, Roosevelt, Churchill (from left to right)

Conference at Yalta, 1945

Map showing the German occupation areas, 1945

| March 1941 | Lend-Lease Act | Aug 14, 1941 | Atlantic Charter | Dec 11, 1941 | Germany and Italy declare war on the US |
| 1941 | Unification of the three great powers in an anti-Hitler coalition | | | Dec 7 , 1941 | Japanese attack on Pearl Harbor |

■ The Advance of the Allies

The German army was forced to retreat on all fronts by the Allied advance from 1943. The successful Allied invasion of the French mainland in June 1944 finally brought the decisive turning point in favor of the Allies.

8 Aftermath of the attack on Pearl Harbor by the Japanese, 1941

As in World War I, the entry into the war of the materially superior United States and its huge manpower in the form of the **❼** US armament industry ensured the downfall of the Axis powers. The European conflict had become a worldwide war following the **❽** Japanese attack on the American naval base at Pearl Harbor and the subsequent declarations of war on the United States by Germany and Italy on December 11, 1941. The overwhelming strength of the Allies pressing against the German occupation

troops from the west and south from 1943 onward put them on the defensive and forced them to retreat back to the borders of Germany.

Following the German-Italian surrender in North Africa, the Allies invaded **⓫** Italy in July 1943. The Fascist government fell apart when Mussolini was overthrown on July 25, 1943. Italy's new government surrendered and then joined the Allies in the war against Germany. Beginning in 1943, the German allies Romania and Bulgaria had been forced suc-

11 US troops in Naples, 1945

cessively by the Allies to accept a cease-fire, and German troops had had to evacuate Greece and parts of Yugoslavia. Soviet troops stood outside East Prussia in August 1943.

The second front in the West that Stalin had demanded was established with the landing in

9 Omaha Beach, cemetery for American soldiers in Normandy

Normandy of an enormous **⓬** Allied force on June 6, 1944. In an immense military operation, 326,000 soldiers with more than 50,000 vehicles went ashore on the French Atlantic Coast within five days, suffering **❾** heavy losses in the process, as 10,000 aircraft secured the airspace above. On August 25, 1944, **❿** Paris was retaken with the support of French troops—who were evacuated to Great Britain before the German occupation in 1940—and the French resistance movement. In the East, the Red Army had advanced to the German border.

Nevertheless, the Germans continued to offer determined resistance despite the hopelessness of the situation. The Nazi leadership mobilized the population to "total war." Only the bloody conquest of all of Germany could end the war.

7 Poster promoting the recruitment of American women for industry, 1943

10 German soldiers surrender in Paris, August 25, 1944

D-Day

The Allied invasion in France was the largest military operation of the war and went down in history as "D-Day." The term does not stand for "Decision Day" or "Disembarkation Day," as is often assumed, but rather is the military convention for denoting the first day of a military operation. The capitalized D, being the first letter of "day," is used to emphasize this. The actual name of the operation was "Operation Overlord."

Eisenhower talking to soldiers of the Allied forces, June 1944

12 Landing of the Allied force in Normandy, June 6, 1944

| **Jul 1943** | Landing of the allies in Italy | **Jun 6, 1944** | Landing of the allies in Normandy ("D-Day") | **Feb 4–11, 1945** | Yalta conference |
| **Jan 14–24, 1943** | Conference at Casablanca | **Jul 25, 1943** | Fall of Mussolini | **Aug 25, 1944** | Allied reconquest of Paris |

Air Warfare

The battle in the air, waged with the cutting-edge technology of the day, caused heavy losses on both sides. The Allied bombing raids on Germany in the final stages of the war were primarily intended to demoralize the population.

1
US bombers attack Frankfurt, January 29, 1944

4
Dresden, 1945

2
Nuremberg, 1945

3
London after a bomb attack, 1940

5
After a bomb attack in Dresden bodies are burned because of the danger of an epidemic, February 1945

Aerial warfare had played a decisive role since the beginning of the war. Successfully tested in the Spanish Civil War, the German pinpoint bombing of military targets effectively contributed to the conquest of Poland in 1939 and Norway in 1940. In May 1940, the Germans for the first time destroyed an entire city, Rotterdam. The air war was radicalized by deliberate "carpet bombing," that is, the systematic saturation bombing of an inhabited area. Both si-

des gradually accepted the mass murder of civilians and employed it as an instrument of warfare. The German bombing raids on ❸ London and Coventry during the air war over England in 1940–1941 aimed not only to destroy armaments factories but also to undermine the morale of the civilian population.

By 1943 the Allies, superior both in material and manpower, were forcing the Germans completely onto the defensive in the air war. Well-directed air attacks on German positions on the front lines cleared the way for Allied advances on the ground. From 1942, ❶ American and British bombing raids had been reaching

cities in the north and west, particularly the industrial regions on the Rhine and in the Ruhr Valley, with increasing frequency. In order to break the resistance of the German civilian population, complete ❷ cities were also purposefully destroyed. In both daylight and nighttime offensives, Allied bombing raids had by 1945 reduced to rubble major areas of Cologne, Lübeck, ❻ Berlin, ❹ Dresden, and Hamburg, among others, and had forced the German population to live in overcrowded ❼ air shelters or to flee to the eastern regions of the Reich. Almost two million tons of bombs were dropped; nearly every fifth family was homeless. At war's end, 51 million cubic meters of debris lay in Berlin; in Hamburg, it was close to 36 million, in Dresden 25 million, and in Cologne 24 million. Altogether, ❺ around 600,000 Germans lost their lives in the Allied bombing attacks.

The War at Sea

The Allies had the upper hand in the naval war after 1943. Up until then, the Germans had been able to disrupt the Allies' merchant marine traffic effectively in the Atlantic with their submarines, but in March 1943 the supreme commander of the German navy, Karl Dönitz, broke off warfare in the Atlantic due to the high losses suffered.

Karl Dönitz plans a submarine attack, 1943

6
Anhalter Station in Berlin after its destruction, 1945

7
Homeless families seek shelter in a bunker, 1944

■ Total War and Resistance in Germany

The Nazis began to mobilize the entire population after 1943 despite the hopeless military situation. An attempted putsch on July 20, 1944, failed.

The closer they came to military defeat, the more the Nazi leaders fanatically tried to mobilize the last reserves at home and on the front lines, attempting to force an exhausted and starving population into action in defense of their hometowns. After the defeat at Stalingrad, Propaganda Minister Joseph Goebbels proclaimed the start of "total war." All males between 16 and 65, as well as females between 17 and 45, could be called up in defense of the Reich in order to achieve the "final victory." After August 1943, Hitler Youth members were shipped out of "defense fitness camps" directly to the front. Large segments of the population were conscripted to work in the armaments industry, and forced laborers were more intensely recruited. ❾ "See-it-through" slogans, promulgated either by propaganda posters or over the ❽ Volksempfänger—mass-produced radios for the general populace—were meant to inspire the "home front willing to sacrifice" to maximum performance. Martial criminal law was made stricter; deserters were shot or hanged on the spot by a drumhead court-martial to intimidate the people.

The terror against civilians became more radical once the ❿ German resistance had entered the public consciousness for the first time with a failed assassination attempt on Hitler on July 20, 1944. Germans taking a stand of resistance in the ❿ church and ⓫ political opposition had been struggling since 1933, unsuccessfully, in a police state against a regime that was still supported by a considerable portion of the population. The risks were high and many paid with their lives.

8   *The Volksempfänger*, a very cheap radio; no foreign programs could be received, 1938

9   "See-it-through" slogans, 1945: "Frankfurt will be held!"

10   Court-martial where suspected resisters were condemned, 1944

11   Helmuth James Count von Moltke, founder of the resistance group Kreisauer Kreis before the courtmartial, executed in 1945

12   Dietrich Bonhoeffer, member of the political opposition, executed 1945

From Joseph Goebbels's Sportpalast Speech, February 18, 1943

"The English maintain that the German people are resisting the government's total war measures. They do not want total war, but capitulation! I ask you: Do you want total war? If necessary, do you want a war more total and radical than anything that we can even imagine today?"

Goebbels makes his speech in the Sportpalast, February 1943

The Assassination Attempt of 1944

The bomb attack aimed at Hitler carried out by Colonel Count von Stauffenberg on July 20, 1944, in the Führer's headquarters in Poland had been planned since 1943 by a group of conspirators from all sections of the resistance. It was supposed to launch an immediate overthrow; after the death of Hitler, party and governmental offices were to be occupied and a new government put in place that would end the war. When Hitler survived the attack with only slight injuries, the coup attempt quickly collapsed. About 200 members of the resistance were executed and a further 7000 incarcerated.

above: Colonel Count von Stauffenberg, 1934
right: Hitler shows his destroyed headquarters to Mussolini

■ The Military Collapse of Germany

Germany surrendered unconditionally on May 8, 1945, only after the Allied forces had conquered the entire country. Hitler avoided capture by committing suicide.

1

Members of the Hitler Youth are arrested by the Russians

2

Soviet flag flying over the German Reichstag, April 30, 1945

3

Soviet soldiers in the ruins of the Reich Chancellery in Berlin, May 1945

The last German offensive in the Ardennes in southern France failed in December 1944. American, British, and French troops pushed from the west onto German soil at the beginning of 1945

4

Rubble at the Brandenburg Gate in the capital of Berlin, 1945

and, despite desperate resistance, conquered the contested cities one after another. On April 25, American and Soviet soldiers shook hands at Torgau on the Elbe. The Red Army crossed the German eastern frontier on January 1945 and launched its attack on Berlin. In the course of this assault, brutal acts of revenge for German atrocities committed on the Russian front were carried out on the German civilian population, particular-

ly on women. Despite overwhelming Soviet superiority, the Germans continued to offer heavy resistance. Hitler now had ❶ children, the aged, and the sick armed and sent to the front. Berlin fell on May 2 after a brutal 13-day battle for every street and building; on April 30 the ❷ Soviet flag flew over the Berlin Reichstag. Hitler and ❺ Goebbels had committed suicide in an underground bunker of the ❸ German chancellery: Hitler on April 30, Goebbels the day after. As many as 200,000 Red Army soldiers and around 50,000 Germans lost their lives in the ❹ battle for Berlin alone.

The German army signed the ❼ unconditional surrender of Germany first on May 7 at Allied Headquarters in Reims, and a day later at Soviet Headquarters in Berlin-Karlshorst; it came into effect the next day. All of Germany was occupied, and the entire armed forces became ❻ prisoners of war. World War II in Europe had ended. Japan, however, surrendered only after the first atomic bombs had been dropped in early August.

6

German prisoners of war are transported to the Soviet Union, May 1945

The "Nero Order"

In mid March 1945, Hitler issued the so-called Nero Order, instructing Armaments Minister Albert Speer to destroy Germany completely. With no regard for the civilian population, any installation in Germany that could be used by the enemy in any way—industrial complexes, supply and transport systems—was to be destroyed as the army retreated. The order was generally ignored.

5

Joseph Goebbels's body in Hitler's underground bunker, 1945

7

Field Marshal Keitel signs the unconditional surrender on May 8, 1945

| Dec 1944 | Failure of the Ardennes Offensive | Apr 30, 1945 | Berlin taken by the Red Army / Hitler's suicide |
| Jan 1945 | Beginning of the attack on Berlin | May 8, 1945 | Unconditional surrender of Germany |

Germany in 1945

The Allied victors laid out the political and economic framework for the reorganization of Germany at the Potsdam Conference. Reconstruction from the ruins began.

In accordance with the agreements of the Allied war conferences, the victorious powers divided German territory into American, British, Soviet, and French ❾ occupation zones. Concurrently, Berlin and Vienna were subdivided into four city sectors. At the conference in ❽ Potsdam in July 1945, new US President Harry S. Truman, Stalin, and Churchill—

8

Potsdam Conference in July 1945. Seated from left to right: Attlee, Truman, and Stalin

10

Seat of the Allied Control Council in Berlin-Schöneberg, 1954

11

Boy cycling through the rubble, Berlin, 1945

who was later replaced by the new prime minister Clement Attlee—emphasized their common responsibility for Germany. An ❿ Allied Control Council was to exercise the supreme power of governance. The German economy would be placed under Allied control. The victors agreed upon demilitarization, denazification, and decentralization as the political principles for rebuilding Germany. The principles were later divergently implemented according to the individual ideology in the occupation zones.

Beginning in November 1945, the leading representatives of the Nazi regime were ⓬ put on trial in Nuremberg for war crimes, crimes against humanity, and crimes against the peace (aggression). Most of the representatives were hanged. The examination of every individual German as to his or her involvement in the Nazi system was only halfheartedly pursued with the beginning of the East–West conflict.

As planned in the Allied war conferences, the north of East Prussia was permanently annexed to the Soviet Union and the remaining German territories east of the Oder-Neisse line were made part of Poland. The resettlement of the German population of Eastern Europe was approved. More than 16 million Germans were ⓮ driven out, often brutally; more than two million died while fleeing.

Meanwhile, in the ⓯ ruins of Germany, reconstruction began. Unlike during the period after 1918, the victors supplied fuel and food to the starving. ⓰ Women primarily accomplished the heavy labor of clearing the cities of ⓫ rubble. The first steps toward democracy were taken under Allied control with the reestablishment of the Social Democratic and other political parties in June 1945. ⓭ Culturally there was also a rebirth; newspapers boomed, and the theaters and concert halls were once again overfilled.

9

Guards on the border between the American and the Soviet occupation zones in Berlin

12

One of the main defendants tried in Nuremberg: Hermann Göring, 1945

13

Poster for a café with dancing, among the ruins of Hannover, 1946

14

Refugees arrive in Berlin, 1945

15

Munich in ruins, 1945

16

Women clear the rubble in Berlin, 1945

Jun 1945	Founding of new political parties	**Sep 2, 1945**	Capitulation of Japan
Jul 1945	Potsdam Conference	**after November 1945**	Nuremberg Trials

Glossary

abolition A movement to put an end to something.

alliance An agreement between two or more parties, often countries, made in order to advance a common goal.

aristocracy Derived from a Greek word meaning, "rule of the best," a form of government in which a few elite citizens rule.

bacteriologist A scientist who studies bacteria.

bicameral The practice in government of having two legislative houses.

bourgeoisie A social class made up of the wealthy upper class in a capitalist society.

clergy The leadership within a formal religion.

colonial Referring to the establishment of colonies in one territory by people from another territory.

communism A political idealogy based on common ownership by the people of a country.

conservatism A political philosophy that promotes traditional institutions and supports minimal and gradual change in society.

consulate The office of a consul, the official representative of the government of one state in the territory of another.

coup d'etat The sudden, illegal deposition of a government.

domination Supremacy or preeminence over another party.

economy The labor, capital, land resources, and goods and services of a country.

egoism Philosophy wherein people act in their own self-interest.

expansionism Philosophy promoting economic (and often territorial) growth outside of a country's borders, though not necessarily through military aggression.

fascism Government run by a totalitarian single-party state.

guillotine A device used for carrying out executions by decapitation.

hegemony An indirect form of imperial dominance over another country or countries by implied means of power, rather than military control.

imperialism The creation of an unequal relationship between countries or territories in which one country controls the other.

industrialization The process of social and economic change in which a country (or territory) develops and changes through the use of technology.

laissez-faire An environment in which transactions between private parties are free from state intervention.

liberalism A philosophy based on change within government, often to the detriment of tradition.

monarchy A form of government in which predominant power is granted to a monarch who serves for an unlimited term.

nationalism Political ideology wherein a country's citizens strongly identify as a part of the whole.

radicalization The process in which a group of people go from passivism to revolutionary or militant extremism.

revolutionary Referring to a major sudden impact on society.

secular The state of being separate from religion.

sovereign The quality of having supreme, independent authority over a geographic area.

totalitarian A political system where the state recognizes no limits to its authority.

urban Having to do with city.

For More Information

British Museum
Great Russell Street
London, WC1B 3DG
England
Web site: http://www.britishmuseum.org
The British Museum has a large array of art and artifacts from throughout human history.

Brooklyn Museum
200 Eastern Parkway
Brooklyn, NY 11238-6052
(718) 501-6258
Web site: http://www.brooklynmuseum.org
The Brooklyn Museum houses collections of historical artifacts from across the globe.

The Jewish Museum
1109 5th Avenue
New York, NY 10128
(212) 423-3200
Web site: http://www.thejewishmuseum.org
The Jewish museum is dedicated to preserving four thousand years of art and Jewish culture.

Metropolitan Museum of Art
1000 Fifth Avenue
New York, NY 10028-0198
(212) 535-7710
Web site: http://www.metmuseum.org
One of the world's largest and finest art museums, the Metropolitan Museum of Art has collections that include more than two million works of art spanning five thousand years of world culture, from prehistory to the present and from every part of the globe.

Museum of Jewish Heritage
Edmond J. Safra Plaze
36 Battery Place
New York, NY 10280
(646) 437-4200
Web site: http://www.mjhnyc.org
The museum of Jewish Heritage is dedicated to Jewish heritage and the Holocaust.

United States Holocaust Memorial Museum
100 Raoul Wallenberg Place SW
Washington, DC 20024-2126
(202) 488-0400
Web site: http://www.ushmm.org
A living memorial to the Holocaust, the United States Holocaust Memorial Museum inspires citizens and leaders worldwide to confront hatred, prevent genocide, and promote human dignity.

WEB SITES

Due to the changing nature of Internet links, Rosen Publishing has developed an online list of Web sites related to the subject of this book. This site is updated regularly. Please use this link to access the list:

http://www.rosenlinks.com/wtoh/mod

For Further Reading

Arnold, James R. *The Aftermath of the French Revolution*. Minneapolis, MN: Twenty-First Century Books, 2008.

Bartoletti, Susan Campbell. *Hitler Youth: Growing Up in Hitler's Shadow*. New York, NY: Scholastic, 2005.

Bosworth, R.J.B. *Mussolini's Italy: Life Under the Fascist Dictatorship, 1915–1945*. New York, NY: Penguin, 2007.

Burleigh, Robert. *Napoleon: The Story of the Little Corporal*. New York, NY: Abrams, 2007.

Cates, David. *Karl Marx: Philosopher & Revolutionary*. Minneapolis, MN: Abdo, 2011.

Davenport, John C. *The French Revolution and the Rise of Napoleon*. New York, NY: Chelsea House, 2011.

DiConsiglio, John. *Robespierre: Master of the Guillotine*. Danbury, CT: Children's Press, 2008.

Finkel, Caroline. *Osman's Dream: The History of the Ottoman Empire*. New York, NY: Basic Books, 2007.

Frank, Anne. *The Diary of a Young Girl*. New York, NY: Everyman's Library Classics, 2010.

Freedman, Russell. *The War to End All Wars: World War I*. New York, NY: Clarion, 2010.

Heuston, Kimberly Burton. *Napoleon: Emperor and Conqueror*. London, UK: Franklin Watts, 2010.

Keay, John. *China: A History*. New York, NY: Basic Books, 2011.

MacColl, Michaela. *Prisoners in the Palace: How Princess Victoria Became Queen with the Help of Her Maid, a Reporter, and a Scoundrel*. San Francisco, CA: Chronicle Books, 2010.

Nardo, Don. *The French Revolution*. San Diego, CA: Lucent, 2008.

Opdyke, Irene Gut, and Jennifer Armstrong. *In My Hands: Memories of a Holocaust Rescuer*. South Burlington, VT: Paw Prints, 2008.

Riggs, Kate. *The French Revolution*. Mankato, MN: Creative Co., 2009.

Rossig, Wolfgang. *Karl Marx*. Greensboro, NC: Morgan Reynolds, 2009.

Schomp, Virginia. *Victoria and Her Court*. Salt Lake City, UT: Benchmark, 2010.

Stone, Norman. *World War One: A Short History*. New York, NY: Basic Books, 2010.

Index

SAN LEANDRO HIGH